FI...

(A revised and enlarged edition of
The Pan Book of Great Composers)

'It is quite clear that these accounts of composers … have been based not only on a reading of the authorities, but also on a first-hand acquaintance with the music.' *Times Literary Supplement*

'Every music-lover will be stimulated by the trenchant, witty comments on famous works in every branch of composition.' *Weekly Scotsman*

'As a cavalcade of musical biographies it is the best of its kind I have ever read.' *Music Teacher*

'The book is admirably cross-referenced, and excellent in its provision of historical and topographical background.' *Music and Letters*

'There is much to provoke thought and stimulate interest.' *Manchester Evening News*

Gervase Hughes was born in Birmingham in 1905 and educated at Malvern College and Corpus Christi, Oxford, where he took M.A. and B.Mus. degrees. He conducted for several seasons with the British National Opera Company. A composer in his own right, Mr Hughes is the author of *The Music of Arthur Sullivan, Composers of Operetta, Dvořák: his Life and Music* and *Sidelights on a Century of Music (1825–1924)*. Together with Herbert van Thal, he edited *The Music Lover's Companion*.

FIFTY
FAMOUS COMPOSERS

(A revised and enlarged edition of
The Pan Book of Great Composers)

GERVASE HUGHES

A PAN ORIGINAL

PAN BOOKS LTD : LONDON

First published 1964 as *The Pan Book of Great Composers*. This revised and enlarged edition published 1972 by Pan Books Ltd., 33 Tothill Street, London, S.W.1.

ISBN 0 330 13064 1

2nd (Revised and Re-set) Printing 1972

*Printed in Great Britain by
Richard Clay (The Chaucer Press), Ltd.,
Bungay, Suffolk*

CONTENTS

Chapter

	Preface	vii
1	PALESTRINA	1
2	BYRD	5
3	MONTEVERDI	9
4	PURCELL	14
5	SCARLATTI	19
6	VIVALDI	23
7	HANDEL	26
8	BACH	33
9	GLUCK	41
10	HAYDN	45
11	MOZART	54
12	BEETHOVEN	61
13	WEBER	70
14	ROSSINI	74
15	SCHUBERT	79
16	BELLINI	88
17	DONIZETTI	91
18	MENDELSSOHN	94
19	BERLIOZ	99
20	CHOPIN	106
21	SCHUMANN	110
22	LISZT	115
23	WAGNER	120

Chapter

24	VERDI	130
25	BIZET	139
26	FRANCK	146
27	SMETANA	152
28	BRUCKNER	157
29	BRAHMS	163
30	BORODIN	170
31	SAINT-SAËNS	177
32	MUSSORGSKY	181
33	TCHAIKOVSKY	187
34	DVOŘÁK	192
35	GRIEG	198
36	RIMSKY-KORSAKOV	201
37	FAURÉ	206
38	WOLF	211
39	JANAČEK	215
40	ELGAR	219
41	PUCCINI	226
42	MAHLER	232
43	DEBUSSY	237
44	DELIUS	245
45	STRAUSS	250
46	SIBELIUS	257
47	VAUGHAN WILLIAMS	262
48	RACHMANINOV	270
49	RAVEL	274
50	FALLA	279
	Index	283

PREFACE

The Pan Book of Great Composers, published in 1964 and incorporating small-scale pen-pictures – part biographical and part critical – of thirty-five great composers, was so favourably received by both the press and the public that I have been encouraged to provide an enlarged edition covering a somewhat wider field: there are now fifteen new chapters, and I have seized the opportunity, also, to revise much of the original text. Perhaps not all the fifteen added composers can be reckoned as 'great' in the commonly accepted sense of the term, but in every case their music is sufficiently well known to qualify them as 'famous': hence the book's new title, *Fifty Famous Composers*. Three of the fifty were born in the sixteenth century; eleven survived the First World War and may therefore be said to have belonged to the twentieth, but since the true stature of a creative artist rarely becomes apparent until after the lapse of a generation or two I have shirked the responsibility of weighing the rival claims to fame of those whose contemporary reputations depend entirely (or very largely) upon their achievements during the past fifty years or so.

GERVASE HUGHES,
July 1972

CHAPTER ONE

Palestrina

On a sun-baked hillside twenty-five miles east of Rome (and in clear weather visible from the *autostrada del sole*) there stands a quaint little town called Palestrina – present-day population 9,000 – with a cathedral dedicated to the memory of the obscure Saint Agapit. In the first half of the sixteenth century a respected member of the community was the small landowner Sante Pierluigi; he and his wife Palma, a fellow-citizen, were indirectly responsible for ensuring that the name of their town would become a household word among musicians the world over, for the eldest of their four sons (christened Giovanni) chose to tag his birthplace to his patronymic and be known as GIOVANNI PIERLUIGI DA PALESTRINA.

In fighting which took place all over the region in 1527 when Emperor Charles V (head of the temporal Power known as the Holy Roman Empire) sacked Rome and imprisoned the reigning Pope (Clement VII) the municipal records were destroyed; there is consequently some uncertainty as to the exact date of Palestrina's birth but it may have been 17th December 1525. Thereafter his career is remarkably well documented. As a boy he became a chorister at the church of Santa Maria Maggiore in Rome where he carried on with his studies after his voice had broken. In 1544 he was appointed cathedral organist in his home town and began to tackle composition. Three years later he married; it seems to have been a love match and furthermore his bride, a local girl named Lucrezia Gori, brought as dowry a considerable inheritance from her father which included among other valuables a mule, a house – and a fertile vineyard.* The union produced three sons, of

---

* Those who know their *Gianni Schicchi* (see page 230) will be reminded of 'la mula, questa casa – e i mulini di Signa'. ('The mule, this house – and the sawmills at Signa'.)

whom Angelo and Rodolpho showed musical promise as youngsters but died in their early twenties; Iginio became a doctor of law and later entered the priesthood.

In 1551 Palestrina returned to Rome to direct the Julian choir of St Peter's; already respected as an organist and recognized as a wine-merchant, he soon established his reputation as a composer. Although in due course receiving tempting offers to migrate – in one instance to as far afield as Vienna – he stayed in Rome, for all practical purposes, for the rest of his life. Between 1555 and 1580, under the successive patronage of Popes Julius III, Marcellus II, Paul IV, Pius IV, Pius V and Gregory XIII, he was choirmaster of several important churches and cathedrals in turn; they included San Giovanni Laterano (the 'parish cathedral'), Santa Maria Maggiore (where he had been a pupil) and St Peter's itself. But during the 1570s pestilence stalked the land in the aftermath of another war, sparing neither prelate nor peasant. Palestrina fell grievously ill and, although he himself recovered, during the space of eight years he lost not only his two elder sons but also his wife Lucrezia; in deep distress he applied to Pope Gregory XIII for admittance to holy orders, was accepted, and was allocated to a vacant canonry. Yet almost immediately (and here one perhaps finds a clue to his personal character) he relinquished the tonsure and married a widow named Virginia Dormuli; she was as well endowed as Lucrezia had been thirty-four years before, but now it was profit from the sale not of wine but of furs that augmented his income. During the thirteen years that remained to him, however, he went on composing as hard as ever and – thanks partly, perhaps, to the tactful and flowery dedicatory epistles which prefaced his compositions – his abrupt abandonment of priestly ambitions escaped the censure of Popes Sixtus V, Gregory XIV, Innocent IX and Clement VIII. But early in 1594 he succumbed to a seizure and he died on 2nd February; so nearly to reach three score years and ten was in those days a fairly remarkable achievement, although surpassed (as we shall see in the next two chapters) by both Byrd and Monteverdi.

In the sixteenth century music was slowly beginning to escape from bondage to the Church, which in earlier days had pounced on the troubadours and still frowned on their successors the lute-players, but it is not surprising that Palestrina, born and brought up in a Papal state and spending most of his life in the shadow of the Vatican, should have concentrated his attention on Masses, litanies and motets. He did also compose secular madrigals, but not many of them rank among his masterpieces; it was in the Masses 'Ecce Sacerdos magnus', 'Aeterna Christi munera' and (above all) 'Assumpta est Maria' that he demonstrated his true genius. Despite – or perhaps because of – the direct and straightforward approach, they possess an other-world quality which has rarely been recaptured. Nevertheless it should be made clear that an apologetic, this-is-a-solemn affair-and-I-must-restrain-myself attitude would here be as inappropriate as it would be in Verdi's Requiem; this music should always be sung with full-throated sincerity.

During the three centuries preceding Palestrina's birth the purely monodic plainsong intoned by the priests had been gradually developed through a primitive form of harmony known as organum to polyphony, an early manifestation of counterpoint, i.e., two or more melodies sung or played *against* one another; the melodies belonged to one or other of the medieval scales – the modes – on which plainsong had been based. A very fair idea of the contrasted modal characteristics can be obtained by playing octave scales on the white notes of a piano: A to A for the Aeolian mode, C to C for the Ionian, D to D for the Dorian, E to E for the Phrygian, F to F for the Lydian, G to G for the Mixolydian. (Since this is neither a history of music nor a text-book there is no need to enlarge on the sub-divisions into Dorian and Hypodorian, Mixolydian and Hypomixolydian and so on.) Palestrina was one of several sixteenth-century composers who were subconsciously responsible for evolving from these medieval modes the modern diatonic major and minor scales, the former being the comparatively rarely used Ionian mode and the latter being based on the Aeolian. Admittedly several

3

of his motets and one at least of his Masses – 'Te Deum laudamus' – harked back to the Phrygian mode, but a critic endowed with a 'tonal' outlook (like Edmund H. Fellowes, see page 7) would have no difficulty in describing the Mass 'Papae Marcelli' as a Mass in C major. (Incidentally, the only modulations – i.e. emphatic digressions to a different key – were to G major, G minor and – once – to D major.) Nor was this the only avenue in which Palestrina showed initiative. In the madrigals *Che debbo far* and *Com' in più negre* and the motets *Paraclito amoroso* and *E, se il pensier* he used a vertical (i.e. harmonic rather than contrapuntal) structure which would appear out of character unless one were prepared to recognize his readiness to experiment. Where he differed from some of his equally enterprising contemporaries was in having the good sense to discontinue such experiments when they proved unrewarding.

In the long run, therefore, Giovanni Pierluigi da Palestrina deserves to be remembered not so much for having been an innovator as for having been a consolidator. He brought Church music to perfection in the idiom of his day; his mastery of that idiom has compelled the admiration of posterity and, moreover, has exerted its own influence on composers who were a hundred, two hundred, three hundred or four hundred years his junior.

CHAPTER TWO

Byrd

Very little is known in detail about the life of WILLIAM
BYRD. He *may* have been born at Epworth in Lincolnshire
(ten miles north of Gainsborough); it is *surmised* that from
1577 until 1592 he lived at Harlington in Middlesex; he
probably spent most of the rest of his life at Stondon Massey
in Essex. Facts (as distinct from conjectures) are that the
year of his birth was 1543; that in 1563 he was appointed
organist of Lincoln cathedral; that in 1568 he married
Joanna Birley who subsequently bore him at least five
children; that during his thirties and forties his activities
centred largely on London where he was partly responsible
for the directorship of the Chapel Royal; that he was later
involved in continual law-suits concerning his property at
Stondon Massey (a village lying midway between Brent-
wood and Ongar); that, although sometime organist of an
Anglican cathedral and generally in good favour at the
Protestant court of Queen Elizabeth I, he was occasionally
in trouble as a staunch Roman Catholic; that he died in
1623 at the age of seventy-nine or eighty. Turning from con-
jecture and fact to criticism it would be fair to say, with all
respect to Christopher Tye, Thomas Tallis, Thomas Morley,
John Dowland, Thomas Campion, Thomas Tomkins, John
Wilbye, Thomas Weelkes and Orlando Gibbons (one is
tempted to add old uncle Tom Cobley and all), that among
the many stars of this golden age of English music the star
of William Byrd shone the brightest.

For the Catholic Church Byrd composed three Masses
and more than two hundred motets, most of the latter being
published in four collections entitled *Cantiones Sacrae* and
Gradualia. For the Anglican Church (whose form of worship had been established by the Act of Uniformity, 1549) he
composed two complete Services, a handful of shorter

liturgical settings and about sixty anthems. In the secular field he was equally prolific, for he wrote some fifty songs (with string or lute accompaniment) and nearly double that number of madrigals. (I use the familiar and well-understood term madrigal rather than follow Byrd himself with his 'songs of sundrie natures' and so on.) Nor was this all : he left a surprisingly large quantity of chamber music for strings and about a hundred harpsichord pieces. (Strictly speaking they were written for the virginal, an instrument built on the harpsichord principle and played in the same manner, but as a rule smaller in size and slightly more restricted in compass.)

Of Byrd's Masses one was written for three voices, one for four and one for five; when there was an extra voice-part or two to play with he was able to provide greater aural contrast than in a three-part work. In the four-part Mass, for instance, separate sections of the 'Agnus Dei' were set for two, three and four voices respectively, while in the five-part Mass he exploited almost every possible threefold, fourfold and five-fold permutation of soprano, alto, tenor, baritone and bass. Of the two complete Anglican Services one was 'short' (i.e. a straightforward word-for-word setting of the liturgy) and the other 'great' (i.e. an extended setting giving more scope for musical treatment). The 'short' Service was four-part; the 'great' Service was the most elaborately contrapuntal of all his works (although not one of the most inspired), being written for a double choir of ten voices and here and there incorporating ten separate vocal lines. His (Latin) motets and (English) anthems were all in anything from three to nine parts, but it is noticeable that what might be called the subsidiary parts were sometimes allotted not to voices but to viols. Byrd's sacred music was often similar in style to that of Palestrina but at times showed a healthy open-air robust-ness more closely associated with his native land than with Italy. The 'Gloria' and 'Credo' from the five-part Mass; the motets *Vigilate, nescitis enim* and *In resurrexione tua*; the anthems *Make ye joy to God* and *From Virgin's womb this day did spring* : these clearly exemplified that trend – which was also apparent in some of the secular madrigals (e.g. *The Nightingale so pleasant* and *Come, jolly swains*).

His chamber music, taken as a whole, has been unduly neglected. It consists of some thirty pieces for three, four, five, six or seven viols (of varying shapes and sizes), all of which are playable on a suitable combination of modern violins, violas and cellos. Some would appear to be little more than madrigal transcriptions, but two at least of the 'quintet-fantasies', all five quintets grouped together as 'In nomine' and the *Pavan and Galliard* (a sextet) are one hundred per cent instrumental in conception – and furthermore ahead of their time. In keyboard music Byrd was no less of a pioneer; indeed in that field he stood alone among his contemporaries of any nationality. His output may be roughly divided into (*a*) dances and marches, and (*b*) airs with variations, the airs used being sometimes traditional (*The Carman's Whistle*, for instance) and sometimes original (*Go from my Window*). These forms he treated with astonishing freedom, often more suggestive of the late seventeenth century than of the Tudor era.

Byrd, being some twenty years younger than Palestrina, did even more than his predecessor to establish the characteristics of major and minor tonality while the medieval modes were gradually falling into disuse; he simultaneously continued to enlarge the range of 'chromatic' expression. This important aspect of sixteenth-century music was thoroughly examined by R. O. Morris in his *Contrapuntal Technique* (1925, revised 1939), by the Danish musicologist Knud Jeppesen in *The Style of Palestrina and the Dissonance* (1927, revised 1946) and by Edmund H. Fellowes in his *William Byrd* (1936, revised 1947) – especially in chapter 15 of that indispensable work. Certainly the 'sourest sharps and uncouth flats' of Byrd's madrigal *Come, woeful Orpheus* give the music a modern *look*, but there is nothing sour or uncouth in their *sound* – and this is far from being an isolated instance. One is therefore inclined to cavil slightly at Fellowes' tendency to couch his valuable remarks in 'tonal' terms. Here are two quotations from his book, the

7

first concerning a passage from the five-part Mass, the second the opening of the motet *Vide, Domine.*

> Following a cadence in D major, the modulations run rapidly through G, B flat, F, and A, ultimately arriving at a full close in C major.

> The main key is D minor, but the opening phrases are in D major, soon leading to a close in F major. After passing through B flat, a plagal cadence in E flat is reached.

Comment of this sort would be entirely appropriate if applied to the work of any composer from Vivaldi to Falla, who when modulating rapidly from D major through G, B flat, F, and A to C major would do so in the full realization of the effect of relative key-contrasts in a particular context. Byrd, I submit, had no key-structure, as such, in mind: although in his capable hands the language of music admittedly became more complex, more chromatic, the real motivation was still the polyphonic interweaving of strands of melody. That in Byrd's case this interweaving led to subconscious mastery of what has since become known as modulation does not mean that in that or any other respect he can be judged alongside Vivaldi, Falla, or any intermediary: he belonged to an earlier age. It would therefore be pointless to argue about his stature as compared with that of Handel or Bach, let alone with that of Haydn or Mozart: he merits not a different standard of criticism but a different application of the same standard. Direct comparison with Palestrina (whom we have already met) and with Monteverdi (to whom we shall very soon be introduced) would be almost equally unprofitable: whereas the two Italians excelled in specialized fields, William Byrd was essentially an all-rounder. In the gallery of illustrious sixteenth- and early seventeenth-century composers he would occupy a niche all on his own, did it not perhaps deserve to be shared by a few compatriot contemporaries such as Thomas Morley, Thomas Weelkes and Orlando Gibbons.

CHAPTER THREE

Monteverdi

CLAUDIO MONTEVERDI was born in 1567. He was the eldest of four children of a doctor named Baldassare Monteverdi who practised at Cremona, a fair-sized cathedral-town on the left bank of the river Po lying roughly in the middle of the triangle whose apexes are Milan, Parma and Mantua, three cities which in those days vied with Verona, Bologna, Ferrara, Padua and Venice as centres of the cultural renaissance which had had its roots in northern Italy. As a youngster Claudio's musical promise fell little short of precocity and before he was out of his teens – probably while still studying with the local choirmaster Marc' Antonio Ingegneri – he published four volumes of sacred and secular madrigals. Few held signs of immaturity; often (as in *Baci soavi e cari*) they showed greater awareness of the harmonic implications of the new tonal system than had the Palestrina examples cited on page 4. Two more volumes of secular madrigals – among which *Stracciami pur il core*, at least, marked a further advance – appeared soon after Monteverdi had taken up a permanent post as viol-player at the court of the reigning Duke of Mantua in 1591 or thereabouts. Then followed a remarkable episode which I believe has no parallel in the career of any other famous composer.

In 1595 Emperor Rudolf II (third in succession to Charles V, mentioned on page 1) called upon Monteverdi's employer, Duke Vincenzo of Mantua, to play his part in resisting Ottoman encroachment on the Holy Roman Empire, for the Turks (who sixty-five years earlier had been driven back to the Balkans from the very gates of Vienna) were again surging westwards to threaten the Christian dominions over which the Emperor held sway. Duke Vincenzo was a loyal liege but he was also a keen musician; when he set out to do his master's bidding he took singers and an orchestra along with him. Monteverdi and the rest had to journey, perhaps on foot, over the Brenner Pass to Innsbruck and then through Upper Austria, Bohemia, Moravia and Hungary. As a military exercise the campaign was inconclusive and possibly futile (for the Turks won a major battle and then withdrew!), and the return journey through Lower Austria, Styria and Carinthia must have been somewhat of an anti-climax. But all along, in moments of both despair and triumph, Monteverdi and his colleagues provided their Duke with the entertainment he required.

A few years later Monteverdi was once more off on his travels, accompanying the Duke on an equally lengthy but this time more peaceful and no doubt more pleasurable excursion north-westwards, in the course of which they penetrated as far as Antwerp. (Meanwhile he had married Claudia Cattaneo, a singer, also employed at the ducal court; she died in 1607, after presenting him with three children.) In 1602 he realized a long-standing ambition when he was appointed choirmaster; as such he was in charge of all court music at Mantua, choral and instrumental, sacred and secular, and the salary was higher than any he had earned hitherto. This was a turning point in more ways than one, for from that date onwards one finds traces of genius as well as of talent in his compositions. The next three volumes of madrigals showed increased assurance in technique (e.g. in *Voi pur da me*) and, moreover, displayed an extraordinary range of emotional expression; it is interesting to compare, for example, the languishment of *Sì ch'io vorrei morire* with what his biographer Leo Schrade pertinently called the frightening intensity of *Era l'anima*. Then came his first two operas, *La favola d'Orfeo* (1607) and *L'Arianna* (1608).

Although the long history of opera is generally taken to have begun with Jacopo Peri's *Dafne*, produced in 1597 at Florence, it is worth recording that at Mantua itself, during Monteverdi's viol-playing days, the then choirmaster Orazio Vecchi had provided Duke Vincenzo with *L'Amfiparnaso*, a 'comedy with music'. *L'Amfiparnaso* consisted merely of a succession of madrigals and, although Peri's *Dafne* was more serious in intent and more ambitious in conception, it would be fair to say that Monteverdi's *Orfeo* established a precedent in that it was deliberately planned to combine appropriate music with stage scenes and action, the object being to forge the whole into a dramatic entity. Before discussing *Orfeo* and the works which followed it, however, space must be found to point the significance of another crucial development in the art of music-making which was taking place at the time and was to affect future generations of composers to almost as great a degree as the substitution of tonality for the modes (which has already been briefly referred to in the preceding chapters).

Towards the end of the sixteenth century realization began to dawn that not even serious music need necessarily be polyphonic; that after all there was something to be said for the troubadours who had accompanied their love-songs with at the most a few simple chords on a lute. When music became a permanent feature of gracious living in royal and ducal households all over western Europe, the despised travelling lutenist was supplanted by the useful resident harpsichordist – or organist. He was a boon to composers who adopted the new (or strictly speaking revived) style, for his all-round musicianship encouraged them to fit their melodies with only a bass line – hereinafter referred to as *basso continuo* or just *continuo*; the harpsichordist or organist himself had to fill in the gaps to the best of his ability, for as a rule he could rely only on shorthand indications – sometimes not even that – of the composer's intentions. (It was therefore in the early seventeenth century rather than in the jazz age that the art of 'vamping' was first developed.)

Monteverdi took full advantage of the *basso continuo* method of composition in *Orfeo* – especially but not exclusively in the recitative passages. In a pastoral version of the Orpheus legend the librettist (Alessandro Striggio) rather shabbily allotted a minor role to Eurydice, the nominal heroine, concentrating his attention on the hero, on Apollo, Pluto, Proserpine, Charon and the allegorical figures of Music and Hope – backed by a chorus of Dionysian shepherds and shepherdesses. The music – recitative, aria, chorus and ritornello (orchestral interlude) in turn – was lyrical in feeling almost throughout but nevertheless conformed admirably with the stage situation at moments of dramatic tension and bore unmistakable signs of mastery. *Orfeo* and its successor *L'Arianna* were followed by an elaborate and in places beautiful choral work, *Vespro della beata Vergine* (1610) – and by the death of Monteverdi's ducal patron (1612). For a time he was unemployed but a year or so later was appointed choirmaster at St Mark's in Venice, where he signalled his arrival by publishing yet another volume of madrigals (some of them, be it noted, with *continuo* accompaniment) which included a very fine sequence entitled *Lagrime d'amante al sepolcro dell' amata* ('A lover weeps over the tomb of his beloved'). He did not lose touch with Mantua, however, where opera was better received than it was, as yet, in Venice; for the benefit of Vincenzo's successor, Duke Francesco, he wrote the ballet-opera *Tirso e Clori*, which provided evidence of a growing realization that what the public wanted was dancing and singing rather than declamation. Recitatives were reduced to a minimum.

Living in Venice for the rest of his life – he died there in 1643 at the age of seventy-six – Monteverdi went on composing madrigals to his heart's content; among them were such gems as *Zefira torna* and *Hor che'l ciel e la terra*. He also wrote seven or eight more works for the stage, including the operas *Il ritorno d'Ulisse in patria* (1641) and *L'incoronazione di Poppea* (1642); in the last-named his genius came to full fruition. Lyrical inspiration rivalled that of *Orfeo* (witness the lullaby 'Oblivion soave') and even today it is hard to resist the genuinely moving appeal of some of the final cadences, however simple they may appear on paper. Moreover, there was greater merging than hitherto of the distinctive characteristics of sung speech and spoken song. While *Poppea* admittedly contained arias, duets and recitatives, there were also moments when the composer fitted music to the text regardless of formal requirements, moments which impel the listener to ask himself: is this an aria or a monologue? is this a *parlando* duet or accompanied recitative? Such an approach to the problems of opera, then in its infancy, was so highly individualistic as to prove unacceptable to later and more prolific exponents like Handel and Mozart – and indeed has generally speaking found more favour in the twentieth century than it ever did in the late seventeenth, the eighteenth or even the nineteenth. It has only recently become realized, therefore, that in some respects Claudio Monteverdi was three hundred years ahead of his time.

CHAPTER FOUR

Purcell

The sixteenth century was extraordinarily productive of composers, among them such important figures as Palestrina and Monteverdi from Italy, Heinrich Schütz from Saxony, Orlando de Lassus from Flanders, Tomás Luis de Victoria from Spain and the crowd of Englishmen catalogued on page 5. By sad contrast the only composer of real historical significance born during the first half of the seventeenth was Jean Baptiste Lully (1632–87, Italian by birth and French by naturalization) whose ballets and operas earned him fame and favour at the court of King Louis XIV, established major/minor tonality on a sound basis, and helped to bridge the chronological gap between the death of Monteverdi in 1643 and the advent to maturity of Henry Purcell and Alessandro Scarlatti some forty years later.

HENRY PURCELL (1659–95) was born in Westminster and lived there all his life. For many years historians were in doubt about his parentage, but research by Sir Jack Westrup has established conclusively that he was the son of Thomas Purcell and not, as was long believed, of Thomas' elder brother Henry. This Thomas was an accomplished court-musician who under the Commonwealth must have been hard put to it to earn a good living but after the Restoration became a veritable Pooh-Bah – 'gentleman of the Chapel Royal, musician for the lute, viol and voices, composer for the violins, groom of the robes, and musician-in-ordinary for the private music'. Small wonder that young Henry, with this background, should have found himself first a chorister at the Chapel Royal and subsequently assistant keeper of the King's instruments, organ-tuner at Westminster Abbey, and composer-in-ordinary for the violins; even greater honour was in store, for in 1679 he was appointed organist at the abbey, where he officiated at two royal funerals and two coronations – and in due course was buried. Little is known of his private affairs except that he married (in 1681) and had six children, of whom the three eldest died in infancy. (His wife and two of the younger children survived him by many years.) Although he died at the early age of thirty-six Purcell's career spanned five régimes in English history – those of Richard Cromwell, Charles II, James II, William III and Mary, William III *solus*; furthermore his younger brother Daniel, a well-known musician in his day, outlived both William III and Queene Anne and was thus able to welcome our first Hanoverian monarch, George I. Another curious fact worth noting is that Purcell was both preceded and followed as organist of Westminster Abbey by John Blow – best remembered for the masque (i.e. dance-opera) *Venus and Adonis*.

Apart from occasional trips to Windsor and Hampton Court during his keeper-of-the-instruments and organ-tuning days, Purcell (just because he was a Londoner, perhaps) seems never to have ventured more than a mile or two from home; his reputation has travelled much further afield – and deservedly so. His art had a wider range than that of Alessandro Scarlatti (whom we shall meet in chapter 5), since Purcell was not narrowly English in the sense that Scarlatti was, if not narrowly, then at least specifically, Italian. Admittedly Purcell now and again drew on folk-melody and also inherited certain tics of part-writing from the Elizabethan madrigalists; what is of greater significance is that he imparted a cosmopolitan flavour to his music by adapting to his own purposes the Frenchified Italianisms of J. B. Lully.

Yet in the theatre Purcell unquestionably showed his birthright. In only one of his stage-works – *Dido and Aeneas* – were the songs, choruses and dances linked together in the Italian manner by recitative; all the rest (some forty-five) incorporated spoken dialogue, and indeed it is hard to draw a firm line between the few which were operas with dialogue and the many which were plays with incidental music. Whatever one calls them these productions, though often bawdy enough to satisfy prevailing tastes, could be of high literary (as well as musical) calibre. Some were adaptations of Shakespeare – *King Richard II, The Fairy Queen* (from *A Midsummer Night's Dream*), *Timon of Athens, The Tempest*; others of Beaumont and Fletcher – *Dioclesian* (from *The Prophetess*), *The Double Marriage, Bonduca*; John Dryden had a hand in *King Arthur* and *The Indian Queen*; Thomas Shadwell provided *Epsom Wells* and *The Libertine* and William Congreve (then in his early twenties) *The Old Bachelor* and *The Double-dealer*. Several of Purcell's best-known songs were composed for these English dramas and comedies: e.g. 'When I am laid in earth' (*Dido and Aeneas*), 'What shall I do to show how much I love her?' (*Dioclesian*), 'Nymphs and shepherds, come away' (*The Libertine*) and 'I attempt from love's sickness to fly' (*The Indian Queen*). All four, in their differing moods, are representative of his genius; the first, Dido's lament, is something more, being one of the most moving expressions of human sorrow in the whole history of music.

Despite the unassuming charm of some fifty little pieces for harpsichord and a dozen or so 'fantasies' for strings, Purcell's most noteworthy contribution to instrumental music was a set of twenty-two sonatas for two violins and cello – a harpsichord providing the *continuo* accompaniment. All but one of these sonatas incorporated four or five movements in contrasted *tempi*, but they were intended to be played without a break. (In the seventeenth century a sonata was merely a piece of music for sounding – i.e. for playing on instruments – as distinct from a cantata, a piece for singing. It was not until later that cantata came to mean an extended vocal or choral work with orchestral accompaniment and that the word sonata was associated with pieces for a single instrument or two at the most, let alone with 'sonata form' – which will be described in due course. In the Purcell Society's editions the *continuo* of the sonatas was realized for performance on a modern piano: in the first volume by J. A. Fuller-Maitland – with considerable restraint – and in the second by Charles Villiers Stanford – with much greater freedom.)

Some historians believe that Purcell originally planned twenty-four sonatas for this combination of instruments – one each in every minor and major key. That the first eight are paired in relatives – G minor and B flat major (two flats in the key signature), D minor and F major (one flat), A minor and C major (no sharps or flats), E minor and G major (one sharp) – is certainly suggestive, but the remaining four from the first volume, published in 1683, provide the irrelevant mixture of C minor (three flats), A major (three sharps), F minor (four flats) and D major (two sharps); of the ten in the second volume, published by his widow Frances Purcell in 1697, the first two are in B minor (the relative of D major) and E flat major (the relative of C minor), but all the rest are in keys that have already had their turn – one each in C, D and F major, D and A minor, and no less than three in G minor. Therefore Purcell can hardly be credited with having anticipated the zealous logic of J. S. Bach in his 'Forty-eight preludes and fugues for well-tempered clavier' (see page 36) or Chopin's equally consistent approach in his twenty-four preludes op. 28 (page 108). Nevertheless certain features of the key-structure of these sonatas demand comment. First: the separate movements of each sonata were all in the same key except (*a*) the short third movement – hardly more than a connecting passage – of no. 10 in A major, which set out on its little tour of modulation from an emphatic chord of F sharp major, and (*b*) the F minor adagio belonging to the F major no. 9 from the second volume (sometimes known as the 'golden' sonata). Secondly: none of the minor movements finished on a major chord, although contemporary ears were already attuned to the *tierce de Picardie* (a conventional full close in the major which was really a modal survival). Thirdly and *per contra*: no. 12 in D major ended, most unexpectedly, in D minor.

Purcell's sacred works – mostly anthems but also including hymns and canticles – were nearly all written before he consummated his powers in opera (or something like it). They are interesting not so much for their own sake as because they provide a link between the (Anglican) ecclesiastical music of the late sixteenth and early seventeenth centuries and that of the late seventeenth and early eighteenth. The anthems were all based on passages from the Old Testament (generally from the Psalms) and unlike those of pre-Restoration days tended to be in verse-plus-refrain form; in the verse sections Purcell set a fine precedent by following both the sense and the underlying rhythm of the words and inclined to adopt a declamatory style foreshadowing Handel (in *Lord, who can tell how oft he offendeth*, for instance), but taken as a whole his Church music was no more sacred in character than the music of his operas, secular cantatas, 'welcome-songs' and 'odes' – one of which, celebrating St Cecilia's Day 1692 and entitled *Hail, bright Cecilia* – was indeed a splendid outburst of commemoration. It might be added that Henry Purcell himself was the most worthy British-born representative of St Cecilia during a musically rather dim period of our island story which spanned some three hundred and fifty years.

CHAPTER FIVE

Scarlatti

ALESSANDRO SCARLATTI (originally Scarlata) was born at Palermo in 1660; he came of obscure Sicilian peasant stock and of his boyhood little is known. But it *is* known that by the age of twelve he was in Rome (probably living with relations and certainly studying music), that before he was eighteen he married a Roman girl named Antonia Anzalone, that by nineteen he had produced the first of ten children and the first of a hundred and twenty operas, that at twenty-four he moved south to become choirmaster of the royal chapel at Naples. He stayed at Naples until 1702, but then turned his steps northwards; with Rome (once again) as headquarters, he visited Florence, Venice, and Urbino in the eastern foothills of the Apennines – where the choirmaster at the time was his eldest son Pietro. By 1709, however, Scarlatti was back at his old post in Naples and there remained (except for a further three-year period of Roman leave) until his death in 1725. Soon afterwards his fourth son Domenico, who had won considerable renown as an executant on the harpsichord and had already toured Portugal, left Italy to settle in Spain, where he composed many admirable keyboard pieces which today are more familiar to us than anything that his father ever wrote. Nevertheless Scarlatti the elder was a more significant figure in musical history. (Domenico's dates were 1685–1757.)

Before he completed his first opera – *Gli equivoci nel sembiante* (1679) – Alessandro Scarlatti had a bunch of chamber-cantatas to his credit. During the course of his career he composed some six hundred, each consisting of four or five short arias connected by recitative; most were written out only for soprano and *basso continuo* but some had two voice-parts and in a few others the accompaniment acknowledged the existence of violins or even flutes –

although he is said to have disliked wind instruments because 'they are never in tune'. At first Scarlatti was not always sure-fingered in handling what was still a comparatively unfamiliar problem of tonality – the judging of the sense of key-structure imposed by the permanent adoption of the major and minor scales: many arias in the cantatas and early operas seemed unable to make up their minds whether they were in, say, C major or G major. This technical aspect, however, became comparatively immaterial when he presently showed that his strongest suit was melodic invention; he continued to play this hand to good advantage in both cantatas and operas – though less well in Church music, a field in which he was not so prolific.

It was during his first Neapolitan period (1684–1702) that Scarlatti established the classical tradition of Italian *opera seria* with such works as *Olimpia vendicata*, *La Statira* and *Pirro e Demetrio*, the last-named being actually played and published in London during the composer's lifetime. In the English version of the libretto the rhyming quatrain

> Veder parmi
> un' ombra nera,
> cruda e' fiera
> minacciarmi

became the rhyming couplet

> Something bloody and unexpected
> at my bosom seems directed.

On the other hand there were scenes in *Clearco, Teodora Augustin* and *Eraclea* which were *intentionally* comic, where farce jostled impending tragedy as closely as in *Hamlet* and *Macbeth* a century earlier or (which is more to the point) in *Don Giovanni* a century later. These operas all followed a stereotyped constructional pattern: aria, recitative, duet, recitative, aria, etc., up to the formal concluding chorus, which as a rule was not so much a chorus in modern connotation as a short ensemble for the principal characters. By contrast with Scarlatti's cantata manuscripts his operatic manuscripts incorporated fairly frequent hints for the realization of the *basso continuo*; indeed the parts were sometimes written out in full and occasionally one meets the injunction *tutti li stromenti d'arco senza cembalo* ('all the bowed instruments without the harpsichord').

While Scarlatti was travelling round central and northern Italy between 1702 and 1708 he composed the opera which those well qualified to judge regard as his best – *Il Mitridate Eupatore* (Venice, 1707); this was unequivocally serious, with no intrusion to the *buffo* (comic) element, and yet here the composer at last began to develop a flair for musical characterization, a flair which after his return to Naples in 1709 was maintained in *La principessa fedele* (1710) and *Tigrane* (1715). Since he so often demonstrated, even in *opera seria*, that he had a sense of humour, it is surprising that *Il trionfo dell' onore* (1718) was the only one of his extant operas which could be rated as a genuine *opera buffa* (comic opera). Here the composer in some respects foreshadowed the Mozart of *Figaro*, although he did little to establish the characteristics of traditional *opera buffa* in the manner in which he had earlier – in *La Statira* – established the characteristics of traditional *opera seria*. *Il trionfo dell' onore* contained no suggestion of the 'concerted finale' later evolved by his successor Leonardo Vinci (not to be confused with Leonardo *da* Vinci!): each act ended with an ensemble appropriate to the situation but it was only in a quartet from Act III ('Pensa, pensa ben') that vocal counterpoint acquired significance in its context.

I have purposely refrained from cluttering the pages of this book with parenthetical or footnote references to authorities, apart from occasional quotations from the writings of recognized experts, but it would be churlish not to admit that even so brief a survey of Scarlatti as the present one would hardly have been possible without a large measure of reliance being placed on the pioneering research of E. J. Dent, who somewhere about 1900 set himself the task of tracking down records and manuscripts all over Europe. Unfortunately he drew blank everywhere except Berlin, Bologna, Brussels, Cambridge, Darmstadt, Dresden, Florence, London, Milan, Modena, Montecassino, Munich, Naples, Oxford, Padua, Rome, Schwerin and Vienna, but none the less he managed to become acquainted with about one third of the hundred and twenty operas which Scarlatti is known to have completed, and he promptly revealed his conclusions in what might be called the Scarlatti bible – *Alessandro Scarlatti, his Life and Works*, first published in 1905 and reissued in 1960 with factual annotations by his younger but equally erudite and enthusiastic colleague Frank Walker. Meanwhile in 1927 Alfred Lorenz of Munich University published his *Alessandro Scarlattis Jugendoper*, which was Teutonically thorough within its self-imposed limitations and incorporated no less than four hundred music-type examples from eighteen operas dated between 1679 and 1700. Yet to most music lovers Scarlatti remains barely accessible: of the operas only a fistful and of the chamber-cantatas no more than a baker's dozen have been published complete, and very few are readily available. A rhetorical question therefore poses itself. Why have Italian scholars given more attention to his (admittedly very gifted) son Domenico and to his talented but relatively unimportant disciples Leonardo Leo and Nicola Logroscino than to the father and master, so that the world at large (which includes Italy) has to thank Dent from Yorkshire and Walker from Hampshire and Lorenz from Bavaria for persuading it that Alessandro Scarlatti from Sicily was not only a great composer in his own right but also the spiritual forerunner of an even greater composer who hailed from Salzburg?

CHAPTER SIX

Vivaldi

During the late seventeenth century and the early eighteenth Italy was not only the land of opera but also the land of the violin, an instrument whose potentialities were developed to a hitherto undreamt-of degree by such exponents as Corelli (whose name was closely associated with the School of Rome), Torelli (Bologna), Vivaldi (Venice), Somis (Turin) and Tartini (Padua). As well as playing the violin they composed plenty of music for it: Vivaldi's lay neglected for a century or so after his death, but began to attract attention when in 1829, during the revival of interest in J. S. Bach largely stimulated by Mendelssohn (see page 94), it was found that the great man had based an organ piece upon one of Vivaldi's concertos. Presently many other 'lost' works were rediscovered, and over the years they have been played with increasing frequency.

ANTONIO VIVALDI (*circa* 1675–1741) was probably born in Venice and certainly spent his youth there, being taught music by his father, Giovanni Battista Vivaldi, himself a violinist, and Giovanni Legrenzi, organist and choirmaster at St Mark's. At the age of twenty-eight he was ordained as a priest, but he suffered from asthma and very soon decided – or was persuaded – that he was incapable of conducting Mass in a satisfactory manner.* In the Venice of those days there were four big girls' schools – approximating to convents – which had been established by charitable religious organizations for the education – and in particular the musical education – of orphans and the children of poverty-stricken or unmarried parents. (It is good to learn that the

---

* He continued to be known as *il prete rosso* (he had red hair), although his allegedly unclerical conduct, particularly with members of the opposite sex, more than once incurred the censure of Church dignitaries.

authorities were sufficiently enlightened not to refuse admission to illegitimates.) One of these institutions was the Conservatorio dell' Ospedale Pietà on the Riva degli Schiavoni (the site is now occupied by the Instituto Provinciale degli Espositi), and Vivaldi joined the staff there in 1704. Five years later he was appointed head violin-teacher, and in 1716 *maestro de' concerti* with the responsibility of composing two new concertos each month.* He also customarily deputized for the choirmaster Francesco Gasparini, and when the latter neglected his duties (as he often did) Vivaldi had to provide motets and other choral items as well. He was bound by contract to fulfil these obligations even when not in residence and may sometimes have found the task irksome, for although he never severed his connexion with the Ospedale he evidently indulged in extra-mural activities to a considerable extent. It is known, for instance, that from 1718 until 1722 he acted as choirmaster to Prince Philip of Hesse-Darmstadt at Mantua, some eighty miles away; it seems probable that in 1729 he toured Germany with his father and quite possible that he later went on his own to France or Austria or both. There is conclusive evidence that he was back at his post in Venice by about 1735, but in 1738 he was off to Holland where he directed the centenary celebrations of the Amsterdam Theatre, for which he arranged a stage *pasticcio* comprising music provided by himself and half a dozen other contemporary composers. Three years later he visited – or revisited – Vienna, where he died, apparently in poverty.

Despite his travels abroad, Vivaldi had passed nearly the whole of his life in his native land, and for all his preoccupation with his own instrument had also endeavoured to distinguish himself (as did all self-respecting Italian composers of his generation) in the field of opera. He completed about forty operas, the first in 1713 and the last in 1740; some were

* Scholars have traced some four hundred and fifty concertos all told, of which about half are for solo violin and orchestra and half for various miscellaneous orchestral combinations; the majority remain in manuscript (see next page).

produced in Venice, others in Rome, Florence, Mantua, Verona or Ancona. Not one of them is known today – although *L'Olimpiade* (1734) was revived at Siena in 1939 – nor are his two oratorios, *Moyses Deus Pharaonis* (1714) and *Juditha Triumphans Devicta Holofernes Barbarie* (1716).* The bulk of his output is carefully preserved in manuscript at the Bibliotecha Nazionale in Turin, but his posthumous reputation has for practical purposes always depended upon his published compositions for the violin: about sixty concertos with orchestra and forty sonatas with *continuo* accompaniments which have been transcribed for a modern piano. (Four of the best-known concertos are subtitled 'Spring', 'Summer', 'Autumn' and 'Winter'.) Many of these works were obviously intended to be part of a sort of *Gradus ad Parnassum* for his girl pupils at the Ospedale and incorporated passages of varying difficulty on the assumption of a progressive improvement in the student's technical ability, but even in the 'elementary' pieces simplicity was combined with an artistry which matched that of Handel and at times even foreshadowed the manner of Mozart. Antonio Vivaldi's violin music, therefore, is admirably suited for practice and performance by executants at all stages of proficiency.

* Since these words were written, there has been a performance of *Juditha Triumphans* at the Queen Elizabeth Hall, London. According to *The Times*, 'the formal procession of recitative and aria seemed excessively mechanical'.

CHAPTER SEVEN

Handel

GEORGE FRIDERIC HANDEL – his own final choice of spelling –
was born at Halle on 23rd February 1685; his father was a
doctor (a 'barber-surgeon') and his mother, Dorothea *née*
Taust, the daughter of a Protestant priest. One is at liberty
to shrug aside the romantic legend of a curly-headed six-
year-old being discovered late at night divinely playing the
harpsichord by moonlight in a cold attic, but the fact remains that Handel was a child prodigy. His natural instincts
were encouraged by his aunt Anna Taust rather than by
his parents, but eventually his father consented to music-
lessons and even allowed him, at the age of eleven, to go by
himself to Berlin (a week's journey in those days) in order
to attend the unconventional court of Electress Sophia Charlotte, to whom music was all that mattered. Soon afterwards
young Handel was deputy organist at Halle Cathedral and
at seventeen, although supposedly studying law at the university, was appointed head organist. A successful career
in that field appeared to be open to him, but he was beginning to feel the tug of the stage and after a year or so left
the organ-loft at Halle for the opera house at Hamburg,
where between 1703 and 1706 he played in the orchestra and
also secured the production of two operas of his own. Realization that he had found his natural bent then drove him
south to Italy, the land of opera; by what route or at whose
expense (it can hardly have been at his own) has not been
determined.

Although Handel never married, it is believed that during
the three years he spent in Italy he had a love affair with a
young singer; historians have been unable to agree as to
which young singer it was out of the many he must have
encountered while travelling back and forth (several times)
between Venice, Florence, Rome and Naples. What is more

important is that in the course of his wanderings he experimented to good purpose in the chamber-cantata form recently popularized by Alessandro Scarlatti (see page 19) and also composed two more operas – *Roderigo* and *Agrippina*. By 1710, however, he was back in his native land as musical director at the court of the Elector of Hanover and was presently granted leave of absence to visit London, where he stayed for six months and produced *Rinaldo* at the Queen's Theatre, Haymarket. He loved London so much that a year or so later (he was twenty-seven at the time) he returned there, stayed on and – although still nominally on the Elector's pay-roll – accepted an allowance from Queen Anne. Consequently there were some awkward moments when, on Queen Anne's death in 1714, Handel's Hanoverian employer followed him across the North Sea to fill the vacant seat on the English throne. Good standing with the nobility, however, weighed in his favour, and the temporary breach between the two Georges, king and composer, was soon healed. Both lived in London for the rest of their lives, the former becoming British *ex officio* and the latter by naturalization.

Over the next twenty-seven years the story of Handel is the story of his fluctuating operatic fortunes. As manager and artistic director of the King's (previously Queen's) Theatre he did far more than anyone else to establish Italian *opera seria* as a permanent feature of musical life in London. His own contribution included over thirty operas – among them such fine works as *Giulio Cesare, Admeto, Orlando, Alcina* and *Serse* – but up to 1730 or thereabouts he received assistance from the already established composers Attilio Ariosti and Giovanni Bononcini while he himself scoured Italy for the best singers that could be found. For a time all went well (and indeed the policy seemed to be both prudent and enlightened), but without knowing it Handel was stirring up trouble. For one thing Ariosti and Bononcini, who were fifteen to twenty years his senior and had their own partisans, were jealous and uncooperative, doing all they could to undermine their associate's personal position and prestige. For another, there was spiteful rivalry between the two famous sopranos Faustina Bordoni and Francesca Cuzzoni; this reached its climax during a gala performance of Bononcini's *Astianatte* when (egged on by the audience) they indulged in a free fight on the stage with no holds barred and no quarter asked or given. Such goings-on under royal patronage could not pass without comment in an age which (like our own) relished any form of scandal, and they were soon satirized by John Gay in *The Beggar's Opera* (1728, with music arranged from traditional and currently popular airs by Handel's Anglo-German contemporary John Christopher Pepusch); this witty little affair and other ballad-operas which followed it were exactly suited to the taste of the age. In the outcome their influence proved to be short-lived, but it lasted long enough to imperil the future prospects of Handel's venture. With bulldog determination he continued along his chosen road (now alone and unassisted), although from 1732 onwards he found it necessary to vary the exclusively operatic diet with oratorios like *Esther, Saul* and *Israel in Egypt*, and with what might conveniently be called cantatas – *Acis and Galatea* and *Alexander's Feast*. (The oratorios and cantatas were in English, not in Italian, and in the oratorios a very prominent share in the proceedings was allotted to the chorus; but it should be stressed that all these works were given on the stage – sometimes with stage costume and action.) In 1741, however, when financial ruin (not for the first time) stared him in the face, Handel the impresario wisely decided to cut his losses and shut up shop – and Handel the composer abandoned opera for ever.

All this while, when away from the theatre, he had produced a fair quantity of short choral works (e.g. the 'Chandos' anthems) and a large quantity of instrumental music. This included the *Water Music*, some forty concertos (not as a rule concertos in the modern sense of the term, but merely concerted works for various instrumental combinations) and several volumes of harpsichord pieces.

Although most of Handel's keyboard music belonged to his early years and looks comparatively unimportant when set beside the rest of his output, a nodding acquaintance helps one to easy familiarity with the forms of gavotte, bourrée, minuet, courante, sarabande, gigue and fugue – which were exploited to even greater purpose by his twin, Johann Sebastian Bach (see chapter 8). The first six were contemporary dance-measures; in a fugue – *fuga*, literally 'flight' – each vocal or instrumental line entered in turn with the same theme or a slightly modified 'answer' to it (perhaps alongside a 'countertheme'), thereby soon becoming involved in an intricate web of counterpoint. When technique is matched by inspiration a fugue can be one of the most exciting forms of musical expression yet devised; when inspiration is lacking it may be no more than a laborious academic exercise. Many – though not all – of Handel's and Bach's belonged to the former category.

Soon after the collapse of his operatic schemes Handel composed the most popular oratorio of all time – *Messiah* – and then went to Ireland, taking the manuscript along with him. He was rapturously welcomed and the nine months he spent there helped to lighten his depression and stabilize his financial situation: *Messiah* had its world première on 13th April 1742 at the Music Hall (not music-hall) in Fishamble Street, Dublin, where, too, some of his other recent works were much better received than they had been in London. Thenceforth Handel concentrated his attention largely on oratorio, although he also produced the 'Dettingen Te Deum' and the cantata *Semele*; five at least of these oratorios were masterpieces – *Samson, Belshazzar, Solomon, Theodora* and *Jephtha*. It was while he was engaged on *Jephtha* (1752) that his eyesight began to fail; presently he became totally blind. For seven years, with characteristic courage, he went on conducting his own works from memory and actually played the organ at a performance of *Messiah* on 6th April 1759. But by that time he was not only blind but also very ill; a week later, on the evening of Good Friday, he fell into a coma, and he breathed his last before the next day dawned.

As has already been hinted, the dividing line between the

sacred and the secular was not very clearly drawn in mid-eighteenth-century London, and it is significant that of the eight oratorios which followed *Messiah* seven were first given at Covent Garden and one at the theatre in the Haymarket which had been the scene of so many of the composer's former triumphs and disasters. It is even more significant that the practice has been revived of recent years – with stage-performances of such fine works as *Theodora* and *Semele*, which were in danger of falling into undeserved neglect. When revivals of Handel's Italian operas are undertaken, however, there are some tricky problems to be faced.

(1) As in Scarlatti's, the space between the opening and concluding choruses is as a rule filled with a succession of arias and duets connected by recitative, which is normally unaccompanied except by harpsichord *continuo*, although here and there (cf. Scarlatti, page 21), a string orchestra is employed. Eighteenth-century audiences did not think they had had their money's worth inside five hours, while those of the twentieth become restive after two and a half; therefore when Handel's operas are given today ruthless cutting is necessary. It is impracticable to shorten the recitative to any significant extent, since this tells the story, carries on the dramatic action and indeed provides the only logical justification for the work being played on the stage. So inevitably about fifty per cent of the aria/duet content has to be sacrificed, nor can the sacrifice be determined solely on musical grounds: every protagonist must be allowed a due proportion of the vocal say.

(2) In most of Handel's operas at least one of the leading 'male' parts was written for a lyric soprano – or possibly a contralto – who ranked second only to the leading soprano playing the heroine, a procedure later endorsed by Mozart in *Figaro,* Gounod in *Faust* and Strauss in *Der Rosenkavalier*. But Handel's characters were not, as a rule, mere striplings immersed in calf-love like Cherubino, Siebel and Octavian, and one's instinct cries out for masculine representation.

(3) Then there is the problem of casting the roles which

early eighteenth-century convention decreed should be played by *castrati* (male singers who before adolescence had
consented or been forced to undergo castration in order to
prevent their voices from breaking); here the physical attributes of a male-impersonator would often be histrionically
unsatisfying, the penetrating timbre of a falsetto counter-
tenor vocally unsatisfying.

(4) The most logical way out of these difficulties is to take
the bull by the horns and replace all Principal Boys by tenors
and all *castrati* by full-blooded baritones. This involves a
spate of key-transpositions, with consequent re-arrangement
not only of the accompaniments to the arias but also of the
key-sequences in the preceding and subsequent recitative
passages, so that the detailed effect may admittedly in places
be some way from the composer's original intentions; any
compromise solution, however, is unlikely to get much
closer.

Enough has been said, I think, to indicate that anyone
who attempts to prepare a Handel opera for present-day
consumption faces no easy task, but at least he can take
one comfort: so long as he recognizes that neither oboists
nor those who listen to them take kindly to four- or five-
minute sessions of uninterrupted reed-blowing, he will find
that the instrumental balance requires little adjustment:
paradoxically it was in his stage-works rather than in his
concertos that Handel proved himself an early master of
what is nowadays called orchestration, using harps, bassoons,
horns, trumpets and even trombones to obtain quite startling colour-effects.

The expression 'typically Handelian' is often used in
reference to such straightforward evocations of healthy
sentiment as 'For unto us a child is born' (*Messiah*), but in
truth this style was only narrowly typical of Handel himself,
although widely typical of many contemporary composers
among whom he can be seen in retrospect to have been
supreme. The outstanding attribute which earned him supremacy was spontaneous versatility of melodic invention.
'For unto us', let us remember, was followed by 'Rejoice

31

greatly', 'He shall feed His flock', 'Why do the nations' and 'I know that my Redeemer liveth'; therein lay an infinite variety of richness. Nor do some of Handel's other oratorios and cantatas deserve the comparative neglect which has overtaken them. Most of my readers will have had the pleasure, some time, of hearing 'Love in her eyes sits playing', 'Let the bright Seraphim', 'Where e'er you walk' and 'Angels ever bright and fair' – but probably out of their context; few may realize that that they belong respectively to *Acis and Galatea, Samson, Semele* and *Theodora* – although the two last-named (as recorded on page 30) have recently been played on the stage.

Handel's personal character was not untouched by the coarseness of the age in which he lived but he was generous as well as self-indulgent and too sincere, perhaps too obstinate, ever to make a thoroughgoing success of the flair for worldly opportunism with which he is sometimes credited. In any case there was no such element in his approach to his art, which was splendidly and consistently *un*coarse. Inevitably inspiration ebbed and flowed, but for so prolific a composer the pages of tedium or triviality were comparatively rare. He occasionally played down to his public ('See the conquering hero comes' from *Judas Maccabeus* might almost be called a pot-boiler), but his music was rarely unworthy of a reputation which over the centuries has suffered very few ups and downs as generation has succeeded generation, each in turn bringing changes of taste and outlook. Englishmen, at any rate, have never swerved from allegiance to their adopted countryman George Frideric Handel and have always regarded him as an outstanding figure in the history of music. How right they have been!

CHAPTER EIGHT

Bach

During the second half of the sixteenth century and the whole of the seventeenth and eighteenth, the musical life of Thuringia (an area of central Germany roughly bordered by the rivers Werra, Unstrut and Saale) was dominated by the Bach family. No fewer than thirty-eight of the clan – the eldest born in 1520 and the youngest in 1759 – have earned separate articles in *Grove's Dictionary of Music and Musicians*; the first 60,000 or so words of Philip Spitta's standard but unwieldy biography of JOHANN SEBASTIAN BACH (published in 1880) were devoted to the achievements of his great-grandfather, grandfather, father, uncles and other senior relatives; three of Sebastian's own sons (Wilhelm Friedemann, Carl Philip Emmanuel and Johann Christian) distinguished themselves as composers and all-round musicians. Our present concern, however, is with Johann Sebastian himself – the noblest Bach of them all – who was born on 21st March 1685 at Eisenach (midway between Cassel and Erfurt), a medium-sized town nestling in a fertile valley and overlooked by a peak known as the Wartburg (later immortalized as the scene of the song-contest in Wagner's *Tannhäuser*). Today Eisenach is primarily industrial, holds a population of some 40,000 and lies (just) on East German soil; in the seventeenth and early eighteenth centuries it was a noted centre of musical activity, activity in which, almost needless to say, the local branch of the Bachs played a conspicuous part. Young Sebastian probably had his first training, along with the rest, at the local choir-school, but his mother died in 1694, his father in 1695, so at the age of ten he went to live with his elder brother Johann Christoph, recently married, who was municipal choirmaster at Ohrdruf, a smaller town than Eisenach and twenty miles away to the south-east. This Christoph, besides being an organist, was an exponent of the clavichord, an instrument which outwardly resembled the harpsichord but was capable of a small measure of dynamic contrast since the strings were mechanically struck, not plucked, and if the controlling key were pressed down hard the corresponding string continued to vibrate slightly for a few seconds – although not to the same extent as on a modern piano. Sebastian quickly absorbed the technique and it was for the clavichord, as well as the harpsichord, that he later wrote some great keyboard music.

Christoph's family multiplied so rapidly that by 1700 he could no longer give hospitality to his young brother, who, however, was sufficiently fortunate and gifted to win a chorister's scholarship at the Benedictine school of St Michael's at Lüneburg, which lies twenty miles south-east of Hamburg on the edge of Lüneburg Heath.* Bach stayed there about three years and meanwhile developed his powers as instrumentalist (organ, harpsichord, clavichord, violin) rather than as singer or composer. He returned to his home ground in 1703 and for the next four years was organist and choirmaster at Arnstadt (a mere morning's walk away from his brother at Ohrdruf); here he composed a fair quantity of organ music which owed much to the influence of the Scandinavian-born Dietrich Buxtehude, whom Bach greatly admired and indeed travelled to Lübeck to visit, thereby incurring the displeasure of his employers at Arnstadt. Then in 1707 there occurred two events of considerable importance in his career: in June he was installed as organist and choirmaster at the free imperial city of Mühlhausen (fifteen miles north of Eisenach and not to be confused with Mülhausen – now Mulhouse – in Alsace); in October he married his second cousin Maria Barbara Bach – hoping no doubt to ensure that his children would thus be doubly well equipped to carry on the family tradition.

* It was here that on 7th May 1945 General Keitel signed and handed to Field-Marshal Montgomery the instrument of unconditional surrender of all German forces in north-west Germany, Denmark and Holland.

Bach did not stay long at Mühlhausen, for his astonishing virtuosity on the organ was quickly noted in exalted circles and within a year or so he was called upon to join a select musical household at the ducal court of Weimar. (He was still within easy distance of innumerable relatives.) His patron, Duke Wilhelm Ernst of Saxe-Weimar, yielded to none as a feudal overlord, but unlike many other minor potentates of his day he was deeply religious (an austere and indeed ascetic member of the 'pietest' branch of the Lutheran faith); nevertheless he enjoyed his music so long as it was serious in intent and not merely an excuse for irreverent caperings in a dissolute gavotte or licentious minuet. Bach was engaged as court organist and director of chamber music, and it was at Weimar that over the next nine years his talent blossomed into genius; he composed the first thirty or so of his two-hundred-odd Church cantatas and his mastery of at least one branch of composition – organ music – became apparent in such works as the chorale preludes of the *Little Organ Book* and the toccata and fugue in D minor. (I should prefer to call this just the toccata in D minor, because by definition a toccata is a piece of music designed to display executive rather than creative powers; if the composer chooses to round things off with a fugue, well and good, but the fugue remains *part* of the toccata, not a sequel to it. A chorale prelude was in essence an organ voluntary based on a hymn-tune but in Bach's hands it became a polyphonic development of voluntary melodies of such intrinsic worth that the intrusion of the hymn-tune which was its nominal *primum mobile* sometimes, though not always, struck an incongruous note.)

Eventually Bach fell from ducal favour and was passed over when a vacancy occurred in the post of head choirmaster. The reason was a personal one: the strait-laced Duke Wilhelm Ernst had a worldly nephew – Duke Ernst August – of whom he strongly disapproved, and he was furious when he discovered that his organist was on cordial terms with him. The composer's disappointment was short-lived however, for his new friend introduced him to Prince Leopold of Anhalt and before the end of 1717 Bach left Weimar to take charge of the more comprehensive musical establishment which Prince Leopold maintained at his court at Cöthen (equidistant from Magdeburg and Leipzig). His new employer, though no less devoted a churchman than Duke Wilhelm Ernst, was far less bigoted – and indeed was a most enlightened patron of the arts. In this congenial atmosphere Bach set out to tackle instrumental music (almost for the first time) and presently produced some twenty sonatas, either for violin unaccompanied (e.g. the 'chaconne'), for cello unaccompanied, for violin and clavier (a generic term covering harpsichord, clavichord and early types of piano) or for flute and clavier; a handful of orchestral suites; the concerto in D minor for two violins with string accompaniment; above all, the six 'Brandenburg' concertos – so called because they were dedicated to Christian Ludwig, Margrave of Brandenburg. Taken collectively these approximated rather more closely than did most of Handel's to the modern notion of a concerto: although nos. 3 and 6 were for strings and *continuo* only, all the rest had in addition a solo violin, nos. 2, 4 and 5 a solo flute, no. 2 a solo oboe as well, while no. 1 actually called for three solo oboes, a solo bassoon and two solo horns. In no. 5, exceptionally, the clavier-player had a specific part of his own, so that instead of being a mere filler-in he too became a soloist with a laid-down share in the concerting. (No. 1 was in four movements, no. 3 in two, the others in three, and it is interesting to note that all six began and ended in major keys; several of the middle movements, however, were in the relative minor.) Meanwhile the organ was not entirely neglected, for the 'great' preludes and fugues in A minor, C minor and G major belong to the Cöthen period; but during these years Bach's output for a smaller keyboard held greater significance, including as it did the six 'French' suites and the first twenty-four of his famous 'Forty-eight preludes and fugues for well-tempered clavier'. And at this juncture, I fear, there must be a brief theoretical digression.

The sound vibrations which produce musical notes of

varying pitch are attuned to pitch-intervals which are very nearly but not absolutely equal: the interval between E and F, for instance, is not quite the same as that between F and F sharp. The singers and string-players of Bach's day, who had – or should have had – complete control over their intonation, would subconsciously adjust that control when the music modulated from, say, the key of F to the key of E. But when the notes were reproduced mechanically on a keyboard instrument there could be no such almost imperceptible raising or lowering of the pitch, so that a harpsichord or clavichord perfectly in tune for the key of F would become out of tune in the key of E; as a corollary a piece composed for an instrument tuned to F could never modulate to E (nor to any but the most closely related key) without courting disaster. Bach, a traditionalist in many respects, here allied himself with the progressive party which was prepared to sacrifice 'just intonation' in favour of 'equal temperament', i.e. a division of the octave, on keyboard instruments, into twelve identical semitone-intervals. To point the fact he wrote this set of preludes and fugues, twenty-four of them, one each in every major and minor key, and all playable, without disaster, on a single 'well-tempered' clavier.

Bach's stay at Cöthen, which lasted from 1717 until 1723, was extremely productive, but it was clouded by personal tragedy when his wife Maria Barbara died in 1720; she had borne him seven children, of whom four still survived (among them were Wilhelm Friedemann and Carl Phillip Emmanuel). He was one of those who stood in need of a permanent feminine helpmeet, and little more than a year later he married the twenty-year-old soprano Anna Magdalena Wilcken. His second marriage was as happy as the first had been and the union produced thirteen more children; only six survived infancy however (among them was Johann Christian). Meanwhile Bach's patron, Prince Leopold, had himself married a lively young lady named Friederica Henrietta who evidently had little taste for music and no taste at all for the solemnity of chorale preludes, fugues and cantatas; in consequence Bach found himself rather cold-shouldered and sent in his resignation as soon as an opportunity presented itself.

During the remaining twenty-seven years of his life when he was cantor of St Thomas' Church in Leipzig (and as part of his duties had to teach small boys Latin) there must have been many moments when he looked longingly back to his comparatively carefree days at Cöthen. But on the whole he seems to have settled fairly happily to a new way of life, although many tales are told of his disputes with the rector of the school, the university authorities, the Leipzig municipal council and the king of Saxony. Be that as it may, no one could cavil at the quality of the compositions which meanwhile flowed fast from his pen: the best of his Church cantatas; the full-length choral works, the *Passion according to St John*, the *Passion according to St Matthew*, the *Christmas Oratorio* and the *Mass in B minor* (originally conceived as a short Lutheran Mass but later expanded to fit the longer Catholic liturgy); in the secular field the cantatas known as *Phoebus and Pan*, the 'Coffee' and the 'Peasant'; for the orchestra more concertos; for the organ a further set of preludes and fugues including the 'great' B minor, C major and E minor; for the clavier the six 'English' suites, the variations (thirty of them) written for his pupil Johann Gottlieb Goldberg and the second volume of the 'Forty-eight'. At the time of their composition however, these works made little impression on the public (one is inclined to think they might have been better received at Weimar or Eisenach, not so far away to the west in his native Thuringia), and when – like Handel – Bach was stricken by blindness, no one seemed much concerned about it except his wife, Anna Magdalena. His immortal soul went aloft on 28th July 1750 but the burghers of Leipzig apparently cared little, for they erected no monument to his memory and allowed his widow to die in poverty.

Although Handel and Bach were born within a month of one another and spent their boyhood less than a hundred miles apart, they never met: the former's visits to Germany after he settled in London were few and far between, and the latter did not move further afield than Lübeck or Berlin. Bach is unlikely to have been familiar with the music of Handel's maturity and Handel almost certainly never heard a note of Bach's. So although they are inevitably and rightly regarded as twin giants it is not surprising that their music held little in common apart from the easily recognizable harmonic and contrapuntal tendencies which characterized the music of the age rather than that of any individual composer. It has already been stressed that what raised Handel to a higher level than Bononcini and company was an extraordinary gift for varied and contrasted melody; at the risk of over-simplification it might be added that one factor which helped to raise Bach above the level of Buxtehude was an extraordinary gift for varied and contrasted rhythm. At times the initial rhythmic impulse carries a whole movement successfully through to its conclusion – as in the finale of the concerto in D minor for three claviers and strings, and in the short chorus 'Sind Blitze, sind Donner' from the *Matthew Passion*; at others the actual counterpoint seems to spring from the interweaving of rhythmic figures rather than of melodic phrases – as in the prelude in F sharp major from the second book of the 'Forty-eight' and the opening section of the 'Gloria' from the *Mass in B minor*. Bach's technique was indeed so stupendous that now and again he let it be his master rather than his servant, and it cannot be denied that at times his music was in consequence more liable than Handel's to sound uninspired – even dull. On the other hand, when in serious and contemplative mood (which was by no means in Church music alone) he could conjure up a spiritual endowment beyond the imaginings of his contemporary. I shall venture no further on comparative judgement; if Handel himself could have the last word he would no doubt point out that Bach never wrote an opera and that if he had it probably wouldn't have been a very good one.

The oft-quoted affirmation of Robert Schumann that 'music owes as much to Johann Sebastian Bach as Christianity does to its Founder' was the colourful and pardonable exaggeration of an enthusiastic champion (see page 112). One might well concede, however, that the subsequent spread of music owes him as much as the subsequent spread of Christianity did to Saint Paul.

CHAPTER NINE

Gluck

In the early eighteenth century some of the wealthiest men in the Empire (as the Holy Roman Empire had by then become familiarly known) were the princes, archdukes, counts and other notabilities who owned vast tracts of land in both Bohemia and Bavaria; among the many thousands of their retainers was one Alexander Johannes Gluck. He must have been a reliable fellow for he was employed (first as huntsman and then as forester and finally as head forester) at various widely separated feudal estates in turn. That is how it came about that his son CHRISTOPH WILLIBALD GLUCK (1714–87) was born at the Bavarian hamlet of Erasbach in the valley of the river Altmühl (some thirty miles west of Regensburg) and yet spent most of his youth in the woods and fields of northern Bohemia (not far from the Sudeten-land which just over two hundred years later was to earn a measure of unenviable notoriety as a political storm-centre); for a time, too, he studied music at Prague and possibly attended its university. Today therefore, Germans, Czechs and Austrians alike claim Gluck as their own: he was born on what is now West German soil and was nurtured and educated in what is now Czechoslovakia, but both regions were then under Habsburg – i.e. Austrian – domination. Compilers of reference books often sit tactfully on a fence and describe him as Bohemian-German; what matters is that thanks to extensive travel he eventually became a cos-mopolitan European, equally at home in Leipzig, Prague, Vienna, Milan, Rome, Paris, Hamburg and Copenhagen, although not quite so much at home in London – as we shall see presently.

At the age of twenty-two Gluck was made welcome in Vienna under the auspices of his father's employer Prince Lobkowitz, but very soon he discovered a noble patron of his own – Prince Francesco Saverio Melzi, who added him to a private orchestra (in which Gluck apparently played violin and cello indiscriminately) and presently carried him off to Italy, where he embarked upon a lengthy career as composer with the opera *Artaserse* (Milan, 1741). This was followed by nine more operas in the next four years; they were so successful that he was invited to London, where his *Caduta de' giganti* and *Artamene* were produced in 1746 at the King's Theatre, Haymarket. This was after Handel had severed his connexion with that establishment (see page 28), but *Giulio Cesare* and *Alcina* were still remembered, and to London opera-goers Gluck's offerings seemed pale by comparison – as indeed they were. Handel himself was severely critical: 'Gluck knows no more counterpoint than my cook' he asserted (being a gourmet he always chose his cooks carefully), and here he placed a shrewd finger on a weak spot, for Gluck's technique was barely adequate for the tasks which he set himself; the time was yet to come when he would prove that in opera musical technique was not all that mattered.

Dissatisfied with the manner in which he had been received in London he returned to Vienna, where two years later *Semiramide piconosciuta* brought him to the favourable notice of no less a personage than Empress Maria Theresa; thereafter he was *persona grata* in the highest social circles and in 1754 was appointed musical director at the imperial court. Meanwhile he had made further tours abroad (to Italy, Germany, Denmark), composing and producing operas as he went, and in 1750 had married a wealthy Viennese lady named Marianne Pergin. His material future thus assured, Gluck (who never lacked initiative) felt free to indulge in experiment.

On his way from Italy to London in 1746 he had spent some time in Paris, the only western European capital where opera had partially escaped from the shackles of Italian tradition and language – thanks largely to the earnest-minded Jean Philippe Rameau (1683–1764, the outstanding French composer of his generation) and the unassuming

François Philidor (composer of *comédies à ariettes*). Gluck, who had hitherto adopted the pattern of *opera seria* inaugurated by Alessandro Scarlatti (see page 20) and subscribed to by Handel, may well have been impressed by the unconventionality of the (French) libretti which Rameau had chosen and by his unconventional treatment of them – especially in recitative passages. At all events, during the next few years he devoted some of his time to studying poetry, literature and drama, and soon came to the conclusion that what opera needed was closer integration between words and music. Very wisely, instead of rushing in where angels might have feared to tread, he felt his way carefully by first providing the Austrian court with a series of French comic operas *à la* Philidor – of which the first was *Les Amours champêtres* (1755) and the most succesful *L'Ile de Merlin* (1758). Meanwhile he made contact with an enlightened Italian writer named Raniera da Calzabigi, and between them in due course they fashioned *Orfeo ed Eurydice*, which had its first performance at Vienna on 5th October 1762. This was a turning point not only in Gluck's career but also in the history of opera, for in *Orfeo* drama and music were fused to an entity by partial elimination of the formal absurdities catalogued on pages 30–31 (paragraphs 2 and 3), by reduction to a minimum of the incongruous contrast between *recitativo secco* and florid vocalism, and by granting the chorus a larger share in the proceedings than had hitherto been customary. In the next two Calzabigi/Gluck operas – *Alceste* (1767) and *Paride ed Elena* (1770) – the policy of integration was carried a stage further and in 1773 the composer was encouraged by his ex-pupil Marie Antoinette (Maria Theresa's daughter, by now Dauphine of France and presently to be its Queen) to set a French libretto based on Jean Racine's translation from Euripides – *Iphigénie en Aulide*. Accordingly he travelled to Paris, where not only the new work itself but also French versions of *Orfeo* and *Alceste* made a profound impression; ardent nationalists acclaimed him as a worthy successor to their own Rameau and were almost inclined to regard him

43

as a naturalized Frenchman. On the other hand he had to face noisy opposition from the adherents of Nicola Piccinni, a talented Italian composer of conventional *opera seria* and Frenchified *opera buffa*. Over the next few years the Gluckists and Piccinnists made confounded nuisances of themselves by trying to stir up trouble between the two composers, who to their credit refused to join in the acrimonious debates and remained throughout on terms of cordiality, if not of mutual admiration. Gluck conclusively established his artistic supremacy with *Armide* (1777), *Iphigénie en Tauride* and *Echo et Narcisse* (both 1779); he then returned to Vienna, where he lived in extremely comfortable retirement until eight years later, when he died of a stroke at the age of seventy-three.

Despite the fact that for many years 'Che farò senza Eurydice' was accounted one of the world's best tunes, Gluck was in truth no more distinguished as a melodist than as a contrapuntist (although Piccinni never compared his rival with his *chef de cuisine*). What cannot be gainsaid is that he was endowed with the instinct and good sense to realize what was wrong with opera and the diligence and ability to demonstrate in practice how it could be put right. From 1790 onwards old-fashioned *opera seria* gradually fell into neglect in France, the Netherlands and Germany; it even took a back seat in Vienna. The reason was that Christoph Willibald Gluck, with *Alceste*, *Iphigénie en Aulide* and the rest, had in effect inaugurated a new art-form – which no one had as yet had the brain-wave to call music drama.

CHAPTER TEN

Haydn

JOSEPH HAYDN was born on 31st March, 1732 at the village of Rohrau, thirty miles east of Vienna on the verge of that low-lying region round the Neusiedlersee (Fertö Tava) which has always been a bone of political contention between Austria and Hungary. Rohrau, although typically Hungarian in lay-out (single-storied cottages set far back from the grass-lined road), was – and is – on Austrian territory, but the border was not far away and the inhabitants were of mixed racial descent; nor were the elements exclusively Austrian and Magyar, for during the seventeenth century there had been a surge of immigrants to this indeterminate no-man's-land both from 'high Germany' (Baden, Württemberg, Bavaria) and from Croatia (now part of Yugoslavia). It is probable that two at least of Haydn's great-grandparents came from high Germany and that he also had Croatian blood in his veins; be that as it may he was Austrian by birth. Since the local landowner employed his father as a coach-repairer (later as a bailiff) and his mother as a kitchen-maid (later as a cook) he enjoyed, in the words of Hubert Parry, the advantages of a thoroughly plebeian extraction.

When he was six he was sent to live with an uncle (schoolmaster and choirmaster at the nearby town of Hainburg overlooking the Danube) who in 1740 arranged for him to enter the cathedral school of St Stephen's, Vienna; a few years later he was joined there by his younger brother Michael.* They sang in the cathedral choir and meanwhile received a sound education, but Joseph's boyish exuberance continually led him into stupid pranks and as soon as his voice broke – at the unusually late age of seventeen – he was summarily dismissed under a cloud of official disap-

* Michael Haydn became well known as an organist and composer; among his pupils was Carl Maria von Weber (chapter 13).

proval. During the difficult years that followed he scraped a bare living by singing and playing in the streets of Vienna, but was eventually befriended by the stage comedian Joseph Kurz for whom he composed a comic opera (*The Crooked Devil*), by the versatile Niccola Porpora (composer, singer, pedagogue) for whom he acted both as valet and accompanist, and finally by two grandees named Baron von Fürnberg and Count Morzin who in turn engaged him as 'private musician'; between-whiles he augmented his meagre earnings by giving singing lessons. The excellence of Count Morzin's private music brought Haydn to the notice of Prince Paul Anton Esterházy, wealthiest of all wealthy Hungarian noblemen, who promptly offered him the post of assistant musical director at his court at Eisenstadt (twenty-five miles south of Vienna) with a good prospect of presently taking complete control; Haydn jumped at the chance and thereafter his livelihood was assured.

In domestic affairs he was less fortunate: in 1760 he married one of his pupils, Maria Anna Keller, and for the next forty years (she died in 1800) both bitterly regretted it. Haydn, who had little experience in such matters, seems to have been trapped into marriage with a woman who had no intention of giving him wifely help or encouragement and even, by one account, used his scores for curl-papers; in course of time his frequent infidelities (for boyish exuberance never deserted him) drove her to devote herself to good works, which according to his biographer Rosemary Hughes (with whom I cannot claim kinship) consisted mainly of 'entertaining at their house a continuous and distracting procession of clergy'.

Prince Paul Anton Esterházy, as it happened, died a few months after Haydn took up his appointment at Eisenstadt, but his brother Nicolas (who succeeded to the title and estates) was an equally enthusiastic patron; the expected promotion to full directorship of the musical establishment coincided with the building of a magnificent new palace, known henceforth as Esterháza, on the site of a former shooting-lodge at Süttor in the desolate marshland south-east of the Neusiedlersee. Haydn's position in the household was no easy one, for his time was divided between Eisenstadt and Esterháza, he had entire charge of a valuable collection of musical instruments and was furthermore responsible for the behaviour (both on and off duty) of a motley crowd of resident singers and players – to say nothing of guest artists. The routine duties were indeed so onerous that at first he found it a hard struggle to fulfil the clause in his contract which stipulated that he 'should compose at all times whatever works His Highness might require', but he soon evolved a satisfactory *modus vivendi* and over the ensuing period of years no one could have made better use of such golden opportunities. Prior to entering the service of the Esterházy family in 1761 he had produced *The Crooked Devil* and perhaps three dozen instrumental works including string quartets and miniature symphonies. By the time he left it in 1790 (with a generous pension) the number of his operas had grown to fifteen, of string quartets to sixty-two, of symphonies to ninety-one; five Masses, forty-odd piano sonatas (the piano was by then gradually replacing both the harpsichord and the clavichord) and a huge quantity of miscellaneous shorter works had been thrown in for good measure. Many of the delightful string quartets and symphonies of this Eisenstadt/Esterháza period – and at least one of the operas, *L'infedeltà delusa* – have been revived of recent years, but Haydn is still mainly remembered for his subsequent compositions, notably the oratorios *The Creation* and *The Seasons,* the 'Nelson' and 'Theresa' Masses, the last three piano sonatas, the last dozen or so string quartets, a ninety-second symphony (celebrating a visit to Oxford where he was installed as honorary Doctor of Music) and twelve further symphonies (nos. 93–104) written in London at the behest of the concert impresario J. P. Salomon. It was during the 1790s that Haydn, who by that time had retired to Vienna, was twice welcomed in Britain (he had previously never seen the sea) and developed an attachment for the country; besides the symphonies he published six collections of Scottish and Welsh folk-song arrangements (about four hundred all told). After the turn of the century, however, he virtually abandoned both travel and composition, and he died on 31st May 1809 during Vienna's occupation by the victorious troops of Napoleon Bonaparte, then well on the way to becoming master of Europe. It is pleasant to be able to record that the respect due to a musical genius overrode military etiquette: at Haydn's memorial service the guard of honour comprised a mixed detachment of French soldiery and Austrian civil guards.

Haydn lived longer than any other famous composer belonging to the eighteenth century and, moreover, his life spanned an era of change. Born when the Turks, though the Ottoman Empire was by then in decline, still maintained a stranglehold on the Balkans and were therefore a menace to Catholic Austria from the east, he lived long enough to find his homeland prey to aggression from the west; meanwhile he survived the War of the Austrian Succession and the Seven Years' War – and like everyone else in Europe felt the impact, however indirectly, of the French Revolution. On a more peaceful level it should be noted that he was already at school when Handel wrote his *Messiah* and yet lived to hear Beethoven's *Fidelio*. In early days he was profoundly influenced by C. P. E. Bach (see page 37), talented son of a famous father and, moreover, largely responsible for inaugurating that astonishing manifestation of artistic ingenuity known as 'sonata form', a subtle *ABAB* evolution combining the features of binary form (*AB*) and ternary form (*ABA*). Since almost every composer worthy of the name, from the mid-eighteenth century to the mid-twentieth, has at some time or other written pieces in sonata form (or some barely disguised modification of it) the term will crop up time and again in the ensuing pages and it will be as well to indicate, at this juncture, the basic characteristics.

A movement in sonata form starts with an exposition of tune *A*, usually a vigorous and masculine affair, which establishes the tonic (main) key. Next comes a bridge passage, possibly based on *A*, which leads to the exposition of a contrasted and often 'feminine' tune *B* (the 'second subject') in a different but closely related key – e.g. G major against C major or E flat major against C minor. There follows a development section in which *A* and *B*, or fragments of them, are tossed hither and thither in any key the composer chooses (bar the tonic) and their hidden potentialities are exploited to the best of his ability. This eventually leads back to a recapitulation of *A* (often a straightforward repetition) followed by an amended bridge passage and a recapitulation of *B*, which this time however is presented in the tonic key; sometimes a coda (tailpiece) rounds things off.

Historians have been at pains to point out that Haydn did not *invent* either the string quartet (for two violins, viola and cello) or the symphony (for a larger band incorporating both string and wind instruments); none the less he established their basic form of construction. The early quartets of his Fürnberg and Morzin days were nearly all in five movements – fast, minuet, slow, minuet, fast – but presently he discarded the second minuet, thus leaving four movements (as compared with the standard three movements of duos, trios and concertos), in one or two of which at least (an innovation) the melodic outline, rather than being a mere violin solo, was subjected to thematic development on all four instruments. As nearly as I can calculate Haydn composed forty-six string quartets for the exclusive enjoyment (initially) of his Esterházy employers, and it will be worth while to pinpoint some of their structural characteristics. I have omitted from the reckoning op. 51, a set of seven single-movement 'sonatas' for the same combination of instruments transcribed from an earlier orchestral work illustrating *The Seven Words of Our Saviour on the Cross*.)

(1) The forty-six quartets all comprised four movements.

(2) Of their first movements forty-three were fast or moderately fast and in sonata form; three were themes with variations, slow or moderately slow.

(3) The finale (last movement) was invariably fast: in four cases it was a fugue.

(4) One of the two middle movements was always a minuet,

49

which in the earlier quartets was usually placed second but was later more likely to be placed third, thus predicating the traditional order of fast, slow, minuet, fast.

(5) Although the majority of the opening and closing movements were in square time (2/4, 4/4, or 2/2), there were seventeen instances of 3/8 or 6/8 and six (all in first movements) of fairly fast 3/4.

(6) Of the forty-six Esterházy quartets only nine were 'minor' (which means, by convention, that they *started* in a minor key) and two of these nine *ended* in the major; of their eighteen middle movements eleven were in closely related major keys.

(7) In every one of the thirty-seven 'major' quartets the minuet was in the main key of the work and the other middle movement – nearly always slow – in a different but closely related key: twenty in the subdominant major; eight in the dominant major; nine in the tonic minor; none, curiously enough, in the relative minor, which nowadays one would regard as equally logical and which indeed was used by Haydn himself in several of his other instrumental works.

These statistics are presented not for the sake of pedantry but to make clear precisely how much his younger contemporaries – including the most illustrious among them – owed Haydn for evolving such an admirable and reasonably flexible form of construction, which gave opportunity for appropriately varied contrasts of form, tempo, rhythm and key – and, incidentally, was applicable not only to string quartets but also, *mutatis mutandis*, to symphonies.

In the symphonies of Haydn's full maturity – including all twelve 'Salomons' – he displayed that perfection of utterance which one associates with his music at its best. Here and there, as in the magnificent *adagio cantabile* of no. 98, he plumbed unwonted depths of feeling, but perhaps their main attractions lie in the straightforward tunefulness of the first movements and the sheer jollity of the finales – notably those of nos. 97, 98, 100 and 101.

Uninhibited jollity (the boyish exuberance which led him into scrapes at school) was one of Haydn's most endearing traits, and it cropped up as frequently in his string quartets as in his symphonies. Indeed in his Esterházy days he had not always lived up to the tenet which inspired Thomas Dunhill's solemn dictum in *Chamber Music* (1913) that 'there is absolutely no excuse for setting forth music to be played by four trained and sensitive musicians which could as well be interpreted by the average fiddlers of a restaurant or beer-garden'. But the six quartets of ops. 71 and 74 (composed in Vienna between his two London visits) and the eight of ops. 76 and 77 (composed after the second visit there) show that, by that time, Haydn was in agreement with Dunhill that 'there is a certain dignity to be upheld in dealing with the string-quartet form'. Admittedly light-heartedness is the key-note of the whole of op. 74 no. 2 and of many single movements from nearly all the other thirteen, but 'dignified' would be an appropriate epithet to apply to op. 76 nos. 3 and 5 and op. 77 no. 2. In these quartets and the piano trios of the same decade – notably that in D major usually called no. 6 – one feels that Haydn was already beginning to teach Beethoven. (Here I use the word 'teach' to imply example rather than precept, although Haydn did actually give Beethoven a few lessons in composition when the latter settled in Vienna in 1792 – see page 65.)

The oratorios *The Creation* and *The Seasons* were composed during the late 1790s to libretti by Baron Gottfried van Swieten (Dutch by birth, Viennese by adoption, diplomat by calling, *littérateur* and musician by inclination). Van Swieten's *Creation* was based on his own German version of Milton's *Paradise Lost*; *The Seasons* on his own German version of a less well-known poem by the Scottish writer James Thomson (who flourished during the first half of the eighteenth century). Perhaps *The Seasons* should really rank as a cantata rather than an oratorio, for parts of it are distinctly earthy and it is only at the very end that religion comes into the picture; so far as Haydn is concerned it was a rather uneven production which surprisingly showed this sunny composer to best advantage in the winter freeze-up, where the steady tempo and persistent semiquaver accompaniment of 'Let the wheel move gaily' set a precedent for many later spinning-songs – e.g. Schubert's *Gretchen am Spinnrade* (see page 81) and the opening chorus of Act II from Wagner's *Flying Dutchman. The Creation* on the other hand was unquestionably an oratorio and, moreover, a landmark in the history of the genre, for it bridged the gap between Handel's *Messiah* (1742, see page 29) and Mendelssohn's *Elijah* (1846, page 96). In this country *The Creation* is still usually given in van Swieten's own re-translation from German back to (very Teutonic) English, since a scholarly and in many respects acceptable revision of the text by A. H. Fox-Strangways and Steuart Wilson (1930) has been slow to make headway against such lovable absurdities of phraseology as 'Cheerful roaring stands the tawny lion' and 'In long dimensions creeps with sinuous trace the worm'; nor are traditionalists convinced that 'The fields are dressed in living green' marks worthwhile improvement on the more familiar 'With verdure clad the fields appear'. The *musical* creation, from the first open octave of the 'Representation of Chaos' (which, thank goodness, is not a representation of 'chaos') to the last bar of the final fugal chorus, suggests that the heavens were telling Haydn his every move, and rationalists should not scoff when they read that 'he knelt down every day and prayed God to strengthen him for his work'. Let them recall, if they wish, that the humorously descriptive orchestral treatment of the roaring lion and the creeping worm caused the composer a few moments of spiritual unease and drove him to expose his simple philosophy in one short sentence.

I hope that God will not be angry if I am irrepressibly cheerful in my worship of Him.

One is reminded that in the mid-eighteenth century it was still assumed that the primary purpose of music outside church was to *entertain*. Joseph Haydn remained to the end an entertainer; in an era of artistic *Sturm und Drang* he was blessedly unaware of any moral obligation to espouse a cause or join a noble army, being content merely to find out musical tunes. 'Classical' *par excellence*, he stood in sharp contrast to such notable reformers – in their respective fields – as Gluck, Goethe, Schiller and Beethoven, for he was concerned not so much with making the world better as with making it happier.

CHAPTER ELEVEN

Mozart

In the 1750s when Joseph Haydn, expelled from school, was still a struggling Viennese street-busker, there lived a hundred and fifty miles away to the west at Salzburg (on the third floor of the house now numbered 9 Getreidegasse) a worthy musician named Leopold Mozart and his wife Anna Maria, *née* Pertl. Of their six children only two survived for more than a few months: one was a girl, the other a boy. The girl, born in July 1751 and christened Maria Anna, was a clever child who had already learnt to play the harpsichord by the time her brother Wolfgang Amadeus Mozart joined the family circle on 27th January 1756. *His* aptitude for music was even more extraordinary: at the age of three his prowess on harpsichord and piano rivalled that of his seven-year-old sister, and he started to compose when he was five. The pieces Wolfgang wrote in those days were short and simple but, far from resembling the jejune efforts of most infantile composers, they were competent little affairs and would hardly be out of place in (say) the Papageno scenes of *The Magic Flute*, which belonged to his last year on earth.

Presently Leopold Mozart resigned the permanent post which he held at the court of the Archbishop of Salzburg (Sigismund von Schrattenbach) in order to exploit – and who shall blame him? – the precocity of his children. From 1762 until 1766 he exhibited them in turn at Munich, Vienna, Brussels, Paris, London, the Hague, Berne, Zürich – and between-whiles at many other centres of musical culture in western Europe. Everywhere they went, and above all in Paris, the Mozart prodigies were acclaimed and fêted. When they returned to Salzburg 'sister Nannerl' had become a mature young lady of fourteen and Wolfgang an oncoming adolescent of ten. Having already completed many instrumental and choral works which demonstrated instinctive ability and exceptional talent in melodic construction, in harmony, even in counterpoint and orchestration, he was now determined to tackle opera; after a year or so in Vienna (where he composed *La finta semplice* and *Bastien und Bastienne*) his father took him on two tours of Italy (*Mitridate* and *Lucio Silla*).* They were followed, after a short stay at home, by return visits to Vienna and northern Italy (and the composition of *La finta giardiniera*, the most accomplished of his teenage operas). By this time, however, Leopold Mozart had re-entered the service of the Church and the new Archbishop (Hieronymus von Colloredo) held strong views on absenteeism; consequently, when in 1777 Wolfgang, never a time-waster, set out from Salzburg for a second visit to Paris it was his mother and not his father who accompanied him. They broke their journey at Mannheim where he fell in love with Aloysia Weber, daughter of a well-known local musician and herself a promising soprano singer. His feelings appeared to be reciprocated but there was no formal engagement.

Thus far Mozart's career, despite occasional disappointments and difficulties, had on the whole been astonishingly successful; his character had remained unspoilt because he was inwardly content in the knowledge that success had been achieved through hard work and merit. This happy state of affairs was too good to last: in Paris the fickle public which fifteen years earlier had been so eager to applaud an infant phenomenon was now indifferent; Mozart's sole new compositions of any importance were the charming ballet *Les Petits riens* and the 'Paris' symphony. Moreover, for the first time in his life he was brought face to face with personal tragedy when his devoted mother fell ill and died. A few months later he turned his back on Paris for ever and rejoined the Webers – who meanwhile had moved their home to Munich. Here he learnt that Aloysia had just run away

---

* Nannerl was left behind; she later married into the nobility and eventually outlived not only her husband and her brother but also Beethoven, Weber and Schubert.

with an actor; this crowning blow shattered his nerves, and it was a thoroughly disillusioned young musician who slunk back to Salzburg early in 1779. He was only twenty-three but already the wheel of fortune had revolved through a full cycle.

Leopold Mozart helped to restore his son's self-respect by securing him a permanent job as organist at the court of his own employer, Archbishop Hieronymus. This appointment gave Wolfgang a chance to settle down, and rather more than a year later he completed his most ambitious opera yet – *Idomeneo*. The libretto was inept, but it had the practical advantage of having been written by a clerical colleague at the ecclesiastical court, and his new employer viewed the first production at Munich with favour; presently he summoned its composer to join him, not at his palace in Salzburg, but at the more modest establishment which he maintained in Vienna. Here Mozart took his meals in the servants' hall. 'The two valets,' he wrote to his father, 'sit at the head of the table, and I have the honour to be placed above the cooks; during dinner there is a good deal of coarse silly joking, but not with me, for I do not speak a word but what I am obliged, and that with the greatest circumspection.' Not being sufficiently well educated to appreciate the prevailing niceties of social precedence, Mozart complained of his treatment to his lordship's high steward, but the interview had a hurtful ending: according to the historian Otto Jahn the high steward literally kicked him out. ('[Dann] warf er ihn mit einem Fusstritt zur Tür hinaus.') Fortunately however – and partly through the agency of Christian Gottlob Stephanie, a man-of-the-theatre who had an *entrée* to court circles – Mozart's talents were soon brought to the notice of none other than Emperor Joseph II, who was keenly interested in music and saw no reason why operas should nearly always be settings of *Italian* words. Mozart was therefore encouraged to embark upon a *German* opera – to be neither too light nor too heavy – and forthwith produced *Die Entführung aus dem Serail* (libretto by Stephanie) which had it first performance in July 1782.

Although very well received – by the aged Gluck, among others – it failed to break down the long-standing tradition that Italian was the language of opera and, indeed, is itself more generally known (except in German-speaking countries) as *Il Seraglio*.*

After his hasty departure from the arch-episcopal household Mozart had gone to live with his old friends the Webers – now settled in Vienna – and had transferred his affections to Aloysia's younger sister Constanze. A few weeks after the successful production of his new opera (whose heroine was named after her) they became man and wife. Leopold Mozart was furious, for he had always regarded the Weber family with disapproval – and in truth they were a very easy-going and bohemian crowd. When the wedding took place he relented to the extent of sending a conventional message of good wishes, but the closely sympathetic relationship between father and son, which already for some years had been showing signs of strain, was now completely severed. (Leopold, who died five years later, was in many ways a tyrannical parent, but he deserves credit for having done all in his power to promote contemporary world-wide recognition of the incomparable genius whom he had begotten.) Constanze, now Mrs Mozart, was in almost every respect the exact opposite of Mrs Haydn: she was devoted to her husband and genuinely anxious to further his success but far too scatterbrained (and possibly, be it whispered, too intemperate) ever to make a good housewife. Consequently Mozart's marriage, unlike Haydn's, paid reasonable dividends – but it showed little capital appreciation: except when professional engagements took him away from Vienna (to Salzburg, Berlin, Leipzig, Dresden, Prague) he led a disordered existence in frowsy and uncomfortable lodgings. An occasional guest was Haydn – when up in town from Eisenstadt or Esterháza; the two men very properly formed a mutual admiration society, and with Constanze's en-

* *Die Entführung* was, strictly speaking, a *Singspiel* (song-play), that is to say a work in which songs were interspersed with spoken dialogue.

thusiasm outweighing her other shortcomings Mozart set out to produce his finest masterpieces.

Every musician owes a debt of gratitude to the Austrian bibliographer Ludwig von Köchel, who in the early 1860s compiled a comprehensive catalogue of Mozart's works (revised in 1937 by Alfred Einstein). The 'Köchel numbers' are invaluable for identifying pieces with no specific title and are in reasonably accurate chronological sequence. Mozart's output during the first eight years or so of his married life comprised roughly K.390 to K.565 inclusive, and if any student runs his eye down that list he will agree, I think, that it includes most of the works in which the composer touched the heights of supremacy that have assured him of immortality. Here is a selection.

(*a*) The 'Linz' and 'Prague' symphonies (K.425 and 504) where Mozart came strongly under the influence of Haydn and which at the time of their composition were unsurpassed for beauty of melody, clarity of expression and technical assurance.

(*b*) The Fantasy in C minor (K.475) which was the summit point of his music for keyboard alone and was notable for some astonishingly daring harmonic sequences.

(*c*) No less than sixteen piano concertos which are all so excellent that it would be invidious to single out any as pre-eminent; yet at grievous personal risk I venture to suggest that K.453, 466, 467, 488, 491 and 503 are the pick of the bunch.

(*d*) The so-called 'Haydn set' of six string quartets, all of which approach perfection; the superb string quintet in G minor (K.516, five movements) which achieves it; six trios for violin, cello and piano of almost comparable merit.

(*e*) The captivating orchestral serenade entitled *Eine kleine Nachtmusik* (K.525).

(*f*) The operas *The Impresario* (one act), *The Marriage of Figaro*, *Don Giovanni* and *Così fan tutte*. *Figaro*, if played in the right spirit and judiciously cut in Act IV, is the best *opera buffa* ever written – with *Così fan tutte* as runner-up. That *Don Giovanni* is often regarded nowadays as an *opera seria* should not blind one to the fact that it was dubbed by its composer as a *dramma giocoso*. (Although Mozart was not insensitive to Gluck, all these operas adhered, in general, to Italian tradition.)

(*g*) Three works which remain supreme examples of classical symphony: K.543 in E flat major, K.550 in G minor and K.551 in C major (the 'Jupiter'), where Mozart improved upon Haydn's manner with an intensity of feeling which the elder man had never (so far) been able to express.

All these superb compositions (in which his astonishing flair for creating, developing and instrumenting melodies of great beauty reached its apex) belonged to the years 1782–90, a period during which Mozart was enjoying fairly good health, and when in December 1790 he took a somewhat emotional farewell of Joseph Haydn on the eve of the latter's departure for London his sole misgiving was on behalf of his ageing friend who had never previously ventured abroad and might not be able, he felt, to stand the strain of all that tiring travel. Mozart underestimated both the strength of Haydn's constitution (he lived for another eighteen years) and his own unfortunate tendency towards neurasthenia – which now became increasingly evident.

The following summer (Constanze had gone to the country to recuperate from illness) he was at work simultaneously on the clarinet concerto K.622 (a carefree composition), *La Clemenza di Tito* (an operatic *pièce d'occasion*) and *The Magic Flute*, which was the brain-child of a clever and unscrupulous impresario named Emanuel Schikaneder whose pantomimic German libretto appealed to the composer (contradictorily both a practising Catholic and a practising Freemason). Planned, like *Die Entführung*, as a *Singspiel*, *The Magic Flute* contained some of Mozart's most sublime music (as well as some of his most naïve) but all along he was obsessed with a feeling of frustration; presently the taut threads began to snap and he fell prey to morbid depression. When he received a mysterious commission to compose a Requiem from a tall dark stranger (who later turned out to be little more than a leg-puller) the shadows were grievously lengthening and he became convinced that this was to be his own Requiem. And so it proved: on 5th December 1791 (the Requiem still incomplete) he died after a fit of delirium.

There was an element of pathos about it all: old and true friends like his father and Haydn were either dead or far away; new fair-weather friends like Schikaneder and his associates proved broken reeds; Constanze, hysterical with grief, was incapable of coping with the emergency. So Wolfgang Amadeus Mozart, the greatest composer of his generation and perhaps of all time, received a pauper's burial: to this day his grave is unidentified. His memorial lies in his music – the finest memorial anyone could wish for.

CHAPTER TWELVE

Beethoven

When I was a small boy the master who had to correct my fortnightly 'essays' used to insist that they should stress only the best features of the subject under discussion, skirt round any defects and avoid deleterious comparisons. But I think I was unconvinced then as I am now that an essayist should necessarily be an advocate. The putting forward of all points *pro* to the exclusion of those *con* has a proper function in any mutual exchange of views between the knowledgeable few, but when standing alone is liable to produce a false impression on the uninitiated many, who may never hear the other side of the argument and cannot be expected to read between the lines or recognize the significance of what counsel for the defence has (purposely) left unsaid. The reputations of many painters, poets, authors and composers have on balance lost more than they have gained through such well-intentioned but unthinking advocacy, often misinterpreted as implying adulation and thereby laying itself open to superficial counter-attack.

No famous composer has suffered more in this respect than LUDWIG VAN BEETHOVEN. It would be a relatively simple matter to put his enemies to flight and his detractors to shame, did one not simultaneously face the task of saving him from friends blind to his weaknesses and from champions determined to ignore them. Since friends and champions have included such honoured figures as George Grove and Donald Tovey the rescue operation is a delicate one, and it is with trepidation that I propound the theory that both these distinguished essayists followed too closely the precepts of my old English master. Grove was a very trustworthy biographer but some of his more pompous pronouncements on his idol's music should not be taken too seriously. Every student is in debt to Tovey for his six classic volumes of *Essays in Musical Analysis* (nearly all based on extended programme-notes for the Reid orchestral concerts in Edinburgh which he conducted from 1914 until his death in 1940), and in programme-notes he was often justified in eschewing deleterious comparisons; indeed it is fascinating to observe the forensic skill with which he conscientiously made out a good case for composers with whom he was temperamentally out of sympathy – Tchaikovsky, for example. But his warmth of feeling for Beethoven led him to become a skirter-round and even to declare (in another book) that 'what Beethoven does I accept as evidence' – which was surely tantamount to saying that he was prepared to find everyone else out of step. Now although Beethoven was honoured during his lifetime and on his death, he became a puzzle to the immediately succeeding generation and it needed the fervent propaganda of Berlioz and Liszt to spread his fame round the continent in the 1850s and 1860s; in Britain it was not until the George Grove days of the late nineteenth century that he was deified and it became blasphemy not to fall down and pay homage. When the twentieth century was under way the inevitable reaction set in and the *avant-garde* began to denounce him as nothing more than a sacred cow of the Victorians. Fortunately vituperation of this sort, understandable enough in the prevailing climate of musical opinion, caused broadminded scholars to realize that a detached approach was overdue. In 1905 Ernest Walker, a staunch admirer of all that was best in Beethoven, went so far as to admit that 'compared with many of the great composers his output is distinctly unequal'; one work was castigated for its 'uncouth inconsequence'. Walker, though a traditionalist, was a wise and upright judge. His high-pitched verbal comments on a more recent and briefer assessment by my colleague Norman Suckling (incorporated in his valuable study of Gabriel Fauré!) might not be entirely unsympathetic; it would be only a friendly bone that he had to pick with Jean Renoir, who observed that 'Beethoven is positively indecent the way he tells us about himself; he doesn't spare us either the pain in his heart or the pain in his stomach'. (Although Renoir's metaphor was blunt he here scored a shrewd and palpable hit, hammering home that Beethoven, instead of emulating say Bach or Mozart as an objective observer of human emotions, forced his own emotions on a world which was at first too stunned to accept the proposition that he was a superman – and later too stunned to reject it.) Despite the fair-minded Walkers, the sceptical Sucklings and the outspoken Renoirs, many music lovers regard Beethoven as the greatest composer that ever lived – and there can be no complaint about that so long as they don't hold the opinion merely because they have been told to. He was in any case the greatest born between 1756 and 1797 and, moreover, was endowed with definable attributes which set him apart from any predecessor or contemporary – and which must be noted right away.

Beethoven is the first composer we have met who might be described as a rebel, for his career was spent in a struggle not only against poverty and ill-health (common enough adversaries) but also against anything that he rated as unjust in politics or unworthy in art. This outlook drove him to choose an unusual *modus operandi*: in his sketch books (mercifully preserved) one can trace in detail how preliminary jottings-down of a few notes led eventually to the emergence of the finally polished article. They have a further and less technical interest, since they make it clear that some of his finest works, so far from being spontaneous inspirations of the moment, had gradually evolved in his mind, and on paper, over many years. From the outset of the tonal era until Beethoven's day nearly all music held a measure of predictability: every phrase, every bar, sometimes even every note, was an explicit thread in the tapestry; with composers of the Bach/Mozart calibre there was often a *perfection* of seeming inevitability where any alternative phrase or bar or even note would have been unthinkable. Beethoven's was a different sort of perfection and inevitability had little to do with it. His sketch books show that the goal was reached through a slow and painful process of conscious striving; as Romain Rolland put it, 'once he takes hold upon an idea, he never lets it go until he possesses it wholly'. Consequently his music is rarely predictable in the sense that one might apply the term – without any disapprobation – to much of Bach's or Mozart's; indeed, one of Beethoven's outstanding characteristics is his *un*predictability. Bolts from the blue like the 'irrelevant roaring C sharp' (Tovey's phrase) in the finale of the eighth symphony have been and no doubt will continue to be interpreted according to taste as strokes of genius, as good jokes, as bad jokes, or as attacks of indigestion. But whatever else they may have been they were unquestionably part of the essence of Beethoven – which had nothing in common with the essence of Bach. Nor for that matter had it as much in common with the essence of Brahms as has sometimes been made out : the grouping together of these composers as the three Bs was merely a convenient and rather inept analogy favoured by the pious 'Brahmins' of the 1880s (see page 163). No; Beethoven was emphatically not a middleman between Bach and Brahms. On the contrary, he was the propagator of an entirely new line of descent leading through Berlioz and Liszt to Wagner, all of whom were tarred with the same revolutionary brush and adopted much the same approach to the problems of musical composition – with (as we shall see later in this book) varying degrees of success.

Beethoven was partly Flemish by ancestry (please note that he was Ludwig van, not Ludwig von) but for fifty years or so before his birth his grandfather and father had earned their keep by playing or singing at the court of the Elector of Cologne and it was at Bonn (515 – now 20 – Bonnstrasse) that he first saw the light of day on 16th December 1770. Few composers were less addicted to travel : during his teens (when he displayed extraordinary ability as a pianist, particularly in extemporization) he never left his native Rhineland except for a trip to Vienna in 1787; when he went there again in 1792 he realized that the Austrian capital was his spiritual home – and for the rest of his life he lived either there or at nearby Mödling on the edge of the Wienerwald. Somewhat unprepossessing in appearance and brusque in behaviour, Beethoven was no ladies' man, and although he fell in love once or twice he remained a bachelor. For practical purposes, therefore, the record of his life is the record of his music.

He did not take seriously to composition until he settled in Vienna where for a time he studied with Haydn and others, but he was an awkward pupil: he was already in his twenties and when he did not see eye to eye with his teachers he adopted an attitude of aggressive self-assurance; formal lessons were soon abandoned by mutual consent and he came to rely not so much on tuition as on intuition. During the nine years 1792 to 1800 inclusive he composed eleven piano sonatas (the best of which were op. 10 no. 3 and op. 13, the 'Pathétique'), the concert aria *Adelaide* (a fine song, splendidly representative of this early period), four violin sonatas of no more than average merit, two piano concertos each of which held its charm but neither of which was remarkable, six string quartets, one symphony and a host of less important pieces. The quartets (op. 18) were stylistically in the Haydn manner but in all but one of them Beethoven replaced the traditional minuet with a faster 'scherzo' – literally 'joke'. (In no. 4, which did incorporate a minuet, the fugal second movement was *entitled* a scherzo.) His first symphony, too, owed much to Haydn; it is so pleasant to listen to – and in the third movement (designated a minuet but in effect a scherzo) presages such mastery – that it may be captious to point out that it might rarely have been played during the last hundred and fifty years had it been written in a moment of exceptional inspiration (as it possibly could have been, apart from the scherzo) by some talented but less well known contemporary like Johann Schenk or Adalbert Gyrowetz.

It was during the next nine years (1801–9) that *unser echte Beethoven* emerged, the Beethoven who was to stimulate Grove to panegyrics and goad Renoir to fury; the Beethoven of the 'Waldstein' sonata with its frightening prestissimo octave passages; of the 'Kreutzer' sonata, demanding unprecedented virtuosity on the part of the violinist; of the 'Rasumovsky' string quartets which imparted a new look to chamber music; of the 'Eroica' symphony with the calculated false entry at the start of the recapitulation in its first movement and the quixotic opening to its last; of the solitary violin concerto where surprising prominence was given to the kettledrums (with an effect so poetic in the context that not even a Renoir could cavil); of the opera *Fidelio*, the like of which had never before been seen on any stage. Yet recognition of the genius which Beethoven demonstrated during this period does not – or should not – depend solely upon his capacity for puzzling or shocking people, for in retrospect it can be seen that he was often in equally confident mood when *not* doing so. The 'Waldstein' is undeniably a fine sonata, but nowadays many musicians prefer the more serene op. 28, the more ardent op. 57 (the 'Appassionata') and the more descriptive op. 81a ('Les Adieux, l'absence et le retour'). To say that the 'Kreutzer' is with one exception (op. 96) the most satisfying of Beethoven's ten violin sonatas might be a backhanded compliment to its composer, for in eight out of the ten he was not at his best. The three 'Rasumovsky' quartets of op. 59 are great beyond doubt, but hardly greater than the suavely beautiful op. 74 – nor than the two well-contrasted and more conventional piano trios of op. 70. There is no accounting for taste and I have to confess that personally I find the much-admired 'Eroica' symphony, no. 3, apart from its superb scherzo, less attractive than nos. 2, 4 and 6 (which by comparison are sometimes underrated) and less impressive than the famous and popular no. 5. The violin concerto, magnificent up to a point, is, I feel, somewhat marred by a finale in which Beethoven slips perilously near banality. *Fidelio* is unique in conception and contains some wonderfully fine scenes, but taken as a whole it is not really a very good opera in the accepted sense of the term; fortunately Beethoven provided it with no less than four overtures – all of them excellent. The fourth – known as the *Fidelio* overture – was written for a revival some eight years after the original production; thanks to its forthright breeziness it is admirably suited to the theatre, but in the concert hall it yields pride of place to the three earlier *Leonora* overtures – whose slightly varying orchestral treatment of Florestan's lovely aria 'In des Lebens Frühlingstagen' is of absorbing interest to students of technical empiricism. (*Leonora no. 3* must be awarded the palm but the others run very close.) Two out of the three piano concertos dating from these years – the romantic no. 4 in G major and the more vigorous but equally expressive no. 5 in E flat major (the 'Emperor') – leave an impression of genuine spontaneity; in the concerto field these inspired and perfectly proportioned works have rarely been surpassed.

Beethoven, as a social rebel, was enraged that the musicians of his day had to depend for their livelihood upon feudal, political or ecclesiastical patronage; on principle he had no time for Gluck's empresses, Haydn's princes or Mozart's archbishops. Yet he had to live in the world into which he had been born and during his early days in Vienna had not been too proud to accept pecuniary assistance from Prince Charles Lichnowsky, Baron Pasquati and Count Browne – three noblemen whose names would be forgotten had they not befriended a struggling composer who later achieved greatness. In 1809 three other notabilities – Prince Lobkowitz (descended from the one mentioned on page 41), Prince Kinsky and Archduke Rudolf of Habsburg – clubbed together to provide him with an annuity; in the event devaluation of currency (an inescapable phenomenon even in those days) played havoc with their good intentions but nevertheless he was thereby enabled to maintain himself well above starvation level. Unfortunately he had other troubles to face which no patron, however wealthy or well-disposed, could alleviate. One was the onset of deafness and buzzing in the ears, first noticeable about 1798 and from 1812 onwards an increasing cause of distress and frustration. The other cross he had to bear was guardianship of his scapegrace young nephew Karl, whose delinquencies brought dishonour on the family name and were a continual source of worry and expense. It is not surprising, therefore, that

Beethoven's third nine-year period in Vienna (1810–18) was less prolific than those which preceded it – but what it lacked in quantity it made up in quality. In their respective categories the 'Hammerklavier' sonata op. 106, the string quartet op. 95, the violin sonata op. 96, the song-cycle *An die ferne Geliebte* and symphony no. 7 maintained througout a level of excellence comparable with that of the *Leonora* overtures and the two great piano concertos. Symphony no. 8 and the two cello sonatas of op. 102 were less consistent.

To the last nine years of Beethoven's life (1819–27), when his deafness and his nephew were driving him nearly frantic, belong the *Mass in D major*, the symphony no. 9 – which between them took four years to complete and were not finished until 1823 – and five string quartets (ops. 127, 130, 131, 132 and 135) all dated between 1824 and 1826. The Mass has its moments of beauty, notably the marvellous 'Et incarnatus' section where Beethoven catches the spirit of Palestrina; but in the double fugue 'Et vitam venturi sæculi' – as in the choral finale of the ninth symphony – imaginative enthusiasm demands an excess of lung-power and agility on the part of the singers and an excess of intellectual concentration on the part of the audience. However both the first movement of the ninth symphony and its scherzo (placed second and not, as usual, third) are arrestingly vital; the slow movement, too, with its alternations of mood and key, is wonderfully effective. Yet for all its calm dignity it is not so deeply expressive as the 'cavatina' from the string quartet op. 130 or the *lento* from op. 135, both of which remain rare examples of music which bridges the gap between earth and heaven: listening to these sublime strains might surely bring comfort and hope to an anxious soul at the dread moment when it is about to pass from the measurable known to the limitless unknown.

The elusive characteristics of late 'Beethoven, however, are not always so easily communicable: some listeners find the last quartets heavy going and have to ride roughshod over such stumbling blocks as the second movement (*vivace*) of op. 135. *Pace* Donald Tovey, what Beethoven does here one is not prepared to accept as evidence: harsh music remains harsh no matter who put his name to it. Rather therefore than pay the customary lip-service to these extraordinary works (for their mysterious profundity, ethereal grandeur, inspired anticipation of the methods of Béla Bartók, etc.) let us recognize and accept the fact that they are in parts rough-edged and excuse it by recalling that they were put to paper at a time when Beethoven had become *stone*-deaf: it is significant that alongside passages of almost divine beauty (as in the two slow movements already referred to) are some which in theory ought to sound well but in practice don't; others which are so fragmentary in construction that they look (and sound) as though they were preliminary sketches for an orchestral composition on a larger scale. One is driven to assume that many of the shadowy ideas surging through a mind still active but by now out of touch with the world of familiar hearing were beyond interpretation in any known instrumental medium, that the eagerly searching spirit of Ludwig van Beethoven was already in tune with the infinite, that from time to time his inspiration was no longer adjustable to a language of earthly comprehension.

Release from mortal shackles came on 26th March 1827; at the moment of his passing a violent thunderstorm was raging, which might be seen in retrospect as symbolizing the tremendous impact of this remarkable composer upon generations of musicians as yet unborn. Take him for all in all he was a great genius; it is improbable that we shall look upon his like again.

CHAPTER THIRTEEN

Weber

As recorded in chapter 11, W. A. Mozart married Constanze Weber, who came of a musical family. Constanze's uncle Franz Anton Weber did not attend the wedding, but he was very proud of the connexion and conceived an ambition to emulate Mozart's father Leopold as the parental propagandist of a famous composer. Unfortunately the omens were unfavourable: although he claimed noble ancestry and added a 'von' to his name to which he was probably not entitled, he had for many years been a rather disreputable soldier of fortune, twice married but never settled down; by the time he wooed and won his second wife he had found no more remunerative occupation than that of arranging concerts in the small municipality of Eutin, twenty miles north of Lübeck in an isolated part of the grand duchy of Oldenburg. Today the region is incorporated in the West German province of Schleswig-Holstein and, although Eutin lies on the direct rail and road link between Hamburg and Copenhagen via the Puttgarden-Rødyhavn ferry, the only people who stop off there are commercial travellers (or should they be called sales representatives?) and a few music lovers who think it worth their while to cast an eye on 26 Lübecker-strasse, birthplace of CARL MARIA VON WEBER (1786–1826). His birthplace, yes; his home, no. Before he had learnt to walk (and incidentally he never learnt to run, for he was born with a diseased hip-joint) his father recruited a band of actors and musicians – among them several older children by his first wife – and for the next eight or nine years the family travelled all over Germany, entertaining the public at small theatres and playgrounds. Franz was delighted when little Carl showed musical ability and he did what he could, according to his lights and the circumstances in which he was placed, to foster him as a prodigy *à la* Mozart. In 1796, having taught the ten-year-old all he knew, he abandoned a roaming life and found semi-permanent jobs in turn at Salzburg, Munich, Freiberg and Chemnitz (now Karlmarxstadt), where the resident professors of music were better qualified than himself to complete the education of a budding genius. (One of them, at Salzburg, was Joseph Haydn's brother Michael – see page 45.)

By Mozart standards Weber's talents were slow to come to fruition; nevertheless his operas *The Forest Maiden* and *Peter Schmoll*, composed between the ages of thirteen and fifteen, were played with fair success, the former at Freiberg in 1800 and the latter at Augsburg in 1803. In 1804 he was appointed conductor at Breslau, but he was unsuited for the post by reason of youth and inexperience, and furthermore incurred local notoriety by leading a promiscuous life and running up a pile of debts; two years later he was asked to leave. After fulfilling an even shorter-lived engagement of a similar nature he joined the household of King Frederick of Württemberg where his duties were largely secretarial and only partly concerned with music-making. The court at Stuttgart was one of the most dissolute in Europe (which is saying plenty) and while Weber was completing another opera, *Silvana*, he indulged in extravagance and dissipation to such an extent that he got into trouble with the police and was thrown in jail; although ultimately acquitted of the criminal misdemeanour with which he was charged, his unsavoury reputation led to banishment from the kingdom. This humiliating experience had a salutary effect on the young ne'er-do-weel: thereafter he stayed for a year or more with some good friends at Mannheim, where he wrote an amusing one-act comic opera – *Abu Hassan* – and turned over a new leaf by developing his talents as a pianist to such excellent purpose that he was presently able to set out on an extended concert tour of Prussia, Saxony, Bavaria, Switzerland and Austria. On a visit to Prague in 1813 he agreed to take over the artistic directorship of the opera house, which had fallen on evil days and urgently needed an infusion of new blood; he took the task seriously and within three years put the Bohemian capital back on the musical map, but his wayward temperament still occasionally led him to indiscreet behaviour both within and without the theatre walls and eventually involved him in a dispute with the management. Since by now Weber had earned considerable distinction not only as an administrator and an executant but also as a composer of attractive piano, vocal and choral music – and though still burdened with debts was in a slightly less parlous financial position than formerly – he felt justified in taking a firm attitude. Instead of waiting to be pushed out (as he had been from Breslau) or kicked out (as he had been from Stuttgart) he sent in his resignation; as a final gesture of defiance he filched Prague's most popular operatic soubrette – Caroline Brandt – and married her.

In 1817 Weber was placed in charge of German opera at the Dresden court theatre. The post was no sinecure: as a true German he constantly found himself at loggerheads with his Italian colleague, the conductor Francesco Morlacchi, and furthermore was mistrusted by his employer, King Frederick Augustus of Saxony, who was an ardent francophile. (Curiously enough, so was Caroline Brandt; but husband and wife did not allow political differences to disturb the domestic scene and on the whole their marriage was a happy one.) Weber's next four operas, *Der Freischütz*, *Preciosa*, *Euryanthe* and *Oberon*, were all composed between 1820 and 1825 either at Dresden or at his country retreat at Hosterwitz on the banks of the Elbe, six miles upstream from the city: significantly, however, they were first produced not at 'his' theatre but in Berlin, Vienna or London. *Der Freischütz* stands head and shoulders above any other German opera dated between 1805 (*Fidelio*, see page 66) and 1845 (*Tannhäuser*, page 123). *Preciosa* was little more than a play which incorporated an overture and a few songs and ensembles. For *Euryanthe* – the only one of his operas in which accompanied recitative replaced the traditional dialogue of the *Singspiel* – Weber wrote some fine and original music, but the libretto was preposterous. By this time, too, he was reaping the wild oats he had sown so freely in youth and became consumptive; nevertheless he put all he knew into *Oberon*, and after its completion went to London for the first performance. *Oberon* had been specially written for Covent Garden and aroused great interest. On the opening night the composer received an ovation, but at later performances, partly because of atrocious weather, neither attendance nor reception came up to expectations. Disappointment and the British climate between them sabotaged Weber's failing health, and hasty preparations were made for his return to Dresden; before they could be put into operation he died in his sleep at the home of his English host, the organist and conductor Sir George Smart.

At his best Weber coupled melodic inspiration and technical skill almost worthy of Mozart with a flair for capturing in music the comfortable sentimentality so dear to the hearts of his countrymen – yet only in some of his comparatively unfamiliar works did he sink to the maudlin or commonplace. To *Der Freischütz* – and to his other mature operas when librettists allowed him – he brought not only an admirable sense of 'theatre' but also a romantic atmosphere which was very much to the taste of German audiences: the wolf's glen of *Der Freischütz* and the fairyland of *Oberon* were territories hitherto almost unexplored. Away from the stage he composed two dozen or so orchestral and choral works and scores of songs and piano pieces: one is always ready to welcome the 'Concertstück' for piano and orchestra or *Invitation to the Dance* (written for piano but more often heard in Berlioz' brilliant orchestral arrangement). Nevertheless the memory of Carl Weber deserves to be honoured mainly for his German operas: along with Beethoven's *Fidelio* they effectively bridged the gap between the *Entführung* and *Magic Flute* of his cousin-by-marriage and the music dramas of Richard Wagner (which will come up for discussion in chapter 23).

CHAPTER FOURTEEN

Rossini

GIOACCHINO ROSSINI was born on 29th February 1792. One doubts whether his parents deliberately planned that their first and only child should be a leap-year baby and therefore able to celebrate his birthday only once in every four years – or, indeed, whether they wanted a baby at all. (Five months previously there had been what is nowadays called a shotgun wedding.) They lived in Pesaro, occupying two small rooms in the house numbered 334 via del Duomo (later renamed via Rossini).*

Gioacchino's father Giuseppe Rossini was the 'town trumpeter', his mother Anna (*née* Guidarini) a professional singer; he inherited their interest in music and in 1806 was enrolled as a pupil at the Liceo Filarmonico in Bologna. Sexually precocious, he soon suffered his first bout of gonorrhea (it was by no means his last), but apart from that all went well. While he was still a student his one-act *opera buffa* entitled *La cambiale di matrimonio* (*The Marriage Market*) was performed at Venice, seventy miles away, and two years later so was *La scala di seta* (*The Silken Ladder*); its overture is one of the earliest of his compositions familiar to today's listeners. The successful production of these two works set his feet firmly on the operatic highroad and helped to determine the course of his future career.

Presently he established his reputation as a composer of *opera seria* with *Tancredi* and as a composer of full-length *opera buffa* with *L'Italiana in Algeri,* both dated 1813 and

* Pesaro (present-day population not far short of 70,000) lies on the Adriatic coast between Rimini and Ancona in the region of Italy now known as the Marches but then part of the 'Papal States'. In 1796/7 the troops of Napoleon Bonaparte invaded northern and central Italy and the French remained military overlords there until his downfall, when the Congress of Vienna (1815) restored control of the Papal States to the ruling Pope.

both first played in Venice. Over the next ten years he consolidated it with a succession of further operas, some serious, some comic; the best-known names are:

Il Turco in Italia (Milan, 1814)
Elizabetta, regina d'Inghilterra (Naples, 1815)
Il barbiere di Siviglia (Rome, 1816)
Otello (Naples, 1816)
La Cenerentola, i.e. *Cinderella* (Rome, 1817)
La gazza ladra, i.e. *The Thieving Magpie* (Milan, 1817)
Mosè in Egitto (Naples, 1818)
Semiramide (Venice, 1823).

Although Rossini was never to leave Italy until 1822 (see below) it will be noticed that during this prolific period he liked to set his scenes further afield, in England for example, in Spain, or in Egypt. It is also worth mentioning that, by contrast with the immediate success which many of his operas enjoyed, *Il barbiere* – known to countless thousands in English-speaking countries as *The Barber of Seville* and now almost universally acknowledged to be his masterpiece – was received with disapproval when first produced (in Rome) as *Almaviva, ossia l'inutile precauzione*; audiences soon came to their senses, however. In 1822, having by now no fewer than thirty-three operas, all told, to his credit, Rossini married the Spanish soprano Isabella Colbran. She was seven years his senior, had sung the leading roles in many of his operas – and had almost certainly already been his mistress for quite a while. Since she brought him a substantial dowry, jealous ill-wishers were quick to describe this marriage as just one more of his 'cunning business deals'.

A few days after the wedding, bride and groom set out for Vienna to attend a Rossini Festival that was to be held in the Kärntnerthor Theater, and while there the composer paid a call upon Beethoven. The great man congratulated him warmly on *Il barbiere* ('it delights me'), but was less enthusiastic about his *opere serie*. During the next two years it was the turn first of Paris and then of London to pay tribute to the Rossinis and they were royally fêted in both capitals. In August 1824 they settled in Paris, where for French audiences Rossini furbished up a previously unsuccessful Italian opera as *Le Siège de Corinthe* and revised *Mosè in Egitto* as *Moïse*. In 1828 he composed *Le Comte Ory*, an *opera buffa* with a French libretto rather than an *opéra comique*.* In 1829 came the first production of *Guillaume Tell*, a *grand opéra*. (Although this work is rarely staged in its entirety nowadays, does not a casual mention of William Tell call to mind Rossini's familiar overture rather than the figure of Switzerland's national hero himself?)

In 1830 Rossini and Isabella parted company: as already hinted, theirs had been little more than a *mariage de convenance*. About the same time he began spasmodic work on a *Stabat Mater* – which he took ten years to complete – but for the most part was content to rest on his laurels so far as composition was concerned. Meanwhile he found an affectionate and efficient domestic helpmeet in Olympe Pélissier (*née* Descuillers), a lively lady who 'knew her way around' and proved fully capable of ministering to all his creature comforts. They subsequently spent much time in Italy, where Rossini helped to reorganize his *alma mater*, the Liceo Filarmonico in Bologna, which had recently fallen on evil days; it was in Bologna that he and his devoted Olympe eventually became man and wife in 1846. Nine years later they returned to Paris, and thereafter Rossini, who by this time regarded himself as one of music's elder statesmen, led an indolent life. The four birthdays that remained to him – in 1856, 1860, 1864 and 1868 – were no doubt sumptuously celebrated, for he was a great lover of good food, good wine, good cheer and good company. His

---

* *Le Comte Ory* adhered to the tradition of 'Frenchified *opera buffa*' popularized by Piccinni during the 1770s (see page 44). *Opéra comique*, of which the most notable exponent in the 1820s was François Boïeldieu (1775–1834), derived rather from the *comédies à ariettes* of Philidor (see page 43); often, although not invariably, in an *opéra comique*, recitative was replaced by dialogue.

musical output during this period was meagre: it consisted of the *Petite Messe solennelle* – sung privately (to piano accompaniment) in 1864 but not performed in public until after his death – and a quantity of short piano pieces which would probably be forgotten altogether had they not, many years later, provided the impetus for Otterino Respighi's ballet *La Boutique fantasque* and Benjamin Britten's orchestral suite *Soirées musicales*. Rossini died on 13th November 1868; Olympe survived him by ten years.

During the three-quarters of a century or so after his death Rossini's reputation in Britain tottered somewhat: *Il barbiere* was still in demand and found a place in the standard repertory of many opera companies, but his other operas fell into comparative obscurity – apart from some of the overtures: as recently as 1948 a critic whom none could accuse of being a highbrow informed his readers that their music was for the most part 'trivial to the point of monotony'. Over the past twenty years, however, the pendulum of responsible opinion – no less than the pendulum of public taste – has swung back sharply in Rossini's favour: revivals of previously neglected works are frequent – and welcomed. Perhaps only the most fervent of his admirers would go so far as to rate him a 'great' composer in the commonly accepted sense of the term, but there can be no denying that he was an exceptionally talented one who deserved most of the triumphs that came his way. He understood the human voice to perfection and the orchestra nearly as well. He conceived plenty of catchy tunes – a sure passport to popularity – and contrived some admirable ensembles and 'concerted finales'. That *Il barbiere* – a work of near-genius – was completed within three weeks gives one some idea of his resourcefulness when inspiration was in full flow – even when allowance is made for the fact that it incorporated quotations from some of his previous operas as well as a few snippets unashamedly cribbed from Haydn's *The Seasons* and Gasparo Spontini's *La Vestale*. It need not be held to his discredit that he usually appeared at his best in *opera buffa*, where lapses into 'triviality' – although not lapses into

77

'monotony' – may be more easily forgiven than those which occur in *opera seria*. (He himself admitted that he preferred to treat comic rather than serious subjects, but explained that he was obliged to accept any libretto chosen for him by the impresarios.)

All in all Gioacchino Rossini certainly contributed his quota to the musical gaiety of nations, but his achievements need to be set in historical perspective: the works upon which his fame depends were nearly all composed between 1813 and 1828, a brief period which exactly coincided with the bright flowering of Franz Schubert – who was endowed with many of the same gifts and exploited them in other fields to greater purpose.

CHAPTER FIFTEEN

Schubert

Of our nine famous composers whose names are closely associated with Vienna (Gluck, Haydn, Mozart, Beethoven, Schubert, Bruckner, Brahms, Wolf, Mahler) the only one born there was FRANZ SCHUBERT. Today his birthplace – 54 Nussdorfstrasse, ten minutes' walk from the Franz Josef Bahnhof – is a museum in the care of the municipality: very appropriately so, for Schubert never left his native city except for occasional brief trips to the Wienerwald and two visits to nearby Hungary, where in his early days he was engaged to give lessons to the children of Count Johann Esterházy. (The estate of this branch of the Esterházy family lay in what is now Czechoslovakian territory, twenty miles north of Esztergom.)

Schubert's mother, who came from Silesia, was, like Haydn's mother, a professional cook; his father, from Moravia, was a schoolmaster with a taste for music. Franz – born 31st January 1797 – learnt the violin and piano as a small boy and at the age of eleven entered a choristers' seminary, where he soon took to composition. At seventeen he became a junior teacher in his father's school, but after a year of striving to inculcate the three Rs into the thick-heads of the bottom form he abandoned scholastic duties and adopted a more congenial if less secure manner of life, spending the rest of his youth – that is to say the rest of his mortal career – in the company of like-minded bohemians who cultivated wine, women and song in the traditional Viennese fashion. Johann Mayrhofer, one of the steadier of these friends and many of whose poems Schubert set to music, left it on record that 'his character was a mixture of tenderness and coarseness, sensuality and candour' – probably a shrewd appraisal. The leader of the set was Franz von Schober, a wealthy dilettante who genuinely admired Schubert's genius and generously looked after his material welfare. Schober also wrote the words which inspired the lovely song *An die Musik*, but in the long run Schubert lost more than he gained from association with this rich young man and his dissolute companions. That he was often encouraged to have a little too much to drink was neither here nor there, but it was a serious matter when in 1822 he contracted syphilis; thereafter his plump, bespectacled, untidy figure – now crowned by a wig – was more grotesque than ever. If he had had thoughts of marriage (and evidence of any deep-felt attachment is very scanty) he now put them aside, but nothing deterred him from composing until he succumbed six years later to an attack of typhoid. He died at the age of thirty-one on 19th November 1828, only nineteen years after Haydn (who was sixty-five years his senior) and barely nineteen months after Beethoven.

Schubert's industry was prodigious: his earliest known composition dates from 1810 – when he was thirteen – and during the eighteen years that remained to him he completed eight operas or operettas (three others were left unfinished), incidental music for two plays, forty-five cantatas and liturgical settings including six Masses, nearly a hundred short vocal ensembles, thirty-five orchestral pieces including seven symphonies (two others were left unfinished), forty chamber works at least half of which were in four movements, over two hundred and fifty pieces for piano solo or duet including twenty-four sonatas, and about six hundred songs. A comparatively small proportion of this huge output was published or even performed during his lifetime; it was posterity, not the composer, who reaped the benefit.

His faults – how few beside his virtues! – were mainly those of inexperience and youthful exuberance, traceable to the fact that he never grew to know himself. The furious pace at which he lived left little opportunity for introspection: he rarely indulged, like Beethoven, in painstaking struggles to achieve perfection; he must have realized subconsciously that time was short and that he must make full use of it. Small wonder that hundreds out of the thousands of tunes he wrote were undistinguished, since everything welling up inside him had to find immediate outward expression; small wonder that despite his brilliant technique in detail many of his more ambitious efforts (not all) are open to criticism on the ground of structural defects, perfunctory orchestration or excessive prolixity, since no sooner had he finished a work than inspiration was already hard at it elsewhere. (The 'heavenly length' of his compositions in sonata form was due not only to repetition but also to the vast quantity of material which he crammed into the 'second subject'; it was probably Schubert who was primarily responsible for driving musicologists to substitute the term 'second group of subjects'. It should also be noted, in passing, that the key-relationship between the various subjects sometimes marked a departure from traditional practice.) Yet Schubert never worked carelessly: he often wrote three or four songs in a single day (or night), but some of his best are among them and they show no signs of hurried execution; no sooner had he completed the first movement of his ninth symphony than he decided that in its most frequently recurring phrase the second G (the fourth note of the *allegro*) should be replaced by D, whereupon he meticulously made all the hundreds of necessary corrections to the manuscript.

Combining in balanced proportions the outlook of the classic, the romantic and the impressionist, Schubert was a classic in so far as he recognized that the main purpose of music was to entertain, a romantic in so far as he was a composer of subjective moods, an impressionist in so far as he could conjure up atmosphere by the simplest of means (the spinning-wheel of *Gretchen am Spinnrade*, the galloping horse-hoofs of *The Erl King*, the babbling brook of *Wohin?*, the ghostly tread of *Der Doppelgänger*). He nearly always chose the right medium for expression and in that respect went astray only in the early string quartets and piano duets, where one feels that he had an orchestra at the back of his mind. It is significant that the *Grand Duo* was probably sketched in the first place as a symphony; it was orchestrated long after his death by Joseph Joachim (who is remembered as an outstanding violinist but was also no mean composer).

Not all Schubert's stage-works were played during his lifetime and few have ever been revived; they lack the dramatic cohesion which is essential to opera or even operetta, for he was singularly undiscriminating in his choice of either plots or librettists. The earlier pieces, dated 1814–19 and mostly in one act, hold little interest except as curiosities. As for the rest, a few items from *Alfonso and Estrella* (1822) might be rescued from their surroundings – notably the duet 'Von Fels und Wald umringen' where the charming woodwind commentaries show him in characteristically good form – and there are some impressive choral scenes in *Fierrabras* (1823). Yet worthwhile medals can be awarded only to the incidental music for *Rosamunde*, whose delightful entr'actes are supreme examples of light orchestral music and have already outlived by a century and a half the paltry drama which they decorated and enlivened in 1823. At one time Schubert took the theatre very seriously but successive failures caused his interest to wane: for instance, he did not bother to complete the *Alfonso and Estrella* overture until after the opera had been produced and used it instead for *Rosamunde*; he later allocated to that work an overture which had previously done duty for *The Magic Harp* (1820).

If the theatre did not as a rule stimulate Schubert to give of his best, neither did the Church. Much of the sacred music of his teens and early twenties – which included the first four Masses – was second-rate. The fifth Mass (A flat major, 1822) was more accomplished but incongruously light-hearted: the 'Gloria', for instance, which began and ended with something like a *perpetuum mobile* on the first and second violins in unison, was well constructed but hardly in keeping with the solemnity of the text. Perhaps only in the 'Gloria' of his sixth and last Mass (E flat major, 1828), which incorporated a stupendous fugue and a very moving 'Agnus Dei' section, did he come within striking distance of achieving distinction as an ecclesiastical composer. Nor is there much to enthuse about in the secular cantatas and vocal ensembles: they were no doubt admirably in place at family reunions or convivial drinking-parties, but in general they were unrepresentative and it was probably fortuitous that they included occasional gems like the unaccompanied male choruses *Sehnsucht* (no connexion with several songs similarly entitled) and *Ruhe, schönstes Glück der Erde*.

Turning to the symphonies we find ourselves in a different world, although not yet in a world where Schubert's genius always found full expression: symphonic development did not come altogether easily to this child of nature. Nos. 1 to 5 – of which 3, 4 and 5 still hold a place in the standard repertory – were written before he was twenty. The first four were for the most part in the Haydn/Mozart manner, although each opened with a slow introduction owing something to Beethoven and ended with a finale which, by contrast, suggested Rossini. In no. 5 there was no slow introduction and not much Beethoven, Mozart raised his head in the second movement, Haydn replaced Rossini (to great advantage) in the finale, but it would be fair to say that this lovely little work brought Schubert to the fore as a symphonic composer in his own right. No. 6 was less spontaneous and more diffuse; it should be noted, however, that the third movement was a scherzo – not (as in nos. 1 to 5) a minuet or *Ländler* – and was incidentally the high-spot.

In 1821 Schubert sketched a symphony no. 7; it was evidently complete in his mind since a manuscript exists which – although presenting only the bare outlines – covers all four movements. J. F. Barnett (in 1883) and Felix Weingartner (in 1934) each filled in the gaps to the best of his ability and thereby helped to confirm the impression that the first three movements marked a further advance in symphonic responsibility, but Schubert himself set no. 7 aside for no. 8, the 'Unfinished'. This is one of the best-loved pieces of music ever written, and if for that reason anybody should disparage it as hackneyed one might rejoin 'then for heaven's sake give us some more hackneys': more sheer beauty is packed into his half-symphony than is contained in nine out of ten completed ones by any other composer, no matter how illustrious. While several melodies from no. 5 are reminiscent – and worthy – of Haydn or Mozart, the oboe/clarinet unison which at the eleventh bar of no. 8 floats above the delicately vibrating violins and violas (not all conductors, alas, succeed in realizing the delicacy), the haunting second subject allocated to the cellos (and astonishingly punctual in making its appearance), the miraculous modulations at the end of the second movement – these are reminiscent of no one and worthy of Schubert alone. It has never been conclusively established why no. 8 remained unfinished but Schubert left a clue with his sketch for a scherzo: it held out little prospect that the third movement would attain the same perfection as the two which preceded it, and perhaps he did right to leave well alone. Symphony no. 9 (often incorrectly called no. 7) was composed during the last year of his life. To distinguish it from no. 6, which is in the same key, it is known as the 'great' C major – an equivocal caption since, although no. 9 certainly outshines no. 6, it can hardly claim to stand alongside the greatest masterpieces of Haydn, Mozart or Beethoven. Here Schubert's enthusiasm perhaps outran his discretion: the *pianissimo* trombone entry at the end of the exposition in the first movement, although not precisely an oasis in a desert, is a miraculous flowering from comparatively unproductive soil; and neither the cultured panache of the *andante* nor the initial vigour of the scherzo nor the whirling energy of the finale can disguise the fact that all three hold their *longueurs*. (It must be confessed, however, that a superlatively fine performance under the direction of a dedicated interpreter like Sir Adrian Boult nearly persuades one to the contrary.)

Chamber music has been the Achilles heel of many composers, for it is a medium in which the closest attention must continually be paid to a very delicately regulated instrumental balance. It has already been hinted that Schubert's early string quartets (1811–16) were not entirely satisfying because the approach was orchestral, but between 1820 and 1828 he produced five of the best pieces of chamber music ever written – the quartet-movement in C minor, the complete quartets in A minor, D minor and G major, and the string quintet in C major. Here he gave each instrument full opportunity to display its expressive powers, while at the same time using his technique to ensure that the overall effect was exactly what he wanted. The opening of the A minor quartet, for instance, is perfect *string quartet* music; half its magic would be lost if it were played on a string *orchestra*.

Although Schubert was not always successful in combining the piano with other instruments (neither the violin sonatas nor the piano trios nor even the 'Trout' quintet represent him quite at his best, and it is significant that he never wrote a concerto), some of his most attractive music is contained in the piano solos and duets. To strum through the piano sonatas is a practicable and enjoyable way of discovering for oneself how he progressed from immaturity to greatness: the first few are unremarkable; the last four (G major, C minor, A major, B flat major) justify comparison with Beethoven. But to appreciate Schubert's extraordinary key-sensitivity, resource in modulation and freedom from conventional trammels one need only turn to a shorter and more familiar piano piece – the popular impromptu op. 90 no. 4. Very typically, this hovers to such an extent between A flat minor and A flat major that it is impossible to declare with certainty to which of the two keys it properly belongs; in the middle section, which sets out confidently in C sharp minor, everything is comparatively straightforward until the theme is recapitulated in C sharp *major* and extended by four bars of surprising – and beautiful – modulation.

Schubert's symphonies, string quartets and piano sonatas, when taken in sequence, provide ample evidence of the steady growth of his powers; had he written nothing else one might have been tempted to propound a theory that the classical composer of 1811–15 eventually became the romantic composer of 1822–8. His songs, however, refute this hypothesis, suggesting, rather, that he was a romantic or impressionist from the word go: of the four instances of impressionism cited on page 81 *Gretchen am Spinnrade* was written at seventeen, *The Erl King* at eighteen. Many of them are particularly suited for domestic music-making, for they are grateful to sing and the accompaniments are usually within the capabilities of a competent amateur pianist. Nearly all are technically impeccable; moreover Schubert often imparts an individual touch to the simplest strophic measure: in *Heidenröslein* for instance, or in *Ungeduld* – of which the melody should be examined in its entirety, since it is not only perfectly proportioned (like so many of the others), rising to a superb climax at just the right moment, but also incorporates an intriguing rhythmic amibiguity (2/4 – 3/4). He was catholic in his choice of collaborators: there were some forty-five of them all told, including Shakespeare, Goethe, Schiller and a host of his own contemporaries, many of whom were personal friends. He found himself particularly *en rapport* with Heinrich Heine and with Wilhelm Müller, a minor but not negligible poet upon whose verses Schubert based two splendid song-cycles, *Die schöne Müllerin* and *Die Winterreise*. (Müller, nine months younger than the composer, had an even shorter life, predeceasing him by a year.)

Schubert's six hundred songs cover a vast range of emotion: there are hymns to nature (*An die Nachtigall*, *Frühlingsglaube*, *Im Abendroth*, *Am Meer*); there are musical poems evoking the tender coquetry, the hopes, fears and disappointments of young love (*Geheimes*, *Who is Sylvia?*, *Mein*, *Die Post*); there are outbursts of deep passion or suffering (*An Schwager Kronos*, *Die junge Nonne*, *Die Stadt*); there are songs descriptive of resignation or spiritual peace (*Litanei*, *Du bist die Ruh'*, *Der Leiermann*). Not all the six hundred are masterpieces, but it is astonishing how many of them are; indeed Franz Schubert's contributions

to any collection of the world's best songs would surely out-
number all the rest put together – a fair indication of his
supremacy.

CHAPTER SIXTEEN

Bellini

With the solitary exception of Franz Schubert, VINCENZO
BELLINI (1801–35) was the shortest-lived of our fifty composers. During his brief career he was considerably less
prolific than his great Viennese contemporary: a few small-
scale vocal and instrumental works dating from his student
days still survive, but for practical purposes his output comprised ten operas – and nothing else.

Like Alessandro Scarlatti, Bellini was born in Sicily (to be
precise at Catania, where his father was an organist) but he
learnt his trade in Naples. While he was still a pupil of the
then well-known composer Niccolò Zingarelli at the conservatoire there, his opera *Adelson e Salvini* was played at the
San Carlo Theatre and showed such promise that the resident impresario, Domenico Barbaia, invited him to provide
another. When *Bianca e Gernando*, too, was favourably received, Zingarelli's and Barbaia's high regard for his talent
was confirmed, and they pulled strings to secure a production of his third opera, *Il pirata* (1827), at La Scala in Milan.
By now the young composer was well on the road to success
and, although neither *La straniera* (Milan, 1829) nor *Zaira*
(Parma, 1829) made much impression, he enjoyed a great
triumph at Venice in 1830 with *I Capuletti ed i Montecchi*,
based on Shakespeare's *Romeo and Juliet*. (One of the
many admirers of this characteristic work was Richard
Wagner, who later admitted that it was only after attending a performance of *I Capuletti* at Leipzig in 1834, with
Wilhelmine Schröder-Devrient in the leading role, that
he was led to take an interest in Italian opera.) Back in
Milan, Bellini surpassed all his previous achievements with
the lyrically elegiac *La sonnambula* (produced 6th March
1831) and the more dramatically forceful *Norma* (Boxing
Day of the same year); *Beatrice di Tenda* (Venice, 1833),

while by no means a failure, was found to be somewhat lacking in inspiration by comparison with its immediate predecessors.

Presently, ostensibly by way of relaxation but perhaps partly, too, to escape from a love affair with one Mrs Giuditta Turina which was becoming somewhat embarrassing, Bellini decided to visit first London and then Paris. (He was not to know that he would never return to Italy.) Although apt to be unreasonably (and unnecessarily) jealous when an opera by some rival – Saverio Mercadante, for instance, or Donizetti (see next chapter) – was applauded as heartily as his own latest effort had been, he could hardly at this stage bear resentment against Rossini, who had given up operatic composition since the production of *Guillaume Tell* four years previously (see page 76) and could therefore no longer be regarded as a dangerous competitor. At any rate, on reaching Paris Bellini was tactful enough to seek his acquaintance, praise him to the skies, and listen to any advice he might have to offer. Rossini thereupon recommended him to compose an opera specifically for the Théâtre Italien, with which he himself had long been associated. Bellini promptly did so, and in the event *I puritani di Scozia* was rapturously acclaimed at its star-studded Parisian première (25th January 1835); it should be stressed, however, that the brilliant cast included at least four singers of international repute – Giulia Grisi, Giovanni Rubini, Antonio Tamburini and Luigi Lablache – and that in those days it was singers, rather than lesser mortals like composers, who were the lords or ladies of all they surveyed. *I puritani* was Bellini's swan-song: nine months later, when just turned thirty-four, he fell ill and died at the home of an English friend at Puteaux, in the outskirts of Paris.

Since Bellini can be judged solely as a composer of operas, it is right and proper that appreciative mention should be made of the help he received from his regular librettist Felice Romani, who supplied the texts for *Il pirata*, *I Capuletti ed i Montecchi*, *La sonnambula*, *Norma* and *Beatrice di Tenda*: he knew his job a good deal better than the miscellaneous assortment of hack writers with whom Rossini collaborated – few of whom were ever given a second chance. Consequently Bellini's operas, whatever shortcomings there may be in their musical content, can for the most part be effectively staged – with a little care – in the straightforward manner intended by composer and librettist.*

Despite the lively vocal histrionics in such songs as 'Ah! non giunge' (*La sonnambula*) and 'Casta diva' (*Norma*), Vincenzo Bellini did not rely to the same extent upon purely virtuoso effects as did some other purveyors of popular *bel canto* opera – i.e. opera largely dependent for effect upon 'beautiful song'. His melodies often (although not always) held a gracious quality of refinement, distinction even, that almost suggested Mozart, and which with the best will in the world one can rarely descry in those of Rossini or Donizetti; on the other hand he was less skilful than they were in his handling of chorus and orchestra, his workmanship at times appearing somewhat amateurish. This weakness, due partly perhaps to his relative lack of experience, might well have been overcome in due course; it was indeed a sad day for Italian opera when this highly gifted composer died at such an early age, his full potential as yet unrealized.

* Yet perfection is not always attained, even in the world's best-appointed opera houses. The American historian Robert Sabin (general editor of the latest edition of *Thompson's International Cyclopedia of Music and Musicians*) has vividly recalled a performance of *Norma* given at the 'Met.' in New York in the palmy days between the wars. 'The size of Norma's bedchamber approximated to that of the Pennsylvania Railroad Station, the state of the equipment of the Roman army was deplorable, winter underwear showed ludicrously through Pollione's armour, and several members of the chorus of virgins (in dingy-looking robes) exhibited distinct signs of an *embonpoint* which did not speak well for the strictness of the vows of chastity in the temple: obviously, the laxity which Bellini's heroine had shown towards her pledge of eternal purity had spread like wildfire among her followers.'

CHAPTER SEVENTEEN

Donizetti

In the mid 1920s there was published in London an admirably concise yet comprehensive history of music running to some two hundred and fifty pages. The author, W. H. Hadow, commented appreciatively on various aspects of Bellini's art but granted less than two lines to a contemporary composer nowadays often regarded as being of comparable calibre. 'Donizetti,' he wrote, 'was a mere imitator of Rossini and has gone the way of most imitators'; that was all. Twenty-five years later Edward J. Dent recorded that 'Donizetti and Bellini, still national heroes in Italy, are hardly even names to the present-day frequenters of Sadler's Wells'. Yet thanks to a recent resurgence of interest in the *bel canto* tradition (which may or may not prove lasting) these two composers are now much more than names to lovers of opera in this country. Bellini was discussed in the previous chapter, and in today's climate the achievements of GAETANO DONIZETTI, that 'mere imitator of Rossini', also demand attention. His dates were 1797–1848 and he was therefore four years older than Bellini, but I have allowed the younger man chronological precedence because Donizetti's international reputation was not really established until the successful production of his *Anna Bolena* (1830), which *followed* Bellini's *I Capuletti ed i Montecchi*; indeed several of his best-known operas were not composed until after Bellini's death.

Donizetti was born at the house now numbered 14 borgo Canale, lying in a poor quarter of Bergamo's hilly and picturesque *città alta* which overlooks the modern part of the town from the north-west; he was the fifth of the six children of Andrea Donizetti and his wife Domenica. (The legend, at one time accepted as genuine, that Donizetti's father was the son of a Scottish adventurer named Don Izett has since been disproved.) As a youngster Gaetano received great encouragement from the composer Simone Mayr (German by birth but Italian by adoption), and thanks largely to his interest and help was accepted as a pupil at the Liceo Filarmonico in Bologna, where Rossini had studied music several years previously (see page 74). Thereafter for the rest of his life he was constantly on the move, composing operas for production at Venice, Naples, Milan, Rome, Palermo, Genoa and Florence in turn, and also in Paris and Vienna; many of them enjoyed great success. (Several of those originally played in Paris were settings of French libretti: hence *La Fille du régiment* rather than *La figlia del reggimento* and *La Favorite* rather than *La favorita*.) In 1828 Donizetti married Virginia Vasseli, daughter of some good friends in Rome; their only child was still-born, and his young wife's death in 1837 left him utterly grief-stricken. A few years later he became subject to intermittent attacks of mental disorder; besides this, from 1845 onwards he suffered from partial paralysis.

Over the twenty-five years 1818–43 Donizetti completed more than sixty operas, some serious in intent, some frankly light-hearted or even farcical, and some conveniently described as *semi-seria*. Like Rossini, he appeared to best advantage in *opera buffa*: indeed *L'elisir d'amore* (1832), *La Fille du régiment* (1840) and *Don Pasquale* (1843) merit comparison, even though in the event it may be slightly unfavourable comparison, with *Il barbiere* and *Le Comte Ory*. One has mixed feelings about his more pretentious works like *Lucia di Lammermoor* (1835, and including the famous 'mad scene') and *La Favorite* (1840), in which one rarely comes across a tune as genuinely expressive as that of, say, 'Una furtiva lagrima' from *L'elisir d'amore*. Perhaps the speed at which Donizetti worked was partly responsible for the fact that the quality of his melodic invention rarely seemed to match the quality of his economical and yet extremely capable workmanship. This feature of his talent was very much to the fore in *buffo* scenes such as those which occur frequently throughout *Don Pasquale* (for example), where the orchestra provides an appropriate and often charming accompaniment of its own as a background to the situation on the stage; in this respect he was Rossini's equal and superior to Bellini.

One further point concerning Donizetti's operas, taken collectively, requires a mention. In his enterprising search for suitable 'settings' he cast an even wider topographical net than did Rossini: here is a selection from the varied and perhaps somewhat arbitrarily chosen *locales*.

Siberia: *Otto mesi in due ore*.

Northern France: *Gianni di Calais, L'assedio di Calais, Gianni di Parigi*.

Burgundy: *Enrico di Borgogna*.

The Alps: *Linda di Chamounix*.

The Pyrenean foothills: *Francesca di Foix*.

The Iberian peninsular: *Zoraide di Granata, Alahor di Granata, Dom Sébastien di Portugal*.

The Caribbean: *Il furioso all'isola di San Domingo*.

Warwickshire: *Elizabetta al castello di Kenilworth*.

'The mountains near Liverpool' (? Walton-on-the-hill): *Emilia di Liverpool*.*

For the sake of completeness, it must be added that in his early days this hard-working composer produced a few symphonies and a fair quantity of chamber music; that when Vincenzo Bellini died he provided a Requiem Mass in honour of his memory. And it is pleasant to be able to record that, according to all contemporary accounts, Gaetano Donizetti, despite his many triumphs, remained one of the most modest and good-natured fellows that anyone could wish to meet.

* This little-known opera was granted a rare revival in 1957 – at Liverpool.

CHAPTER EIGHTEEN

Mendelssohn

Almost alone among famous composers FELIX MENDELSSOHN underwent no struggle to achieve fame or fortune. Born in 1809 in the outskirts of Hamburg and brought up in Berlin, he was the son of Abraham Mendelssohn, a wealthy banker who was better placed than the impecunious Franz Weber (see page 70) to attend to the requirements of a child prodigy in the Mozart class. Whereas in boyhood Carl Maria von Weber had picked up hints from strolling musicians, young Felix Mendelssohn was sent to the most expensive teachers in Berlin and Paris – and moreover was supplied by his fond parents with a private orchestra which he could conduct whenever he wished; he was soon composing sonatas, symphonies, cantatas, operas even, some of which are still preserved in manuscript. As it turned out many were competent little works deserving recognition on their merits, and when at seventeen Mendelssohn startled everyone with the *Midsummer Night's Dream* overture even the sternest moralist had to admit that he had used his worldly advantages to excellent purpose.

He was never obliged, as was Weber, to seek regular employment. Indeed when pressed to accept resident directorships he often declined them, and the only permanent post which he occupied for more than a year or two was that of conductor at the Leipzig Gewandhaus; as a rule he preferred to indulge in the extensive travel which he could well afford. Not that he was ever idle; far from it: he helped to rescue the name of J. S. Bach from oblivion by reviving that great master's works all over Germany, and furthermore composed, played and conducted his own music wherever he went, whether it was Austria, Switzerland, Italy, France or Britain – to which he paid no less than ten visits and where he found himself completely at home. He toured the remoter parts of Scotland and Wales and was enchanted with their scenery; as for London, he compared it favourably with Naples ('it is indescribably beautiful when the roses of Piccadilly gleam in the sunshine'); he even went so far as to write that he was 'delighted' with Birmingham: no wonder our countrymen hailed him as a genius. But the strain of continual wayfaring in all sorts of weather – by crowded stage-coach, bumpy post-chaise, tossing channel-boat – eventually undermined a constitution which had never been robust and he died in 1847 (at Leipzig) at the age of thirty-eight.

Apart from being a composer Mendelssohn was a man of letters, a classical scholar, a fine linguist and a painter of considerable ability. Jewish by race and German-Protestant by religion, he cherished family affection and was particularly devoted to his elder sister Fanny, an accomplished pianist who married the artist William Hensel. Instinct drove him to play down his wealth and avoid any show of extravagance, and although friendly by nature and lionized wherever he went his character remained unspoilt; by contrast with many of his colleagues he was the epitome of upper-middle-class respectability. In 1837 he married Cécile Jeanrenaud, eighteen-year-old daughter of a Lutheran minister from the Swiss-Jura village of Môtiers in the val de Travers (canton Neuchâtel); she proved a good wife – and he a good husband. But although excessive popularity never corrupted the man it tended to demoralize the composer: success came so easily that in course of time he lost the power of discrimination, and since his intuition was less sure than Weber's he slipped more frequently into melodic triviality and the facile use of harmonic clichés; he knew that his admirers were not interested in unconventional modulations (*à la* Schubert) or surprising strokes of dynamic originality (Beethoven) – and he was careful not to offend their susceptibilities. It was not so much that he prostituted his talent in return for public recognition as that he let it develop along lines which ran parallel with contemporary requirements; he did not sin against the Holy Ghost, but he sinned sufficiently to have incurred some measure of retrospective disapproval.

Mendelssohn's technique was admirable (few composers before or since have better understood an orchestra), and professional *expertise* was apparent even in such early works as the *Rondo capriccioso* for piano (1824), the string octet (also 1824) and the *Midsummer Night's Dream* overture (1826). This youthful masterpiece was later surpassed only by the *Hebrides* overture (of which more presently), and so far as orchestral pieces are concerned was matched only by the *Midsummer Night's Dream* scherzo and nocturne (composed sixteen years after the overture), the 'Italian' symphony, and possibly by the 'Scottish' symphony and the violin concerto – which is still the standby of every virtuoso violinist. (Neither of the piano concertos is of comparable merit.)

For about eighty years Mendelssohn's *Elijah* (first produced at Birmingham in 1846) was almost as regular a feature of a British music festival as Handel's *Messiah*. Recently it has failed to stay the course, but despite a tendency to squareness in the part-writing it is certainly the most satisfying of his choral works. 'Is not his word like a fire?' remains a fine piece of declamation, the lyrical charm of 'For the mountains shall depart' is still apparent, and our grandfathers were not far off the mark when they acclaimed the conclusion of Part I ('Thanks be to God') as the most stirring climax in all oratorio. Of the string quartets perhaps only that in E minor exploited the medium to advantage – and few people would suggest that Mendelssohn was an outstanding song-writer. On the other hand much of his piano music, if judged by appropriate standards, is excellent. The *Songs without Words* are admittedly uneven in quality, but it would be unfair to dismiss them out of hand as pretty trifles; not all of them are trifling and I see no objection to prettiness – in moderation. The *Variations sérieuses* display unexpected authority in a specialized field, and the prelude and fugue in E minor (op. 35 no. 1) – closing with a chorale in E major – is masterly. (The keys of E minor and

E major often brought out the best in Mendelssohn: it is no coincidence that of the self-contained works which I have singled out for praise about half are in either one or the other – or a mixture of both.)

That Mendelssohn is normally assigned to the romantic school of composers is largely because he appeals to cosy sentiment; he was not a romantic in the true sense of the term, since he always – or nearly always – preserved a classic sense of detachment. One rarely comes across a subjective expression of emotion such as one often finds in Schubert (especially in the songs), and the attempts to evoke atmosphere *à la* Weber usually have a touch of artificiality about them – not that they are necessarily for that reason any the less effective in their context. The fairy music from *A Midsummer Night's Dream* is captivating, but it suggests not so much fairies as a well-drilled troupe of dainty ballerinas; Bottom, when translated to Eeyore, is not written down an ass – he is a stage comedian wearing an ass's head. Yet elsewhere Mendelssohn proved that besides being a classic (a romantically inclined classic, if you insist) he was also a superb impressionist. Nobody who, like the composer himself, has been to Fingal's Cave on the isle of Staffa (off the west coast of Mull) – and few of those who haven't – could deny that the *Hebrides* overture, while perfectly fitting the concept of sonata form, was at the same time the first great tone-picture in music and therefore a landmark in the history of the art; not even Wagner or Debussy later surpassed its imagery – the eternal swell of the ocean, the surging of the waves round the rocks, the intermittent calm and storm, the cry of the sea-birds overhead. (Mendelssohn exploited the same flair, though less consistently, in the concert overture *Calm Sea and Prosperous Voyage*, which is a finer work than the more familiar *Ruy Blas*.)

A crowd of Mendelssohn's compositions – including the oratorio *St Paul*, *Walpurgisnacht*, the *Hymn of Praise* and the 'Reformation' symphony (all highly esteemed in the nineteenth century) – are already as good as dead; in course of time *Elijah*, too, may sink into further and undeserved oblivion and pianists no longer think it worth while to expend their energies on the *Rondo capriccioso* or the *Songs without Words*; even the enchanting *Midsummer Night's Dream* music may eventually find itself out of favour in the brave new world of Benjamin Britten. But for the sake of the *Hebrides* overture, if of nothing else, the name of Felix Mendelssohn will surely be honoured so long as mankind remains capable of recognizing consummate artistry.

CHAPTER NINETEEN

Berlioz

HECTOR BERLIOZ (1803–69), the greatest French composer of his generation (whether by birth or adoption), was rather more than five years older than Mendelssohn and therefore, were birth-date the sole criterion, would be entitled to chronological precedence. But his powers were comparatively slow to develop; all but one of his best-known works were dated long after Mendelssohn had lost that first fine careless rapture – and in any case he outlived his contemporary by more than twenty years.

Berlioz was born at La Côte St André, an attractively situated but rather poky little town on the marches of Lyonnais and Dauphiné. (His birthplace is now the Musée Berlioz, 69 rue de la République, which guards many private letters as well as the manuscript scores of *Benvenuto Cellini* and *L'Enfance du Christ*.)* We have it on the authority of the composer himself, whose humour was dry, that he came into the world quite naturally, unheralded by any of the signs which in poetic ages preceded the advent of remarkable personages. His father was a physician, a man of culture and well esteemed in La Côte St André where for a time he held the office of mayor; broadminded, with no strong doctrinal beliefs of his own, he did not demur when his wife, a devout churchwoman, insisted that their children be brought up as Catholics. The splendour of Church ritual appealed to Hector and he never forsook the faith – although in later life he found himself in general sympathy with his father's live-and-let-live attitude towards religion. Sent to

* Motorists on their way to the *côte d'azur* should note that La Côte St André lies on the N 518, which winds its way from Lyon to Die (Drôme) through the lovely region of Vercors and is a more spectacular and less frequented route than the direct N 75 through Grenoble.

Paris at the age of eighteen to study medicine, his first sight of a dissecting laboratory so repelled him that he abandoned forthwith a half-hearted attempt to follow in parental footsteps and turned aside to music – which Berlioz *père* had encouraged as a hobby but viewed with suspicion as a profession. To the credit of both father and son neither forfeited mutual respect during the difficult years when Berlioz *fils* was striving, on a meagre financial allowance, to justify his choice of career.

His musical aspirations derived mainly from a youthful veneration for Gluck; he visited the library of the Paris Conservatoire (open to all), copied out the score of *Orfeo* (see page 43), studied it at his leisure and wrote a modelled cantata which he showed to J. F. Lesueur (an enlightened professor of composition), who was genuinely impressed but had to point out many technical defects. Berlioz was unable to secure immediate admission to the Conservatoire because his impetuously insubordinate behaviour in its library had permanently estranged its director Luigi Cherubini (Italian-born composer of *The Water Carrier* and *Anacréon*, who had settled permanently in Paris in 1788), but he studied privately with Lesueur and others and meanwhile composed exuberantly in a garret. Recognition eluded him, but much of this early outpouring was refurbished later – a form of economy which he never ceased to practise. One work that does survive intact from this period is the sonata-form overture to an unfinished opera, *Les Francs juges;* the second subject has a disarming lilt characteristic not only of Berlioz in his most genial mood but also of Beethoven and Schumann in theirs, recalling the second subject from the finale of Beethoven's symphony no. 1 and foreshadowing the second subject from the finale of Schumann's no. 4.

When at last in 1826 Berlioz (to use his own phrase) cracked the barriers of the Conservatoire, he immediately entered for the Prix de Rome.* But he went the wrong way

* The Prix de Rome was awarded annually by the French Academy of Fine Arts for the best student-composition of the year; it entitled the recipient to a period of free study in Rome.

about it: instead of adhering to the (admittedly antiquated) regulations he asserted self-confidence by disregarding them and thereby alienated the examiners. He eventually won the prize at his fifth attempt, in 1830, with a work which for once fulfilled academic requirements without exhibiting any disturbing symptoms of alien influence. (Beethoven and Weber were still looked upon by everyone in Paris – except Berlioz – as dangerous foreign revolutionaries.) Meanwhile an intense admiration for Goethe led to a setting of *Eight Scenes from Faust*, which brought a first small measure of material success. Goethe soon yielded place to Shakespeare, and Berlioz fell violently in love at a distance with Ophelia as personified by Harriet Smithson, Irish member of a visiting theatrical company from Britain. The emotional fluctuations of this (as yet) entirely one-sided affair prompted completion of the *Symphonie fantastique* ('Episode de la vie d'un artiste'), a very personal and therefore romantic expression of youthful fervour followed by disillusionment, and by any standard a remarkable composition for a twenty-six-year-old. Descriptive rather than impressionistic, it displayed many features commonly associated with typical Berlioz: loose construction, a puckish and Beethoven-like addiction to the unexpected, attractive but often inconsequential flights of melodic fancy, crude-at-first-glance harmony (with an apparent obsession for chords in 'root position'), flimsy counterpoint, a brilliant battery of orchestration. (W. H. Hadow, who did much to inculcate appreciation of music in Britain, once wrote that 'the harmony, counterpoint and form which Berlioz learnt from the best teachers in Paris are very frequently defective, while his most indisputable title to immortality lies in the orchestration, for which he had no master at all'. Hadow was right to stress the paradox, but one regrets that he did not on mature consideration cross out the words 'his most indisputable title' and substitute 'one of his titles'.) A good deal of the *Symphonie fantastique* was written before Berlioz had so much as heard of Harriet Smithson, but passion impelled him to set himself a precedent by announcing a programme. I reproduce it (condensed), because apart from programmatic interest it provides a key to the composer's temperament, and in the enigmatic words of Donald Tovey (for whom see page 61) 'only very silly people take Berlioz seriously but they are not so silly as the people who don't'.

A young musician of morbid sensitivity is in love; he has the strangest of dreams wherein his sentiments are translated into musical ideas. The Beloved has become a Melody – an *idée fixe* – which he hears everywhere. First he remembers the volcanic love which she instantly inspired. Next he meets her in the tumult of a ball. But when he goes to the country [even a Berlioz symphony must have a slow movement] the gentle sound of the wind in the trees gives a new calm to his turbulent heart. Presently, however, he dreams that he has killed her in a fit of jealousy, that he is condemned to death and led to the scaffold; finally that he is at a Witches' Sabbath, where the Melody of the Beloved is transformed into a vulgar dance-tune.

By the time the symphony was completed Berlioz had found a more tangible mistress than Ophelia in the young pianist Camille Moke, who accepted his loving farewells before he set off for Rome in February 1831; in April she married a fellow-pianist, Camille Pleyel.* Apart from a *crise de nerfs* when he learnt of this perfidy (which sent him scurrying to Nice – and then back), Berlioz' stay in Rome passed without incident. He satisfied the authorities of the Conservatoire by periodically sending them watered-down versions of back-dated works and meanwhile ran riot in the concert overtures *Rob Roy* and *King Lear* (Shakespeare again, one notes) and in *Lélio* (a sequel to the *Symphonie*

---

* This good lady seems to have had a *penchant* for illustrious composers. Once Chopin, while on holiday, lent his Paris flat to Liszt; he returned earlier than expected and found that his tenant had installed Madame Pleyel alongside. (That she bore the same Christian name as her cuckolded husband was a coincidence: 'Camille' is no more indicative of male or female than is 'Evelyn'.)

fantastique which had most of the faults and few of the virtues of its predecessor). Of greater artistic merit was a fine setting of Victor Hugo's poem *La Captive*, later revised and expanded as a concert aria.

Still devoted to his father, Berlioz broke his return journey from Rome at La Côte St André and did not reach Paris until November 1832, when almost immediately he had a chance social encounter with his Ophelia, Harriet Smithson. On the instant love revived – and was reciprocated; within three months they were betrothed, within a year they were married, within two years they were parents of a son. For Berlioz all this meant hard work since his actress wife, now past her prime, made no contribution to the family budget. To augment his income he took to regular journalism (pungent articles on music in the Paris press); four of his major compositions date from the same period. First came the symphony *Harold in Italy*, vaguely based on Byron's *Childe Harold*. The virtuoso violinist Niccolò Paganini, who was a very good friend to Berlioz, had recently acquired a Stradivarius viola and urged a prominent solo part for that normally neglected instrument; for its benefit the composer retrieved a few tunes from discarded earlier works, including one which in *Rob Roy* had been allotted (more appropriately) to the cor anglais. Next: the Requiem (where the valour of a gigantic chorus and orchestra could hardly help outrunning the discretion imposed by such items as the beautiful 'Sanctus'), and the spirited but in places rather pretentious opera *Benvenuto Cellini* (revived at Covent Garden not long ago but mainly remembered for its overture and an orchestral transcription known nowadays as *Le Carnaval romain*). These were followed by yet another programmatic symphony, *Romeo and Juliet* (incorporating voices); it was characteristically disjointed but here and there the music caught to perfection the spirit of the words, notably in the passage inspired by

Good night; good night; parting is such sweet sorrow
That I shall say good night till it be morrow.

Meanwhile Berlioz' own connubial bliss had faded away in scenes of personal recrimination, and from 1841 onwards he often escaped from Paris and conjugal ties in the company of a pretty but untrained soprano named Marie Recio. Over the next fifteen years he established his reputation abroad: still unappreciated in France (which he likened to 'a forest inhabited by anxious men and ravening wolves') he and his music were acclaimed in Britain, Belgium, Germany, Austria, Hungary and Russia, although the distressing vocal inadequacy of his endearing young charmer was a constant source of embarrassment. During this period of travel and consolidation (consolidation of two separate urges) Berlioz wrote his classic *Treatise on Modern Instrumentation and Orchestration*; compositions included the delightful song-cycle *Nuits d'été*, the concert overture *Le Corsair* (dedicated to the music critic of *The Times*), the cantata *The Damnation of Faust* (which incorporated the original *Eight Scenes* and from which the dance of the sylphs and the Racockzy march were promptly popularized in Britain by the conductor Charles Hallé) and the oratorio *L'Enfance du Christ*. Perhaps because the approach was here more austere than usual, *L'Enfance* was better received in Paris than most of his works, but the nervous excitement of his disposition was once again mirrored in the incongruous variations of style, which ranged from the calm loveliness of a duet for Mary and Joseph at Bethlehem to the picturesque exoticism of a cabbalistic dance (in 7/4 time).

All this while Berlioz had honourably provided financial support for Harriet; when she died in 1854 he made an honest woman of Marie Recio and started work on a new five-act opera, *The Trojans*, which took four years to complete; production difficulties were immense and only part of it was played during his lifetime. Just as the *Symphonie fantastique* holds the quintessence of youthful Berlioz so *The Trojans* represents his full maturity. One is conscious of the same vivid imagination and flashes of brilliance, often coupled with the same diffuseness and gaucherie, but despite some weak threads the tapestry as a whole is woven with greater assurance and the choral sections (as in *Faust*) show uncommon mastery. Those who enjoy the Trojans' March and the Royal Hunt and Storm (who doesn't?) should also take note of passages where a subtle touch of poignant sound is added to melodies which on paper may look undistinguished.

While struggling vainly to secure a complete production of *The Trojans* Berlioz wrote a cheerful but uneven light opera, *Beatrice and Benedict*, a final tribute at the shrine of his beloved Shakespeare (*Much Ado about Nothing*). Thereafter he concentrated on literary work – notably his memoirs – but when his second wife died in 1862 he began to age prematurely. He visited La Côte St André for the last time and had a romantic meeting with a sweetheart of his adolescence, but he was already a sick man and the death of his son Louis (a sea-captain) at Havana in 1867 was a crippling blow; he himself died two years later.

Berlioz has always been a controversial figure. Of recent years one of his most ardent protagonists has been the American musicologist Jacques Barzun, whose factual conclusions, based on exhaustive research, may certainly be regarded as definitive. Other biographers, including his compatriot Adolphe Boschot, while commenting with appreciative discernment on many aspects of his work, have by my interpretation of their writings been more concerned with debunking him. Boschot himself has in turn been effectively debunked by Barzun, but it would be fair to agree with the former's comment that Hector Berlioz refuses to fit into any familiar category, a refusal that surely might have been expected from such a disconcertingly unconventional genius.

CHAPTER TWENTY

Chopin

FREDERIC CHOPIN was born at the village of Zelazowa Wola, near Warsaw; whether the date was 1809 (as some authorities maintain) or 1810 (officially accepted) matters little. What does matter is that his father, although bred in Lorraine (which had close historic ties with Poland), had been a Polish citizen since 1787 and earned a fair living as private tutor to the sons and daughters of the nobility; that his mother, gentle and well educated, was one hundred per cent Polish; that he himself was Polish not only by birth and upbringing but also by outlook and temperament. A child prodigy, he earned public recognition at the age of eight both as pianist and composer, and his choice of career was never in doubt. After a course of study in Warsaw with Joseph Elsner – an honoured figure in Polish musical history – he presented himself in Vienna where he played his own compositions to appreciative audiences. That was in 1829. A year later he was back there again, purposefully *en route* for Italy. But Italy, like Poland, was in the throes of political upheaval, and perforce his second visit to Vienna lasted longer than intended. Eventually he abandoned the idea of going south and instead made for Paris, which he reached by way of Munich and Stuttgart in the autumn of 1831.

In Paris Chopin soon established his reputation as a brilliant pianist, a tactful mentor to the young hopefuls of the aristocracy, and an *émigré* composer with out-of-ordinary ability. Though handicapped by a frail constitution he also undertook several concert tours in Germany and one in Britain; everywhere he went his pale and interesting good looks and charming manners captivated the ladies, but his only serious love affair at the time – with a fellow-Pole, Marie Wodzinska – was terminated by mutual agreement in 1837. The same year, however, saw his first meeting with a remarkable woman who had been christened Aurore Dupin and had married a dull provincial named Casimir Dudevant, by whom she had two children; she is known to posterity by her pseudonym as an authoress, George Sand. Having for a time lived openly with the poet Alfred de Musset, she now took Chopin under her wing and carried him off to spend the winter of 1838-9 in Majorca. As it happened he was in an even poorer state of health than usual and the trip was not an unqualified success, but thereafter he was a constant guest at her country-house at Nohant (Indre), where he could relax in quietude and carry on with his composing; consequently he soon came to regard Nohant as his home. (The château and its grounds, today no less gloomy and derelict than most of their kind, adjoin the N 143 twenty miles south of Châteauroux and three miles north of La Châtre.) It is acknowledged by all that George Sand was a generous patroness and Chopin a grateful *protégé* with whom she had much in common; few will agree with the good people who have convinced themselves that this close friendship, which lasted for ten years, depended solely upon a shared enthusiasm for intellectual pursuits. Be that as it may, the permanent cuckoo eventually became a source of embarrassment even in this most unconventional of nests, and the régime finally broke itself on a violent family quarrel in which George Sand sided with her son Maurice (who had always resented the intruder) against Chopin and her daughter Solange (with whom he had remained on cordial terms). Frustrated and depressed, he paid another visit to Britain, where he stayed for seven months and despite the onset of tuberculosis gave four concerts; in the autumn of 1848 he returned to Paris too ill to make any further public appearance, and he died there a year later.

Apart from two concertos, both belonging to his early Warsaw days, all Chopin's works of any importance were written for piano alone: it will be convenient to refer to them in generic groups, identifying individual pieces by *opus* numbers. These indicate sequence of publication rather than of composition, but a rough guide would assign ops. 1-22 to the Warsaw-Vienna period of 1825-31, ops. 23-34 to the Paris period of 1832–8, ops. 35-65 to the Nohant period of 1839-47. (Ops. 66-74 are posthumous publications, their composition-dates ranging from 1825 onwards.) It must be stressed that this division of Chopin's active career into three periods is purely for the sake of easy chronological reference and has little if any stylistic significance. One has heard the view expressed that he 'was at his best in the polonaises and mazurkas which belonged to Poland, while his later and more popular *salon* works were tainted with Parisian mannerisms and affectation'. This is nonsense. All the well-known polonaises and at least two-thirds of the mazurkas were composed after Chopin reached Paris, while many of the more popular *salon* works date from before he ever set foot there – among them the inescapable nocturne in E flat major op. 9 no. 2, the luscious *étude* in E major op. 10 no. 3 (nowadays incorporated in the ballet *Les Sylphides*), the big waltz in E flat major op. 18, and the unique slow waltz in A minor published later as op. 34 no. 2. Even in the twenty-four preludes op. 28 – one in every major and minor key and which, taken collectively, may perhaps convey a superficial impression of conventionality – there are fewer signs of Parisian mannerisms and affectation than of Slav influence. (See especially nos. 2, 4, 12, 18 and 22.)

Emphasis on his consistency must not be taken to imply that Chopin the artist stood still, that op. 65 showed no advance on op. 1; nevertheless the progressive development of his powers was largely a matter of technique rather than of style. As befitted an outstanding exponent of lyrical romanticism in music he had an inborn flair for varied melody – graceful, passionate, rhapsodic; to this in due course was added a sense of harmonic colour-contrast beyond contemporary imaginings (glance through the chromatic sequences of the polonaise in C minor op. 40 no. 2) and a growing realization that brilliant pianism should cease to be mere decoration and become welded to the melodic scheme; the *leggierissimo* passages of the scherzo in C sharp minor op. 39, for example, were an integral part of the whole conception. Furthermore, from about 1835 onwards Chopin tackled larger forms with greater assurance. Admittedly he never completed a wholly satisfying sonata (for even op. 35 in B flat minor, funeral march and all, was thrown off balance by the brevity of its demoniac finale), but he was at his best in the scherzo in B flat minor op. 31, the *ballade* in A flat major op. 47, the fantasy in F minor op. 49 and the polonaise-fantasy in A flat major op. 61 – all of which are much more massive in scale than their titles would suggest. Nevertheless Frederic Chopin also deserves our heart-felt gratitude for bringing us perfection in miniature (e.g. the preludes op. 28 nos. 7 and 20), as well as for raising the modest mazurka and the ball-room waltz to a level of artistry hitherto undreamt of.

CHAPTER TWENTY-ONE

Schumann

Both Berlioz and Chopin were among those who demonstrated, in their different ways, that a secondary feature distinguishing romantic from classical music was a tendency to reflect more closely the personality of its composer. The unquestionably romantic music of ROBERT SCHUMANN was an exception which neither proved nor disproved the generalization. The man, despite a fund of good nature, was unsociable and wayward, liable to fits of depression and even to mental instability; it is true that his music was always good-natured, but it was rarely wayward and never depressing or unstable. One hesitates to hail him as he himself hailed Chopin – 'hats off, gentlemen, a genius!' – but he had immense talent which he used to splendid purpose.

This most unreliable of men and most reliable of composers was born in 1810 at Zwickau (equidistant from Weimar, Leipzig and Dresden), today an industrial centre with a population of nearly 100,000 but then a typical Saxon market-town with perhaps one-tenth that number of inhabitants. His father was a publisher and bookseller, and although Robert showed precocity in music he was also an avid reader of Goethe and Schiller – as well as of E. T. A. Hoffman and Jean Paul (J. P. F. Richter), who took romanticism in literature to a level of extravagant fantasy. On the death of his father (who had encouraged artistic ambitions), his mother (who hadn't) sent him to study law at Leipzig, where he attended a few lectures but spent most of his time hob-nobbing with musical friends who gave him lessons in harmony, counterpoint, piano-playing – and wine-bibbing; one of his mentors was Friedrich Wieck, whose pretty nine-year-old daughter Clara, he noticed, was a very promising young pianist. Presently, however, Schumann decided he was getting nowhere; so did the university authorities, who readily agreed that his student's registration should be transferred to Heidelberg. His intention was to study law and music side by side, but bouts of drunkenness soon made him unpopular even in that traditionally free-and-easy academy and he was eventually dismissed on the ground that he had not paid his fees. Back, then, to Leipzig, where having thrown away his legal books and permanently injured two fingers in a foolish scientific experiment, Schumann finally abandoned all hope of becoming either a barrister or a concert pianist and devoted himself entirely to composition and journalism. (It was at this stage that he founded *Die neue Zeitschrift*, which under his editorship continued for many years to print pithy comment, both pertinent and impertinent, on contemporary personalities and events in the musical world.) In due course, after a short-lived engagement to one Ernestine von Fricken, he became seriously enamoured of Clara Wieck, but his old piano-teacher did not fancy him as a son-in-law and the wedding was postponed until she was on the verge of attaining the age of twenty-one.

Up to now Schumann had composed only piano music: notably the very original *Carnaval* ('Scènes mignonnes sur quatres notes'), the more conventional but equally attractive *Etudes symphoniques*, and many shorter but by no means trivial pieces published under collective titles like *Fantasie-stücke* and *Noveletten*. His bride, however, urged him to seek new pastures, and the next four years were given over in turn to songs, orchestral works, chamber music and oratorio. In 1840, the first year of their married life, Schumann completed the song-cycles *Frauenliebe und Leben* and *Dichterliebe*; in 1841 two symphônies (the second of which was afterwards revised and became known as no. 4), *Overture, Scherzo and Finale* (in effect a symphony in three movements) and a fantasia for piano and orchestra (later expanded as a full-length concerto); in 1842 half a dozen miscellaneous chamber works with or without piano; in 1843 *Paradise and the Peri*.

Thanks largely to conjugal understanding and devotion this was the happiest and most placid phase of Schumann's career. Unfortunately, over the next six years or so the physical and mental strain of visits to Berlin, Vienna, St Petersburg and elsewhere (giving concerts at which Clara played divinely and he himself demonstrated his incompetence as a conductor) caused a succession of nervous breakdowns. Nevertheless he composed two more symphonies (nos. 2 and 3), a concerto for cello and another for four horns, incidental music for Byron's *Manfred* and Goethe's *Faust*, the opera *Genoveva*, and some further piano pieces including two admirable collections dedicated to youthful executants (our old friend 'The Merry Peasant', etc.). Most of these works were penned at Dresden, where the Schumanns maintained a *pied-à-terre* during their travels, but in 1850 they settled in Düsseldorf. Here they lived very quietly, for by that time Schumann had become a psychiatric case; his later compositions – apart perhaps from two violin sonatas – were unrepresentative. After an unsuccessful attempt to commit suicide he was placed at his own request in a private asylum in the outskirts of Bonn; it was there that in 1856 he died in the arms of his beloved Clara – who for forty long years of widowhood continued to play and teach the piano and remained her husband's most faithful champion.

Although Schumann studied music with many respected professors of the art in Zwickau, Leipzig and Heidelberg, there was only one master to whom he owed and owned lifelong allegiance – J. S. Bach. He had little time for Haydn; not a great deal, in his secret heart, for Mozart or even Beethoven (although his music often showed traces of Beethoven's influence): all three, he felt, had chosen to follow easy but ultimately unrewarding byways rather than march boldly forward along the hard high road which Bach had signposted.* This apparently intolerant attitude should not

* He wrote in *Die Neue Zeitschrift* that 'Haydn is like a familiar friend of the house whom all greet with pleasure and with esteem, but who has ceased to arouse any particular interest'.

be ascribed to bigotry; in the 1830s and 1840s Bach was generally shrugged aside as an academic pedant, and Schumann was one of the few who strove (along with Mendelssohn) to force recognition of his true greatness – and to implement it. Admittedly there is not much outward resemblance between, say, the 'Forty-eight' and the *Fantasiestücke*, but Schumann was a throwback to Bach in so far as he adopted the same approach to music's formal problems, and furthermore he was capable of evoking Bach-like clarity in contemporary idiom: although he rarely exploited counterpoint *per se* his pianistic effects, unlike Chopin's, often derived from a cunning flair for treating snatches of melody 'canonically'. Another characteristic feature of his music was a specialized form of syncopation; the rhythm is sometimes cross to the eye rather than the ear – there are passages in the finale of the piano concerto where the poor conductor always looks as though he couldn't keep time with the orchestra – but there is no mistaking the aural impact in (for instance) the 'Davidsbündler March' from *Carnaval*.

It has often been said that Schumann appears to better advantage in the recital room (or even *salon*) than in the concert hall, a tenable proposition since undeniably there are many exquisite gems amongst his songs and piano pieces while some of the larger works are clumsily fashioned – and not always well orchestrated. Yet in truth the point at issue is one of medium rather than of scale: that his scoring for strings and woodwind was sometimes insensitive – due mainly to his lack of interest in the aesthetic or technical potentialities of any instrument save the piano (which he loved and understood) – matters relatively little when the piano itself is the principal centre of attraction. Partly if not wholly for that reason the string quartets are less satisfying than the piano trios, the piano quartet and the (splendid) piano quintet; and although *Paradise and the Peri*, *Manfred* and *Genoveva* contain some good music and the symphonies some excellent music, most of us, if allowed only one Schumann disc on our desert island, would plump for the piano concerto – which in any case is a masterpiece in its own right. Although conceived, as we have already noted, in two separate spasms, it is better balanced than Schumann's other works of comparable proportions and is more compact and unified than any of the symphonies, each of which (despite the unifying finale of no. 4) compels admiration not so much *qua* symphony as for the sake of certain individual movements: the sonata-form finale of no. 1, for instance, where the short and somewhat dark-hued development section contrasts so well with the light-hearted Mendelssohn-like melodies of the exposition; the expressive *adagio* (better orchestrated than usual) from no. 2; the stirring *allegro* which opens no. 3; the vigorous scherzo from no. 4.

At first Schumann's music made little impact abroad, and it is still arguable whether his claim to immortality depends upon an instinct for the miniature amounting to genius (in summing up one cannot, after all, escape the word) or upon an unbounded talent which found expression in almost every branch of composition; it is certain that the claim, be it in little or big, is firmly established, and even those for whom German romanticism spells anathema should not grudge him praise for having been, in his day, a manly and at the same time poetic interpreter of its characteristics. Robert Schumann had his failings and his failures, but he never courted easy popularity or wrote a bar of music that marked conscious withdrawal from the highest standards of artistic integrity.

CHAPTER TWENTY-TWO

Liszt

The versatile FRANZ LISZT – for tidy-minded historians an even more disturbing character than Berlioz – came from that Austro-Hungarian borderland where Joseph Haydn had spent much of his life (see chapter 10). He was born in 1811 at Dobrjan, ten miles south of Sopron in the extreme west of Hungary, where his father was employed as bailiff by Prince Nicolas Esterházy, son of Haydn's patron. (The village now lies in the Austrian province of Burgenland and is called Raiding.) As a small boy he demonstrated such musical ability that his parents took him to Vienna, some fifty miles away, for they decided that there – and there alone – could his talent be brought to fruition. Their confidence in him was justified: at the age of twelve he started a long and successful career as pianist – and a long but more chequered career as composer.

From 1823 till 1837 Liszt lived in Paris and from 1848 till 1861 was director of the Weimar court opera house, but throughout his life he was continually on the move. A succession of concert tours – spread intermittently over half a century and bewildering to follow in detail – led him to every European country except Sweden and Norway: his virtuosity was acclaimed with equal fervour in Constantinople and Kiev, Lisbon and Liège, Milan and Manchester, Hanover and Heligoland. During the course of his travels he became acquainted with nearly every musician of contemporary importance as well as with some who belonged to previous or subsequent generations: for instance he met Beethoven, forty-one years his senior, at Vienna in 1823; he met a promising young Norwegian named Edvard Grieg, thirty-two years his junior, at Rome in 1869; he met the eighteen-year-old Isaac Albéniz (from Spain) at Budapest in 1878. He was on particularly friendly terms with Berlioz,

Chopin and Schuman, to all three of whom – and to many others – he gave practical help by transcribing, playing or conducting their works and by arranging concerts at which they could play or conduct their own. Generosity to fellow-artists was indeed Liszt's most endearing personal characteristic; among his favourite *protégés* were Peter Cornelius (the underrated composer of *The Barber of Baghdad*), Joachim Raff (now only remembered, poor fellow, for a cavatina) and Richard Wagner (who eventually became his son-in-law, see page 125). During his declining years Liszt suffered from dropsy, but it was of pneumonia that he died – rather suddenly – while attending the Bayreuth Festival of 1886. (For Bayreuth also, see page 125.)

No account of Liszt's career would be complete without a reference to what Eric Blom – in the admirably laconic style which he adopted throughout the strictly factual *Everyman's Dictionary of Music* – called 'his 2 great and innumerable minor love affairs'. A footnote on page 120 has already drawn attention to a minor one; the 2 great were with the golden-haired Countess Marie d'Agoult (which lasted from 1834 till 1844 and produced three children) and the cigar-smoking Princess Caroline Sayn-Wittgenstein (1847 till 1863). The second of these protracted *liaisons* might have led to marriage had not Pope Pius IX (to Liszt's secret relief) refused in 1861 to sanction Caroline's divorce. As it happened her husband died three years later, but by that time her lover had chosen to immerse himself in religious mysticism; after two years devoted to study and meditation he received the tonsure as a lay priest – and thereupon resumed his roving. Ernest Newman in *The Man Liszt* (1934) once and for all dispelled the myth that he was a romantic *galant* who treated his mistresses with unfailing chivalry and renounced the pleasures of the flesh on becoming an *abbé*.

Most of Liszt's original compositions for piano – some three hundred pieces all told – were written between the ages of twenty and fifty and fall into three groups: the Chopinesque; the Hungarian; the truly Lisztian. The source of inspiration for the bulk of his waltzes, mazurkas, *études* and *consolations* (in effect nocturnes) was obvious, but only now and again – e.g. in the *étude de concert* in D flat major and the *consolation* in the same key – did he capture the poetic sensibility of his Polish contemporary. On the other hand his only piano sonata (in B minor) was original in conception (it is played without a break) and more satisfying than any of Chopin's. He took great interest in the gipsy music of his native land, but not even in the vigorous Hungarian rhapsodies (among which it would be snobbish to disparage the ever-popular no. 2) did he fully exploit its essential characteristics: an Italian flavour was apt to overwhelm the Magyar. More truly Lisztian, or so one would like to believe, were the short pieces published under such collective titles as *Apparitions*, *Harmonies poétiques et religieuses*, and *Années de pèlerinages*; the third volume of the *Années*, belonging exceptionally to his sixties, displayed a flair for impressionism (e.g. in 'Les Jeux d'eaux à la villa d'Este') which hitherto had often been clouded by flashy showmanship. It is interesting to note that the famous *Liebestraum* (the third of a set of three) started life as a song – *O lieb', so lang du lieben kannst*; as a song-writer Liszt was rarely at his best, although a handful of Victor Hugo settings – notably *Enfant, si j'étais roi* – were unaffectedly charming.

Until he was about forty-five Liszt, although a conductor, was curiously insensitive to orchestral values; he was actually driven to call in outside help when orchestrating the first few of his dozen or so symphonic poems. Confined to one movement, these were more consistent in style and less diffuse than the *Symphonie fantastique* and *Harold in Italy* of Berlioz (which provided programmatic precedents) but hardly matched them in spontaneity of inspiration; *Les Préludes* (1848, revised 1854) is the most familar, but *Hamlet* (1858) is more concise and contains finer music. Liszt's most noteworthy orchestral work, however, was the full-length *Faust* symphony – character-pictures of Faust, Gretchen and Mephistopheles – dated 1857; here his descriptive powers reached their summit-point. The two piano concertos came comparatively early (although each was later revised); the emphatic opening of the first (in E flat major) can still make an audience sit up and take notice but both works are uneven: there are passages of dignity and indeed of beauty, but the brilliance of the treatment (with Liszt a matter of theme-transformation rather than symphonic development) cannot hide the poverty of much of the material. A shorter piece for piano and orchestra (strings only), the posthumously published *Malédiction*, probably written when he was about thirty, incorporated some startling harmonic progressions typifying a lifelong struggle to prove himself an innovator which reached its climax in the selfconscious modernity of *Via Crucis* (1879), for four soloists, choir and organ. Among his sacred works this does not rank so high as the impressive and indeed masterly oratorio *Christus* (1867), where he cut his coat in accordance with his cloth and showed that he was not the mountebank that some of his harsher critics have made him out to be; honourable mention should also be made of the admirable setting of Psalm XIII for tenor, chorus and orchestra (1859), with its unexpected initial juxtaposition of the common chords of C major and G sharp minor.

Finally, a word about Liszt's piano transcriptions. Although virtuosity was their motivation it would be unfair to dismiss them as mere show-pieces, for he had an extraordinary knack of interpreting for his own instrument the more diversified expositions of abler composers: one feels that Mozart, for instance, would have enjoyed the 'paraphrase' of *Don Giovanni*, Schubert the wordless *Winterreise*. To attempt a piano-solo reduction of Beethoven's symphonies may have been presumptuous; in the outcome it was not only a stupendous technical achievement but moreover focused public attention on their greatness, at the time not fully recognized. And furthermore, where lesser composers were concerned, the Liszt version often transcended the original in artistry.

By all accounts Liszt was the finest pianist of his age;

unfortunately he could leave no tape-recordings and so his prowess in that field must remain a legend. As a man he deserves to be remembered not so much for his exploits as a lady-killer as for the goodwill he showed to contemporary musicians with fewer worldly advantages. In Franz Liszt the composer there burned a flame of genius; though often flickering, it nevertheless shone brightly enough to light the stairway to the master-musicians' gallery.

CHAPTER TWENTY-THREE

Wagner

RICHARD WAGNER (1813-83), who rode the seas of nineteenth-century music with a stormy bluster worthy of any flying Dutchman, was the ninth child of Johanna Wagner, *née* Patz, whose husband, an actuary at the Leipzig police court, died in a typhoid epidemic which swept the city after the crushing defeat there of Napoleon's army by the Prussians and Russians in October 1813. On his death she took her children (Richard was six months old at the time) to Dresden, where Ludwig Geyer, a well-established singer and actor, generously assumed responsibility for their upbringing. Johanna married him in 1815 and soon afterwards presented him with a daughter, Cäcilie. Cäcilie Geyer (or Cäcilie Avenarius as she became when she married a book-publisher) will not reappear in this narrative, but it is worth noting that throughout his life Wagner remained on affectionate terms with his half-sister – if indeed she was no more than a *half*-sister: research has revealed good grounds for belief that Geyer, who for many years had been a close friend of the family, was also responsible for Richard himself. (The available evidence has been set forth fully and fairly by the indispensable Ernest Newman in his monumental *Life of Richard Wagner*, Vol. I pages 17-24, Vol. II pages 560-65, Vol. III pages 524-8 and Vol. IV page 597 footnote 9.) There was always a touch of irony in the thought that a police servant had fathered such an uncompromising rebel against authority – in politics, art and morals.

Any attempt to assess Wagner's true worth as an artist continually finds itself up against the problem as to how far his work reflected a half-digested intake of the writings of Arthur Schopenhauer, for he aimed at being a philosopher, an author and a poet as well as a composer (he wrote all his own libretti), and even when his music apparently illustrated to near-perfection a straightforward dramatic situation he had to expound the inner meaning in characteristic jargon.

(a) In Elsa I saw my desired antithesis to Lohengrin – yet not so absolute an antithesis as that which is included in his general nature and forms the necessarily longed-for complement. Elsa is the Unconscious, the Undeliberate, into which Lohengrin's conscious, deliberate being yearns to be redeemed; but his *yearning*, again, is itself the unconscious, undeliberate necessity in Lohengrin, whereby he feels himself akin to Elsa's being. (*A Communication to my Friends*, 1851.)

(b) The necessity of prolonging beyond the point of change the subjection to the tie that binds Wotan to Fricka – a tie resulting from an involuntary illusion of love, the duty of maintaining at all costs the relation into which they have entered, and so placing themselves in hopeless opposition to the universal law of change and renewal, which governs the world of phenomena – these are the conditions which bring the pair of them to a state of torment and lovelessness. (Letter to August Röckel, dated 25th January 1854.*)

(c) The grand concordance of all sterling Myths, as thrust upon me by my studies, had sharpened my eyesight for the wondrous variations standing out amid this harmony. Such a one confronted me with fascinating clearness in the relation of Tristan to Isolde as compared with that of Siegfried to Brünnhilde. Just as in languages the transmutation of a single sound forms two apparently quite diverse words, so here, by a similar transmutation or shifting of the Time-motive, two seemingly unlike relations had sprung from the same mythic factor. Their

* Röckel was a close associate of Wagner's (in both music and politics) at the time of the 1849 revolution (see page 124); they remained friends until 1868, when Wagner accused Röckel of trying to make mischief between himself and his by then established mistress, Cosima von Bülow (page 125).

intrinsic parity consists in this: both Tristan and Sieg-fried, in bondage to an illusion which makes this deed of theirs unfree, woo for another their eternally pre-destined bride, and in the false relation hence arising find their doom. (*Epilogue to The Ring of the Nibelung,* 1871.)

Perhaps all one really gathers from (*a*) is that Elsa was a romantically minded young lady and Lohengrin a very romantic lover, from (*b*) that Wotan was an adulterous husband and Fricka a nagging wife, from (*c*) that Wagner was not too happy about having used the same plot twice over. I shall not argue the points further; for present purposes I prefer to confine myself to a condensed summary of his career and brief comment on the *musical* content of his operas – or music dramas.

For the first twenty years of his life Wagner did not stray farther than eighty miles or so from Dresden; his time was divided between Dresden itself, Eisleben (nearby), Prague, and his birthplace Leipzig. Brought up in a household whose bread and butter depended upon opera and drama and where he was left largely to his own devices, he at first concentrated youthful attention on the theatre's literary side (Sophocles, Dante, Shakespeare, Schiller) and took little serious interest in music until he was about fifteen. At that age he discovered Mozart, Beethoven and Weber, and thereafter there was no holding him. All other studies were put aside; during the next four years he composed two piano sonatas, a handful of concert overtures and a sym-phony, and started work on two operas – *The Wedding* (which he did not finish) and *The Fairies* (which he did finish but which was never performed during his lifetime). In 1833, at the age of twenty, he was appointed chorus-master at the Würzburg opera house and in 1834 musical director of a recently inaugurated municipal theatre at Magdeburg. Here he completed another opera, based on Shakespeare's *Measure for Measure*; intended to be a glori-fication of free love, it was named *Das Liebesverbot* – diplo-matically rendered in nineteenth-century Britain as *The*

Novice of Palermo. Meanwhile he had fallen in love with the company's leading lady, Minna Planer, and when the Magdeburg venture foundered for want of support the two young people went to look for work in the Baltic port of Königsberg – where in 1836 they were married. But Wagner was heavily in debt and his bride, appalled at the prospect of unrelieved poverty and insecurity, soon became the mistress of a local business worthy who could afford to indulge her extravagant tastes. Wagner threatened divorce, but when Minna was discarded by her wealthy lover he took her back rather than let her go on the streets. It was a rewarding gesture: over a long period of years she showed her gratitude – and, let one add, some nobility of character – by sharing with equanimity the uncertain fortunes of a husband whose budding genius can have been but small compensation for his profligacy. Privation was the order – privation aggravated by travel: from Königsberg to Riga; from Riga by sea to London and thence via Boulogne to Paris (where they continually had to shift their lodgings because they rarely paid any rent); from Paris back to Dresden, where in 1842 Wagner at last found regular employment as deputy conductor at the opera house.

During three unhappy years in Paris he had composed *Rienzi* (here and there showing prophetic signs of originality), *The Flying Dutchman* (nearly all the best of which was incorporated in the overture, a fine piece of tone-painting which owed something to Mendelssohn's *Hebrides* – see page 97) and the very effective *Faust* overture (intended as the first movement of a symphony). Settled once again in Dresden, with a reasonable stipend, he was able to tackle composition in better heart. There he completed *Tannhäuser* (1845) and *Lohengrin* (1847) which presently, thanks to the patronage of Franz Liszt, brought him to the notice of a wide public; both operas are still deservedly popular although it can now be seen that neither marked such an advance on *Der Freischütz* or *The Huguenots* as some ardent Wagnerites would have us believe. (For Weber's *Freischütz* see page 72. *The Huguenots* was a typical grand opera by Giacomo Meyerbeer – originally Jakob Beer – who had settled in Paris in 1825 and six years later had a sensational success with *Robert the Devil*; he befriended Wagner in Paris and later received contumely in return.) It is true that Weber's flair for atmosphere was brought neatly up to date in the *Tannhäuser* overture and Venusberg scene, and that in the duet between Ortrud and Frederick in Act II of *Lohengrin* the Meyerbeer convention was pushed aside when the orchestra was allowed to play its part in the unfolding of the drama; but although these two operas do indeed hold moments of rare beauty one may be oppressed by the monotonous rhythmic background: relief from 2/2 or 4/4 time comes only in the pilgrims' chorus from *Tannhäuser* and the ensemble 'Mein Herr und Gott, nun ruf' ich dich' from Act I of *Lohengrin*. (Wagner eventually outgrew this weakness: many of the lyrical passages in *The Ring* and *The Mastersingers* are in flowing 9/8 time, and it is significant that for the 1861 'Paris version' of *Tannhäuser* – see page 127 – he recast some 4/4 choral sections in 3/4.)

Back in 1830, as a rioting Leipzig student, Wagner had had his first brush with the police. When in 1849 he was faced with imprisonment as an active political revolutionary (his friend Röckel – see page 121, footnote – paid that penalty), he fled ignominiously from Dresden with a forged passport and sought asylum in Switzerland. For many years thereafter his career again became picaresque: he was always moving on, sometimes to fulfil professional engagements but as often as not to escape imminent arrest as a dangerous mutineer against governmental authority or as an accomplished bilker of importunate creditors. It would take too much time and space to recount his travels in chronological and topographical detail; suffice to record that being barred from his native Saxony he was mostly resident in tolerant Switzerland where he continued to compose, while also visiting (among other cities) London, Paris, Bordeaux, Venice, Vienna, Budapest, Prague, St Petersburg and – from 1864 onwards – Munich. At Munich (and at the royal retreat at Starnberg on the nearby Würmsee) he was a frequent guest of the young King Ludwig II of Bavaria, to whose personal interest and financial support he owed the privilege and satisfaction – on his fifty-ninth birthday – of laying the foundation stone of the Festival Theatre at Bayreuth (about thirty miles north-east of Nuremberg) which until very recently has been consecrated exclusively to performances of his music dramas.

Meanwhile in the domestic world chaos reigned and poor Minna's patience was sorely tried. Her position became well-nigh intolerable during Wagner's typically passionate but more-than-usually protracted love affair with Mathilde Wesendonck (wife of one of his most sympathetic admirers), but the final break did not come until about 1864 when he entered into a permanent *liaison* with Cosima von Bülow, the illegitimate daughter of his lifelong patron Franz Liszt by Countess Marie d'Agoult (see page 116) and the wife of his good friend the conductor Hans von Bülow. When Minna died two years later Wagner established himself with Cosima in idyllic surroundings at Triebschen on Lake Lucerne and he married her in 1870 as soon as von Bülow obtained a divorce. (Their villa, now a museum full of interesting relics, should not be missed by any music lover who finds himself in Lucerne; it is barely two miles from the town centre.) They stayed at Triebschen until 1873 when they moved to Bayreuth – the villa Wahnfried – but from 1876 onwards spent much of their time in Italy. With Cosima by his side – and, thanks to King Ludwig, a fairly full purse – Wagner found travel less exhausting than it had been with Minna thirty-five years before: there was no despair, no privation; southern sunshine and good living were objectives both attainable and attained. In September 1882 they settled in Venice where he died the following February, aged sixty-nine.

Before being driven from Dresden in 1849 Wagner had written the libretto of a projected music drama entitled *The Death of Siegfried*; several years later he made it the starting, or rather finishing, point of the mighty tetralogy which we now know as *The Ring of the Nibelung*. By 1856 he had completed both words and music of the first two sections, *The Rhinegold* and *The Valkyrie*, and had begun work on the third, *Siegfried*; at that stage, prompted by Mathilde Wesendonck, he slipped aside to *Tristan and Isolde* (1857–9). It was not until after he had also written and composed that great operatic comedy *The Mastersingers of Nuremberg* (1862–7) that he returned to his Nibelung: *Siegfried* was eventually finished in 1869 and *The Twilight of the Gods* in 1871; the forging of *The Ring* had thus taken him nearly a quarter of a century. *Parsifal*, a sublime hotch-potch of esoteric Christianity, medieval legend, eroticism and panto-mime magic, occupied him from 1877 until 1882.

The Ring, Tristan, The Mastersingers and *Parsifal* belong to a different world from Wagner's earlier operas, which broadly adhered to the convention of separate arias and ensembles connected by recitative or something like it (al-though the composer was careful to explain that no single passage in *Lohengrin* was strictly speaking a recitative). The structure of his later music dramas, by contrast, depended almost entirely upon the interlinking of significant *Leit-motive* (guiding themes), each of which represented or sug-gested a place, a person, a particular aspect of a person's character, or some abstract idea. Though a risky method of musical composition and apt to invite irreverent lampooning, one is almost persuaded of its rightness by Wagner's masterly treatment of literally scores of *Leitmotive*; at times they undergo symphonic development, at others they are recapi-tulated at a climax in a different context or in new guise – often with overwhelming effect. For instance: one of the great moments in Act III of *The Valkyrie* is Sieglinde's ecstatic outburst when she learns from Brünnhilde's lips that the child in her womb is destined to be the mightiest hero in the world (Siegfried), but nothing more is heard of this noble theme until Act III of *The Twilight of the Gods*, where it reappears, transfigured, in the course of Brünn-hilde's final lament, and from the words 'Das Feuer, dass mich verbrennt' onwards dominates the scene. This *Motiv* is said to typify 'Siegfried as redeemer', but listeners should not concern themselves too much with the *Motiv*-ticketing of erudite analysts. It scarcely matters how one labels a certain magical passage from the love duet in *Tristan* (at the change of key-signature marked *immer mehr ruhig*); what matters a lot is that when Tristan lies close to death, anxiously awaiting the ship that brings Isolde to Brittany, its recollection weaves itself in and out of his feverish dreams with a poignancy that almost tears human heart-strings asunder, and that when the ship at last arrives and Isolde hurries to his side the same theme acquires new urgency (in 5/4 time) as the dying man, with a sudden access of strength born of delirious excitement, raises himself from his couch and staggers forward to embrace her. There is no more moving scene in all opera; Wagner – Wagner in his prime – alone could have contrived it.

Aside from his more massive achievements there are two minor works which deserve appreciative comment – the 'Venusberg music' and the *Siegfried Idyll*. The former was written for a Paris production of *Tannhäuser* in 1861 (ostensibly to provide the ballet-girls of the Opera with a chance to show their paces and their charms); by that time Wagner's matured artistic perception enabled him to give added point to several of the already suggestive themes. (Many years ago an eminent conductor confided to me his opinion that this gorgeous bacchanale incorporated a perfect representation in music of the physical sensations of sexual intercourse.) The *Siegfried Idyll*, an orchestral piece composed in 1870 as a surprise birthday offering for Cosima and a tribute to their son Siegfried (then eighteen months old), is largely but not entirely based on tunes drawn from Act III of *Siegfried*; lasting only about fifteen minutes and scored with unusual restraint for single woodwind, horn, trumpet and strings, this of all the jewels in Wagner's crown is the smallest – and perhaps the brightest.

Today there is a widespread impression (not only widespread but inescapable, since apart from anything else his ostentatious *Kaisermarsch* celebrated the foundation of the German Empire in 1871) that despite Wagner's having been during much of his life *persona non grata* in his fatherland his work, taken as a whole, had a pan-German quality which later well served Nazi propaganda. The phase may pass, for Wagner the poet is dead, Wagner the philosopher is dead, Wagner the conceivable stimulator of an abhorrent régime is dead – or so we hope. Still very much alive, although possibly receiving fewer encomiums than hitherto, is the extraordinarily talented and ambitious schemer who conceived and created *Lohengrin, The Ring, The Master-singers* and the rest as entities. Unquestionably immortal is the consummate artist who clothed with exquisite music the rapture of Elsa and her anonymous bridegroom, the unconsciously incestuous passion of Sieglinde and Siegmund, the warm humanity of Hans Sachs. Purists maintain that it is unfair to Wagner's memory to present purple patches from his music dramas at orchestral concerts, although all but the most hidebound admit the suitability of the overtures and a few interludes like 'Siegfried's Journey to the Rhine' (which is a magnificent piece of music but in the opera house merely serves to keep the audience interested while the scene-shifters are noisily dismantling the Valkyries' rock and setting up the hall of the Gibichungs). Many of us would go further, believing that Wagner was in the broadest sense of the term a *symphonic* composer, at his best when concentrating on the music and away from his best when giving equal rein to literary or philosophic urges. In the great works of his full maturity the exposition and development of the all-important *Leitmotive* is almost entirely orchestral and the singers, who should be the true unfolders of the saga, are left at a disadvantage; far too often for comfort the vocal line – which is dramatically essential – fits the pattern awkwardly and thereby becomes musically redundant. Then there are those long metaphysical discourses: to assert that King Mark and Gurnemanz are crashing bores might involve excommunication from the diminishing band of perfect Wagnerites but devotees, even, go so far as to concede that there *are* patches of tedium in *Tristan* and *Parsifal* – to say nothing of *The Ring*. The eminent philosopher Friedrich Nietzsche once wrote that he loathed Wagner's music but could no longer listen to any other; less inhibited folk might affirm that they like Wagner's music but prefer it in small doses. One therefore feels free to put forward the proposition that as a composer Richard Wagner wrought better than he knew; that thanks to his incomparable musical genius his sound-pictures do not require the simultaneous visible enactments which he himself regarded as essential for their understanding but which in practice nearly always fall short of one's imaginings. While good performances of *Tannhäuser, Parsifal, Tristan, The Mastersingers* and *The Ring* remain unforgettable experiences, let us be thankful that if we wish to do so we can relax in a concert hall or by our own fireside and there (with closed eyes, perhaps) savour to the full the sensuous delights of the Venusberg or the searing anguish of Amfortas' spear-wound, share the last mortal longings of the dying Tristan, dance with a jolly crowd of youngsters in the streets of sixteenth-century Nuremberg, or march with the gods into Valhalla.

CHAPTER TWENTY-FOUR

Verdi

In the age which witnessed the bright flowering of Weber, Schubert and Mendelssohn, *bel canto* opera had been kept very much alive by Rossini, Bellini and Donizetti (see chapters 14, 16 and 17). Next in line of succession came GIUSEPPE VERDI. Had he died like Bellini at thirty-four, his name might now be forgotten. Had he died like Donizetti at fifty, he might be remembered only as one who carried on the existing tradition of conventional Italian opera. Had he died at the traditional three score and ten, an age by which Rossini was dead in all but the purely physical sense, posterity would at least have acknowledged that he had been able to improve upon that tradition. But in the event the gods, although they loved Verdi dearly, refrained from calling him home in youth – that is to say at thirty-four, fifty or seventy; it was when he produced his two finest works between the ages of seventy and eighty that he raised himself alongside Wagner, who was the elder by five months and had already been dead for three years by the time his close contemporary established himself as a giant of comparable magnitude, a giant demanding comparable attention.

After the defeat of Napoleon at the battle of Leipzig, from which baby Wagner emerged unscathed but officially an orphan (see page 120), Austrian and Russian troops were sent to occupy the Napoleonic Kingdom of Italy, an area covering (roughly) the regions now known as Lombardy, Venetia, Emilia-Romagna and the Marches; during the course of the operation a marauding band of undisciplined soldiers massacred half the population of the hamlet Roncole – two miles south-east of Busseto and about midway between Parma and Cremona (birthplace of Monteverdi). Among those who escaped were the tavern-and-store-keeper Carlo Verdi, his wife Luigia and their few-months-old son

Giuseppe – who had been born 10th October 1813. The Congress of Vienna (1815) left them citizens of the duchy of Parma, *de jure* an independent state but *de facto* under Austrian domination, like Lombardy, until forty-five years later. For the peasants of Roncole life was hard, and weekly services in the village church provided their sole respite from the laborious task of wringing a bare livelihood from the soil; Carlo Verdi, as a licensed victualler supplying their necessities, may have been slightly better off than his neighbours, and for Giuseppe the church meant only one thing – music. He was no infant prodigy but by the age of twelve had proved himself a capable organist; since he was also a sensible and intelligent lad his parents sent him to school at nearby Busseto where he came under the notice of Antonio Barezzi, a prosperous wine-merchant who was also a keen amateur musician. Thanks to his help and encouragement young Verdi soon became a prominent figure in the musical life of the little town: he conducted the brass band (for whose benefit he tried his hand at composition) and from time to time deputized for the organist and choirmaster, Ferdinando Provesi. It was Provesi who had charge of his musical education; he was an unconventional preceptor and also instilled in his pupil a profound distrust of clericalism. Between the ages of eighteen and twenty, with a local grant and an allowance from Barezzi, Verdi continued his studies in Milan (about sixty miles away); he was adjudged too old to enter the Conservatoire, but found an excellent private teacher in Vincenzo Lavigna, senior accompanist at La Scala Theatre.

By the autumn of 1834 he was back in Busseto, where eighteen months later he married Margherita Barezzi – daughter of his benefactor – and became choirmaster in succession to Provesi, although the ecclesiastical authorities insisted upon having as organist a rival candidate for the two posts (normally combined) whose religious orthodoxy was less suspect. Verdi relinquished this equivocal appointment in 1838 and returned to Milan where Bartolomeo Merelli, director of La Scala, commissioned him to compose an *opera seria* and an *opera buffa*. *Oberto* (1839 and serious) was well received, but *Un giorno di regno* (1840 and comic) was an utter failure. Hereabouts, too, Verdi's career was clouded by personal tragedy: his elder child Virginia had died in infancy; the same fate overtook his little son Romano while *Oberto* was in rehearsal; to crown all his wife died of meningitis while he was at work on *Un giorno di regno*. By the time his twenty-seventh birthday came round, therefore, he was alone in the world and in deep despair, but with characteristic resolution he soon pulled himself together: in 1842 *Nabucco* set him on the road to international fame and by 1848 not only Milan but also Venice, Rome, Naples, Florence, London, Paris and Trieste had each in turn welcomed a Verdi première. With part of his rapidly growing fortune he bought an estate at Sant' Agata, just north of Busseto. Having had the villa – almost a *castello* – completely refurbished and the surrounding farmland cleared of rubbish, he took possession three years later, and apart from holidays and occasional visits to Milan, Rome and other Italian cities (as well as to Paris and London) he stayed there for the rest of his life. (Like his birthplace five miles away on the other side of Busseto, the 'villa Verdi' at Sant' Agata is now a national monument in the care of the Italian Ministry of Fine Arts.)

By this time Verdi had recaptured domestic happiness. In his early Milan days he had been friendly with Giuseppina ('Peppina') Strepponi, a fine singer and actress from La Scala; when they met again in Paris in 1847 she became his inseparable companion and remained so until her death forty years later. Despite the wagging of busy tongues and the occasional misgivings of Peppina (a devout Catholic), Verdi with his sturdily independent outlook for long opposed any civil or religious binding of a union which had been entered into freely and with full recognition of its implications. When Barezzi, his generous patron and father of his late wife, not unnaturally made inquiries, Verdi replied with dignity.

I have nothing to hide. In my house there lives a lady, free, independent, like myself a lover of the country, the possessor of a private fortune which places her beyond the reach of need. Neither of us has to account for our actions to anybody. I will say this, however: in my house she is entitled to the deference due to myself – nay, more. On no consideration whatever must this be forgotten, for her conduct and her character give her a special claim to the consideration which she never fails to show to others.

Neither Verdi nor Peppina ever disclosed to the world why it was that in 1859, after twelve years of 'living in sin', they decided to bow to common usage; it is perhaps significant, however, that they chose to be married not at Busseto but at the village of Collonges on the Savoy/Switzerland border, while they were spending a summer holiday at Geneva. Meantime Verdi was playing an active role in political affairs; he was an ardent supporter of Cavour and the *risorgimento*, and many of his early operas contained tendentious allusions which landed him in trouble with the Austrian censors. In 1861, after the liberation and unification of Italy, he became for four years a member of parliament – an unusual sideline for a composer.

There has recently been an upsurge of interest in this country in Verdi's early operas, which for many years previously had languished in comparative oblivion. The enthusiasm with which revivals have been received is very gratifying to lovers of *bel canto* as such, but one has doubts as to whether Verdi's reputation has thereby been enhanced. Admittedly an unquenchable flow of melody was already apparent in those days, but apart from a healthy vigour not untouched by vulgarity *Nabucco*, *Ernani*, *Macbeth* and the rest made little real advance on Rossini's *Semiramide*, Bellini's *Norma* and Donizetti's *Lucia di Lammermoor*. (In *Macbeth* as we know it today, Act II opens with a fine soprano aria 'La luce langue' which would not be out of place in *Aida*, but this is not part of the original, having been composed in 1865 as substitution for the somewhat common-place 'Trionfai! securi alfine'.)

The next group of Verdi operas (1850–67) includes some more distinctive works, many of which show greater initiative than their forerunners. In *Rigoletto* uninhibited and eminently singable tunes are again in evidence, but one is also conscious of a growing power of musical characterization never realized by Rossini, Bellini or Donizetti (as in the masterly quartet 'Bella figlia dell' amore') and of a tendency to break away from conventional design ('Pari siamo'). Its successors *Il trovatore* (despite some stirring moments) and *La traviata* (for all its captivating bravura) appear slightly retrograde by comparison, although both have always been able to attract capacity audiences on a Sunday night in Italy or even on a Saturday night in Britain.* That *Simon Boccanegra, Un ballo in maschera* and *La forza del destino* did not immediately acquire equal popularity may have been due to *dramatic* weaknesses. Verdi certainly did the best he could with rather unpromising material by continuing and developing the *Rigoletto* approach; moreover, the music allotted to the page Oscar in *Un ballo* displayed a delicacy which was as unexpected as it was welcome, and the comic friar Melitone in *La forza* gave the composer a chance to prove, almost for the first time, that he could incorporate a sense of humour alongside a sense of drama. Unfortunately all three works suffered from faulty construction. So did *Don Carlos* (based on Schiller and written for the Paris Opéra) in which Verdi made an attempt to reconcile his own manner with the methods of Meyerbeer (see pages 123–4); in the event only a few items – notably the final duet – held the qualities which his many admirers had by then come to expect.

* I am surprised that an eminent music critic should recently have asserted that Act II of *La traviata* 'reveals to us a new Verdi, a fine-fingered musical psychologist'. If this opera does anywhere reveal such a new Verdi, it is surely in the justly famous aria 'Ah, fors'è lui' at the close of Act I, in which Violetta, disregarding coloratura precedent, recalls word for word and note for note Alfredo's previous outburst 'Di quell'amor, quell'amor ch'è palpito'.

Although *Boccanegra*, *La forza* and *Don Carlos* were later revised to good purpose (and thereby perhaps achieved greatness without having been born great), neither they nor *Un ballo in maschera* (which has had a measure of greatness thrust upon it by distinguished interpreters of its leading roles) have ever found as secure a place in the repertory as the last opera of Verdi's youth which he completed in 1871 when a mere fifty-seven. Of all grand operas *Aida* might be called the grandest; here Verdi flirted with *Leitmotive* (and in the prelude combined two in counterpoint), but whatever was said at the time Wagner's influence was in no other respect observable: vocal melody, lyrical melody, was still the order of the day, although there was more variety than hitherto in the orchestral accompaniments, where tum-tum and arpeggios were on the way out. Perhaps the most striking feature of *Aida*, however, was a new assurance in harmony, the emergence indeed of a recognizable and individual harmonic style. Students should examine in particular Amonasro's appeal 'Ma tu Re, tu signore possente' from the second-act finale, where the consecutive 'six-four' chords in the seventh bar look so startling on paper and yet sound so perfectly right in performance. They should also consider the contrasted effects of the frequent straightforward transitions from minor to major. (In this respect Verdi certainly learnt something from Schubert – see page 85.) In the trio from the first scene there is a wonderful moment where, coinciding with a change of key from E minor to E major, Aida's voice joins the others and floats above them in a *cantabile*; the same hovering of tonality acquires a bitter-sweet taste in the last few bars of 'Ritorna vincitor' and adds an appropriately exotic flavour to 'O cieli azzurri'. Two and a half years later Verdi used the same device again at the beginning of the Requiem; here the sudden shift from A minor to A major is neither bitter-sweet nor exotic – just sublimely beautiful.

This Requiem (dedicated to the memory of the author and poet Alessandro Manzoni, whom Verdi much admired) was paradoxically the first unquestionable masterpiece of a composer whose name is always associated with opera. That Verdi, an unbeliever, should have been at the top of his form in an extended piece of Church music is perhaps no more surprising than that a century and a half previously J. S. Bach, a staunch Lutheran, should have excelled himself in a Mass acceptable to Catholics: it was simply that Verdi – like Bach – found the traditional liturgy the only possible vehicle for a burden of self-expression. Admittedly much of the music of the Requiem was in the mood of *Aida* and such outbursts as the 'Dies irae' were unconventionally dramatic; yet there was nothing *theatrical* about this remarkable work, which leaves one with the conviction that it was composed in a spirit of profound reverence.

After the Requiem (if one disregards revisions of two earlier operas) Verdi wrote nothing at all until *Otello*, produced in 1886; *Falstaff* followed in 1893. Both libretti were splendid adaptations of Shakespeare (*Othello* and *The Merry Wives of Windsor*) by Verdi's friend and fellow composer Arrigi Boito, who deserves high praise for having given his elder and more illustrious colleague the opportunity to crown his career with a two-fold triumph. What is so astonishing is that throughout twelve years of virtual silence Verdi's latent powers had evidently been developing subconsciously: *Otello* marked an advance on *Aida* which could have been no greater had the gap between them been filled with half a dozen operas, each a finer work of art than the one which preceded it. Thus, despite superficial appearance to the contrary, *Otello* and *Falstaff* stand in direct line of succession from *Oberto* through *Rigoletto*, *La forza del destino* and *Aida*. (Apart from *Falstaff*'s other unique attributes its six scenes last on average less than twenty minutes each and it is one of the few operas ever written that leaves one regretting that all is over so soon.) During his eighties Verdi composed four short choral pieces of which two at least, the *Ave Maria* based on an 'enigmatic scale' and the *Laudi alla Vergine Maria* (words by Dante), possess a singular loveliness; they are still played now and again. (So is the attractive string quartet, dated 1873.) After the death of his beloved Peppina in 1897 Verdi knew the loneliness of old age; in the autumn of 1900 he was taken from Sant' Agata to a comfortable hotel in Milan, where he breathed his last on 27th January 1901.

'I am not a very learned composer but I am a very experienced one', was Verdi's self-assessment. In truth his learning was far from negligible (witness the fugal passages in the Requiem) and instinct rather than experience dictated that even in his last two operas the orchestra should be the servant and not (as in Wagner's music dramas) the master of the singers. But it was experience which eventually drove him to abandon the old operatic formula of stylized arias and ensembles in favour of a more homogeneous framework and so enabled him to contrive (for example) the unconventional but exquisite love duet which ends Act I of *Otello*. Experience, too, brought in its train a new sense of artistic values: *Otello* and *Falstaff* were entirely free from the vulgarity which had reared its head frequently in his very early operas – occasionally even in *Il trovatore* and *Aida*. Experience, moreover, led to the superb musical delineations of Iago's villainy, Pistol and Bardolph's roguery, the swagger of Sir John Falstaff himself. What other composer could so perfectly have portrayed corpulence as Verdi did in *Falstaff*, Act I scene 1, at the words 'sul fianco baldo, sul gran torace, sul maschio pie, sul fusto saldo, erto capace'? Note, too, the difference between his treatment of the jealous raging of the Moor, ending in tragedy, and his treatment (except perhaps in one short scene) of the jealous raging of the comic butt Master Ford. By contrast he had a curious habit – which only a genius could have exploited to such good purpose – of applying the same technical process to achieve varied emotional effects. An instance has already been cited, on page 135, concerning *Aida* and the Requiem. In that same passage from the Requiem there is also a characteristic little chromatic twirl in the accompaniment, which reappears not only at a moment of deep pathos in *Otello* (Act III, nineteenth bar after first letter I) but also at a moment of teasing charm in *Falstaff* (Act II scene 2, fifth bar after figure 41).

I shall not presume to pass judgement on whether *Otello* is a greater masterpiece than *Tristan and Isolde* or *Falstaff* than *The Mastersingers*; too much depends upon the listener's temperament. Yet since in the previous chapter the mature Wagner did not escape criticism it is only fair that the mature Verdi should also be brought under the microscope. While *Otello* is never boring – as *Tristan* is in places for any but the most ardent devotee – a sensitive musician cannot fail to notice that nearly all the terrific climaxes are built on a chord which he views with suspicion (the diminished seventh) and that there are a few – a very few – passages where the composer's melodic inspiration seems to desert him. Of *Falstaff* it might be said that here Verdi's melodic inspiration was almost *too* overpowering: the delightful little tunes follow one another so rapidly that sometimes there is hardly time to make their acquaintance. But criticism on this score would be criticism run wild, for such fluency was really a sign not of weakness but of strength, providing further evidence of the integrity with which the composer faced every problem as it presented itself. One is left with a single rhetorical speculation: would not Verdi have done better to have scored *Falstaff* for a smaller orchestra?

The humble innkeeper's son from Roncole who became a national figure in politics and an international figure in music had his personal shortcomings like everyone else: he was evidently something of a domestic tyrant and in moods of depression was notoriously liable to behave like a naughty schoolboy and growl at all around him like a sore-headed bear. But his collaborator Boito was on the mark in recording that in every moral and social sense Giuseppe Verdi was a true Christian. On his death at the age of eighty-seven the world lost a great composer – and a great man.

CHAPTER TWENTY-FIVE

Bizet*

Twenty-two of our famous composers spent the whole or a large part of their working lives in either London, Vienna or Paris, but among the twenty-two the only born Londoner was Henry Purcell, the only born Viennese Franz Schubert and the only born Parisians Camille Saint-Saëns (see chapter 31) and GEORGES BIZET, who drew his first breath of Montmartre air at 26 rue de la Tour d'Auvergne on 25th October 1838. His father (a hairdresser turned singing-teacher) came from Rouen and his mother from Cambrai, and so the point can be made that Bizet, remembered above all for his evocations of the sun-drenched south, was in fact a French *northerner*.

Both parents encouraged a youthful aptitude for music, and at the age of ten he was enrolled as a student at the Paris Conservatoire where in due course he became a pupil of Fromental Halévy (composer of the fine opera *La Juive*) – whose daughter Geneviève he was to marry in 1869. At seventeen Bizet wrote a symphony, at eighteen two operettas – *La Maison du docteur* and *Le Docteur Miracle* – the second of which tied for first place in a competition organized by Jacques Offenbach (uncrowned king in that realm) and thereby secured public representation. Soon afterwards, at the second attempt, he won the coveted Prix de Rome (see page 100, footnote); while in Italy he composed, alongside some conventional student pieces, a third and more ambitious operetta – *Don Procopio* – but this did not, as he had hoped and expected, earn a renewal of the prize, and before the end of 1860 he was back in Paris. During the

* Bizet was younger than Franck, Smetana, Bruckner, Brahms, Borodin and Saint-Saëns. I have given him precedence over them because many of their best-known works were not composed until after his death at the early age of thirty-six.

next ten years he worked hard but spasmodically (in truth he was never a very steady character), spending much of his time making piano transcriptions for the publishing firm of Choudens et Cie. The only really significant compositions belonging to this period were the operas *The Pearl Fishers* (1864) and *The Fair Maid of Perth* (1867), each of which incorporated tunes lifted from *Don Procopio*. (This was a justifiable procedure on the composer's part, seeing that the earlier work had made no headway; it was neither played nor published until thirty years after his death.)

Of all the music which Bizet composed during his teens and twenties nothing is more attractive than the very early symphony in C major which was rescued from oblivion when it had its first performance (under the baton of Felix Weingartner) at Basle in 1935; since then it has made friends all over the world. In its uninterrupted flow of melody – coupled with a tendency to long-windedness in the two middle movements – this charming work recalls Franz Schubert, but it also owes something to Charles Gounod's symphony in E flat major.* Bizet's symphony should not be taken as a model, for although the eager young student carefully adhered to convention (sonata form for the first movement, etc.) he was no master of thematic development. Nor does one find many traces of typical Bizet, except perhaps in the second movement where the pseudo-oriental colouring presages *Djamileh*. But there is an abundance of tunes (which is what really matters), most of them very good, some fairly good, none bad. This spontaneous and unsymphonic symphony was certainly a remarkable achievement for a seventeen-year-old.

Of the three operettas (all early) *Don Procopio* is the best; in some respects it is Italian *opera buffa* rather than French *opéra bouffe*, but one can trace here and there the emerg-

---

* Gounod (1818–93), who for many years was a very good friend to Bizet, is famous for *Faust* (1859) and deserves to be remembered also for some of his other operas (among them *Romeo and Juliet*), two full-scale symphonies and a 'petite symphonie' for wind instruments; for a reference to his choral music see page 146.

ence of an individual style. In the more serious and more renowned *Pearl Fishers* and *Fair Maid of Perth* Bizet tried too conscientiously to emulate the ideals of his friend Gounod as exemplified in *Faust* and *Romeo and Juliet*. *The Pearl Fishers*, a work of considerable technical accomplishment, is marred in places by a barely successful attempt to capture an Asiatic atmosphere, but it retains considerable popularity in France and elsewhere at the expense of *The Fair Maid*, which has no specifically Caledonian pretensions and deserves occasional revival.

On the outbreak of the Franco-Prussian war in 1870 Bizet enlisted in the National Guard (roughly corresponding to our own Home Guard during the Second World War). This did not involve service in the field but it did involve long hours of routine training and sentry duty, especially (as events turned out) during the siege of Paris and the subsequent Prussian occupation. Nor was the part-time composer and part-time militiaman free from domestic worry, for Geneviève Bizet, *née* Halévy, had a domineering and possessive mother and was herself somewhat neurotic; she was hardly attuned to cope with an easy-going husband who seems to have indulged in casual promiscuity as a matter of course. On a woman of her temperament the hardships of the siege perhaps pressed deeper than on housewives more accustomed to privation. At any rate Bizet wrote to Ernest Guiraud (who was later to compose recitatives for insertion in *Carmen*) that 'a kind friend brought us a few horse-bones which we shall share; every night, however, Geneviève dreams chicken and lobster; for myself I dream that we are all at Naples, living in a charming villa under a purely artistic government composed of people like Michelangelo and Shakespeare'.

By the time things had returned to something like normal Bizet, now in failing health, must have realized subconsciously (like Schubert before him) that not many years were left to him, for he concentrated much harder on composition than before the war. Within little more than three years he completed (apart from a fair quantity of comparatively unimportant works) the set of piano pieces entitled *Children's Games*, the symphonic suite *Roma* (based on the earlier *Souvenirs de Rome* of 1868), the one-act opera *Djamileh*, comprehensive incidental music for Alphonse Daudet's play *L'Arlésienne*, the concert overture *La Patrie* and finally *Carmen*. *Roma* is rather dull and *La Patrie* neither inspired nor inspiring; many of the *Children's Games*, on the other hand, are charming, though taken as a whole they are perhaps not so attractive as the *Dix pièces pittoresques* of Bizet's younger contemporary Emmanuel Chabrier, with which they have certain features in common. *Djamileh* – based on the same poem by Alfred de Musset as was Edouard Lalo's ballet *Namouna* – was Bizet's best opera so far, but its compromises with exoticism have militated against wide popularity. With *L'Arlésienne* and *Carmen* however he came into his own; it would hardly be an exaggeration to say that each outshone anything that the talented Lalo and Chabrier had ever written or were ever to write.[*]

When travelling from Paris to Rome in the winter of 1857–8 Bizet had arrived on Christmas Day at Avignon, at that time the terminus of the PLM railway. From Avignon to Toulon, his next objective, was a mere eighty miles by road and I find it hard to believe that the young composer, had he so wished, could not have covered that distance by stage-coach in a day or so. Instead he took *four* days, following a circuitous route which enabled him to visit (among other famous antiquities of Provence) the *maison carrée* at Nîmes, the château at Tarascon and the Roman theatre at Arles. Like many others before and since he succumbed to the fascination of the region – and it was probably his nostalgic recollections of that journey which encouraged and inspired him, fourteen years later, to compose music for *L'Arlésienne*, all of whose scenes are set either in the town itself or in the surrounding countryside. Bizet, although only here and there using traditional dance tunes (e.g. in the far-

---

[*] I reviewed the careers and achievements of Lalo and Chabrier, as well as Halévy (see page 139), in *Sidelights on a Century of Music* (Macdonald, 1969; St Martin's Press, 1970).

andole), was completely successful in capturing the authentic Provençal atmosphere. Moreover the orchestration was brilliantly original throughout – and not just because he used a saxophone, either : in the *andantino* section of the prelude, for instance, the cellos play a *legato* version of the vigorous main theme against a sonorous horn counterpoint while two bassoons scamper all over the place with *staccato* triplets. As for the 'adagietto' (actually marked *adagio* in the score, and only thirty-four bars long), one admirer of Bizet, at least, finds it a perfect – and moving – example of what Ernest Newman once called the small poem in music. (Most listeners are familiar with *L'Arlésienne* through two popular orchestral suites. The first of these was transcribed by the composer himself and played during his lifetime; 'suite no. 2' was arranged by Guiraud after Bizet's death and incorporates excerpts from both *L'Arlésienne* and *The Fair Maid of Perth*.)

Among regular opera-goers there are some queer fish. On the one hand is a hard core which interests itself in opera to the exclusion of all else in music and is ready to undergo considerable discomfort in order to attend any performance of (say) *Il trovatore* or *Tannhäuser* without ever having realized, apparently, that Verdi wrote a superb Requiem and Wagner the incomparable *Siegfried Idyll*.* Then there are those whose taste is so uncatholic that they resent Rossini's *Barber of Seville* because it isn't Mozart's *Marriage of Figaro*,

---

* Somewhere about 1930, while standing in the gallery queue at Covent Garden for a performance of *Don Giovanni*, I got into conversation with my neighbour, who turned out to be just such an opera 'fan'. Inevitably the talk turned on Mozart and it was soon clear that he knew his *Figaro*, *Don Giovanni* and *Magic Flute* from A to Z. When I briefly referred to the 'Jupiter' he interjected 'What's that? An opera called *Jupiter*?' Somewhat taken aback I explained as tactfully as I could that the 'Jupiter' was not an opera but a symphony. 'Oh,' came the reply, 'I've never heard a symphony; I thought it was only Bach and Handel who wrote anything of that sort.' At that moment the doors opened and we surged forward to the diminutive box-office; after climbing those interminable stairs I was cowardly enough to seat myself on a bench as far away from him as possible.

Weber's *Freischütz* because it isn't Beethoven's *Fidelio*, Richard Strauss's *Rosenkavalier* because it isn't Johann Strauss's *Fledermaus*. (Or vice versa.) Yet many of these good people, I think, would agree with the rest of us that Bizet's *Carmen* is one of the seven operatic wonders of the world. (Devotees of Mozart, Beethoven, Weber, Rossini, Wagner, Verdi, the Strausses, Puccini and who-you-will are at liberty to argue to their hearts' content about which are the other six.)

For *Carmen* Henri Meilhac and Ludovic Halévy (Bizet's cousin-by-marriage), whose names had previously been associated only with operetta, between them forged a very good libretto out of Prosper Mérimée's short story – which incidentally is worth reading for its own sake. Bizet took full advantage and gave the world a galaxy of good tunes, inevitably not all of the very highest quality but all appropriate in their context. In their different ways the seguidilla, the quintet, the 'card trio', Micaela's aria 'Je dis que rien ne m'épouvante', these – and not these alone – entitle their composer to world-wide recognition as a master of his craft, yet true genius is equally in evidence in the musical treatment of the drama as a whole, the steady progression through situations which, though clearly dangerous, do not at first look likely to prove fatal, but lead ultimately to the tragedy which throughout the course of the last act is seen to be inevitable.

It has never been conclusively established whether the cool reception at first accorded to *Carmen* was due to the reluctance of the Parisian public to accept a virago as an operatic heroine or to the antagonism of a pressure-group of musicians who for one reason or another cherished a measure of animosity against the composer; possibly it was a bit of both. However that may be, Bizet was greatly distressed and three months later he died – on 3rd June 1875. Not of a broken heart, for such a phenomenon is unknown to medical science; his worthy doctor reported, no doubt with clinical accuracy, that 'he succumbed to a cardiac complication of articular rheumatism'.

Bizet worked subjectively and can therefore be accounted a romantic, but his subjectivity was less personal, less individual, than that of, say, Berlioz. He was one of those (Wagner perhaps was another) who rather than interpret the mood or *milieu* in which they found themselves at the time – as Berlioz had in the *Symphonie fantastique* – found it more aesthetically satisfying to interpret the mood or *milieu* in which they would have *wished* to find themselves. Therein lies the explanation of the apparent paradox pointed in this chapter's first paragraph. Georges Bizet the man was a Parisian to his fingertips; his finest music, by contrast, belonged to those lands of southern sunshine and song of which he used to dream during the careworn days and nights when his native city lay blockaded and besieged.

CHAPTER TWENTY-SIX

Franck

CÉSAR FRANCK (1822–90) was born in Liège (at 13 rue St Pierre, within a stone's-throw of the Prince-Bishops' Palace) but, like his fellow-townsman André Grétry eighty years earlier, he left his native Belgium while still a youngster and spent most of his life in Paris. It is no good pretending, however, that he was French by anything but naturalization and adoption, and indeed he was only just Belgian, for his father came from the indeterminate borderland west of Aachen and his mother was German by birth. César showed youthful precocity as a pianist and did well at the Paris Conservatoire but then disappointed his parents (who had great ambitions on his behalf) by declining to follow in the steps of Franz Liszt as a virtuoso. He again disappointed them by marrying Félicité Saillot, daughter of an actor and actress, and yet again by adopting the unglamorous career of organist and teacher of music.

Franck even pursued the smooth tenor of his way – although inevitably losing a few pupils – during the siege of Paris and the *commune*. Meanwhile he had produced a fair quantity of instrumental and choral music superficially comparable in style and quality with that of his colleague Charles Gounod (whose achievements in those fields are often underrated), but it was only when at the age of fifty he was appointed a professor at the Conservatoire that his compositions began to make an impact. Since his reputation depends almost entirely upon the piano pieces, chamber music and orchestral works which he wrote during the eighteen years that remained to him it is perhaps both unfair and inaccurate to dub him – as disparagers are wont to – as an organ-loft composer.

Yet one can see the disparagers' point of view, for Franck's music does display features which one tends to associate with composers who spend their working lives in the service of the Church: sincerity of approach, thickness of instrumental texture and an addiction to square-cut rhythmic figures (although this last never became such an obsession as it did with his fellow-organist Anton Bruckner whom we shall meet in chapter 28). What eventually set Franck apart from Gounod and the younger Jules Massenet (with whom also he had certain characteristics in common) was an extremely individual exploitation of chromatic harmonies which in his day could be interpreted as a genuine attempt to widen the musical horizon but in which later generations have found evidence of mannered artificiality: many of us have to make a conscious effort to put ourselves in the right frame of mind before we can appreciate Franck as he deserves to be appreciated – but the effort brings worthwhile rewards.

The oratorio *Les Béatitudes* (completed in 1879) and three symphonic poems – *Les Eolides* (1876), *Le Chasseur maudit* (1882) and *Les Djinns* (1884) – were not altogether successful, mainly because Franck's style, unlike Bizet's, was so personal that it allowed little scope for musical characterization; *Les Djinns* was the most typical, and noteworthy for incorporating a part for solo piano not so much for the sake of virtuosity as to provide tone-contrast with the orchestral forces. The fact remains that the works which hold Franck's quintessence number precisely seven; in order of composition they were:

a piano quintet (1879)
Prelude, chorale and fugue for piano (1884)
Symphonic Variations for piano and orchestra (1885)
a violin sonata (1886)
Prelude, aria and finale for piano (1887)
a symphony (1888)
a string quartet (1889).

All adhered to classical formulae, though the quintet and the symphony were each in three movements rather than the four which might have been expected; for a composer who adopted a highly flavoured harmonic idiom such restraint was appropriate and commendable.

The piano quintet (in F minor) is a fine piece of work. It admittedly has weaknesses: the first movement is both diffuse and disjointed, and when the second, after setting out confidently in A minor, suddenly jumps back in its fifth bar to the F minor of the first movement – a curious case of key-insensitivity – both composer and listener are momentarily thrown off balance. But there is far more to be said on the credit side of the ledger: except here and there in the finale, where an orchestra seems called for, the quintet combination is expertly handled; the first movement, for all its faults of construction, rises at one moment to a joyous climax and then dies away in a subtly contrived anti-climax of despondency; the D flat major section of the slow movement (marked *dolcissimo ma cantabile*) takes one to a world of ethereality; the finale, despite its naïvities of despair, admirably rounds off a work which is predominantly gloomy in mood but which an objective critic will place among the three best piano quintets ever written. Nor is this a back-handed compliment: although piano quintets are not three a penny, ten of our fifty famous composers provided twelve between them – and there have been others of considerable merit, notably that of Ernö Dohnányi.

Camille Saint-Saëns (for whom see chapter 31) complained of Franck's *Prelude, chorale and fugue* that the chorale wasn't a chorale and the fugue wasn't a fugue. (He could hardly deny him the right to call the first movement a prelude.) The criticism was justified only from the narrowest academic standpoint, for here Franck (like Mendelssohn before him) was merely adapting eighteenth-century convention to fit nineteenth-century practice. Nevertheless the companion piece *Prelude, aria and finale* is more immediately attractive: the prelude is splendidly masculine and virile, the aria delightfully feminine and yielding; the finale, though the least satisfying of the three movements, is at least lively – and thematically unifying.

The *Symphonic Variations* (in F sharp minor) are based

(*a*) on two short phrases of four bars each and (*b*) on a more extended theme which does not emerge in concise form until about a quarter of the way through. The second of the two initial four-bar phrases one was taught in youth to identify with the words 'get your hair cut', and in all seriousness the bearing-in-mind of this unromantic precept is more helpful than any laborious analysis in enabling one to appreciate the artistry of the work – e.g. in the extraordinarily poetic passage which leads from a beautiful F sharp major variation – marked *molto più lento* – to the sparkling finale. This finale, incidentally, sweeps aside sultry hot-house chromaticism in as exhilarating an open-air display of brilliantine as any barber could wish for; students should take special note of bars 385–99, where woodwind players and violinists in turn get their hair cut – in 4/4 time – while the pianist provides a whirling spin-drier accompaniment that might derive from a Chopin waltz or the last movement of Schumann's piano concerto.

The lovely violin sonata (in A major) was dedicated to the eminent virtuoso Eugène Ysaye – another native of Liège – and stands rather apart from the rest of Franck's representative compositions, for in none of the others does one find such a continuous flow of limpid melody. Spontaneous lyricism is apparent not only in the undulating 9/8 of the first movement and the unconventional 'recitative-fantasia' which does duty as the third (slow) movement but also in the turbulent *allegro* (placed second) – where the violin often seems to be giving added point to what the piano has to say – and in the graceful finale where both the placid theme and its canonic treatment recall Schumann once again.

By comparison Franck's symphony (in D minor) is disappointing. The first movement, which in most symphonies is expected to set a standard for the whole, shows him in a rather poor and artificial light which even an ingenious adaptation of sonata form fails to brighten. The second movement, however, whose middle section is a discreetly abbreviated scherzo, is most attractive; at the risk of enraging Franck devotees I suggest that it might sometimes be rescued from its surroundings and played all by itself as an orchestral intermezzo. As for the third and last movement, that perceptive critic Martin Cooper, champion of all that is best in French music, hit the nail on the head when he wrote that it seems to protest too much that it is the finale of a symphony; one might add that its most satisfying moment comes when a tune from the (outstanding) second movement provides a thumping climax.

The string quartet (in D major) is perhaps Franck's *chef d'oeuvre* for here, while harmonic individualism yields no whit, there is a refreshingly original approach to the formal problems of chamber music; moreover, anyone who has patiently schooled himself to accept the Franck idiom will acknowledge that a touch of genius is evident almost throughout, and that the mastery of the medium puts to flight the notion that he was mentally as well as physically cooped up in an organ loft all his life. The four movements are well contrasted, and some of the harmonic progressions in the third might come near to convincing an unbeliever that Franck's specialized form of chromaticism had something to be said for it after all; it is only in the finale, a rather selfconscious attempt to 'do a late Beethoven', that the composer slightly lets everyone down – Beethoven included.

The string quartet, when first played in public early in 1890, brought Franck a greater measure of applause from the Parisian musicians of his day than had any of his previous works, and it looked as though he might be turning the corner of their esteem. Soon afterwards, however, in a regrettable fit of the absent-mindedness to which he was always prone, he crossed a busy street without looking where he was going and collided painfully with the shaft of a horse-omnibus. Minimizing his injuries, he carried on his way – and indeed for a few weeks carried on his work – but lack of proper medical treatment resulted in the onset of pleurisy and he died the following autumn, one month short of his sixty-ninth birthday.

During the last fifteen years or so of his life César Franck exerted a considerable influence on a younger generation of French composers: among his pupils and disciples were Vincent d'Indy (a good friend but an undiscriminating admirer), Ernest Chausson, Alfred Bruneau and Gabriel Pierné. If since then his reputation has had its ups and downs on the stock exchange of responsible musical opinion it can be seen in retrospect that he was as significant a figure in the musical life of Paris during the first two decades of the Third Republic as Berlioz had been during the Second Empire.

CHAPTER TWENTY-SEVEN

Smetana

From 1620 until the dissolution of the Habsburg Empire in 1918 the Czechs, racially allied with the Russians and inhabiting Bohemia and Moravia, were subject to foreign domination. For all those three hundred years 'national' ideals in politics were (at worst) harshly stamped out or (at best) strongly deprecated, and until 1860 or thereabouts 'national' ideals in art survived only as a picturesque feature of the Empire's provincial backwoods; so far as culture was concerned Prague, the Bohemian capital, was a mere outpost of Vienna. Bit by bit, however, improved communications brought further opportunities for the spread of propaganda abroad: Czech literature at last began to make more than local impact, and meanwhile BEDŘICH (Frederick) SMETANA emerged as the first composer of his race to qualify as 'famous'.

Smetana was born on 2nd March 1824 at Litomyšl, a small town in eastern Bohemia; his father was the manager of a brewery and discouraged him from adopting music as a profession. But Bedřich, who even as a boy had displayed remarkable proficiency on both piano and violin, struck out on his own and at the age of twenty secured a reasonably lucrative post as 'music master' in the feudal household of Count Leopold Thun, who owned one magnificent mansion in Prague and half a dozen others in various country districts of Bohemia. Count and music master parted company in 1848 when Smetana, who all his life was a devoted Czech nationalist, joined other equally enthusiastic compatriots in a demonstrative and well-intentioned but eventually abortive rebellion directed against their Viennese overlords. Presently the young firebrand settled down and married Kateřina Kolařová, daughter of old friends of the Smetana family and herself an accomplished pianist; between the two of them they established a private music school in Prague. This modest venture was sufficiently successful to bring Smetana's name to the notice of musicians outside Bohemia, and in 1856 he accepted the directorship of the Göteborg (Gothenburg) Philharmonic Society. During the next seven years he spent most of his time in Sweden, where he produced his first compositions of importance: three symphonic poems entitled *Richard III*, *Wallenstein's Camp* and *Haarkon Jarl*, all of which paid tribute to Liszt in their manner and to Wagner in their matter.

Smetana's wife Kateřina died in 1859, but about a year later he married again (Barbara Ferdinandi), and in 1863 returned to Prague, where he soon began to play a prominent part in the Czech cultural resurgence which was by then under way. He even composed a Czech opera, *The Brandenburgers in Bohemia*, which after many frustrating delays was eventually produced in January 1866. But although Smetana the man was an ardent nationalist, Smetana the composer was at the time a suspect cosmopolitan: the libretto of *The Brandenburgers* appealed to Czech patriotic instincts, but the music could only be regarded as an attempt to emulate early Wagner; consequently the work made little more impact than a revival of Wagner's *Rienzi* might have done. (It is only fair to add that nevertheless *The Brandenburgers in Bohemia* is still now and again played in Prague.)

Annoyed by the poor reception given to his first opera Smetana, who, let it be admitted, was a hypersensitive and rather ill-tempered fellow, tried to revenge himself on the good people of Prague by dashing off an operetta, a 'trivial affair', which he reckoned that only boors would be likely to appreciate. 'I composed it without ambition, straight off the reel, in a way that beat Offenbach himself hollow.' Whatever Smetana's motives, *The Bartered Bride* showed him in a more favourable light than any of his previous works. This indeed was Smetana straight off the reel: Liszt and Wagner might never have been born; here was jolly folk-style music that the Czech people understood and loved. It should be explained, however, that *The Bartered*

Bride as we know it today differs in many respects from the 'trivial affair' played in Prague in May 1866. In its original form this unassuming stage-piece comprised no more than eight musical numbers, separated by dialogue. For a revival in 1869 Smetana added an opening chorus to Act II, along with Mařenka's aria 'Our dream of love how fair it was' and the dance of the comedians. Later the same year the whole work was reconstructed in three acts instead of two, the furiant being inserted in Act I, the polka in Act II, and the dance of the comedians being transferred to the new Act III. Finally, for a production at St Petersburg in 1870, dialogue was replaced throughout by recitative. (Personally, I think Smetana's judgement was at fault in making this last alteration.)*

In September 1866 Smetana was appointed permanent conductor at the Czech National Theatre in Prague, and to celebrate the laying of the foundation stone of a new theatre building in 1868 was invited to compose another opera. Presumably because he thought this too solemn an occasion for anything but 'music drama' he eschewed the light-heartedness of *The Bartered Bride* and produced another pseudo-Wagnerian essay: *Dalibor* is a better opera than *The Brandenburgers in Bohemia*, standing in the same relation thereto as does *The Flying Dutchman* to *Rienzi*, but a curious light is thrown on Smetana's mentality when one recalls that even at the age of forty-three this ardent Czech nationalist saw fit to adopt a largely alien idiom in a work specially composed to mark a milestone in the progress of a *Bohemian* cultural enterprise.

His next work for the stage was *Two Widows* (1874). Like *The Bartered Bride*, this was in the first instance built on *Singspiel* or *operetta* lines, but Smetana was furious when an indiscreet critic turned his previous reference to Offenbach into a boomerang. To make intentions perfectly clear

* The familiar English title of this opera (or operetta, as I still prefer to call it) is inapposite, for the heroine is neither a 'bride' nor 'bartered'; the French equivalent, *La Fiancée vendue*, is a more literal translation of the original *Prodaná nevěstá*.

he produced a new 'through-composed' version in which once again two acts were expanded to three; in this form *Two Widows* has survived. Though less immediately attractive than its predecessor, it is lively and entertaining. A constructional weakness is the perfunctory treatment of the chorus, which makes only three conventional appearances – at the beginning of Act II and at the ends of Acts II and III; it might just as well have been left out altogether. The overture, following the precedent of *The Bartered Bride*, is in sonata form and incorporates a *fugato*; there is also an excellent polka, and the music is spirited throughout. Smetana's subsequent operas were also all based on Bohemian lore, but as a rule the subjects were historical or romantic rather than humorous, and the touch was sometimes heavy-handed: in parts of *The Kiss* (1876) and in much of *Libuše* (1881) it was evident that he had still not succeeded altogether in casting aside Teutonic shackles. On the other hand *The Secret* (1878) and *The Devil's Wall* (1882) were less pretentious, and the former, at any rate, recaptured to a certain extent the carefree gaiety of *The Bartered Bride* and *Two Widows*.

Apart from his operatic achievements Smetana displayed his early mixed-style talent in many songs and piano pieces and in an excellent piano trio in G minor. He later appeared as a true apostle of Czech musical art in the splendid cycle of six symphonic poems collectively entitled *My Country*, of which *Vltava* is deservedly the best loved, although *Šárka* is an almost equally fine piece of work; the other four are each at least as impressive as any of Liszt's essays in the same field. The unconventional but here-and-there captivating string quartet in E minor, dated 1876 and subtitled *From my life*, is also for the most part Bohemian in character, but about the time of its composition Smetana began to suffer increasingly from deafness, and the doctors of his day could do little to alleviate the distress which this caused him: a second string quartet (1882) was pathetically uneven, and indeed was soon followed by a mental breakdown. He died (in an asylum) on 12th May 1884.

When the whole corpus of his work is taken into account Bedřich Smetana perhaps hardly deserves to be recognized as a 'great' composer. But if one leaves aside the intermittent attempts to emulate Wagner and contemplates, rather, what one likes to think of as his most characteristic works – *The Bartered Bride*, *My Country*, and a handful of the rest – it becomes clear that he established himself as one of the first composers in musical history to earn an international reputation through adopting, consciously and conscientiously, a 'national' outlook.

CHAPTER TWENTY-EIGHT

Bruckner

Seven pages of W. H. Hadow's excellent little book *Music* (Home University Library, 1924, already referred to on page 91) were devoted to Brahms, for whom his adulation stopped not far short of idolatry. There then followed, as in sonata form, a bridge passage leading to the second subject (Dvořák, who was granted two pages).

In Vienna itself there is not much more to tell: there were the two Johann Strausses, much beloved of Viennese ball-rooms; there was an amiable and industrious composer named Anton Bruckner whom his contemporaries endeavoured to place in rivalry with Brahms; there was the true song-writer Hugo Wolf, whose eager and hectic genius wore him out before his time; there was Carl Goldmark, suave, polished and efficient, a typical example of the second order of composition. Of more moment than these was the growth of the Nationalist School in Bohemia, inaugurated by Bedřich Smetana, whose *Bartered Bride* is still upheld as a standard, and continued by his greater disciple, Antonín Dvořák.*

Bruckner, earning this brief mention as amiable and industrious, was at least luckier than Mahler who earned none at all, although the author admitted such relatively undistinguished contemporaries as Charles Martin Loeffler and Edward Macdowell and was sufficiently up to date to deal with Arnold Bax and Sergei Prokofiev. Hadow typified the outlook of his generation, for Bruckner's name (let alone

* For Brahms see chapter 29, for Wolf chapter 38, for Smetana chapter 27, for Dvořák chapter 34; for Johann Strauss the younger recall *Die Fledermaus*; for Johann Straus the older and Goldmark let Hadow's comments suffice. (For Goldmark see also page 258.)

Mahler's) appeared very seldom on British concert programmes until 1930 or thereabouts and it is only of comparatively recent years – in this country – that his stock has risen to present heights: it is significant that in the third edition of *Grove's Dictionary of Music and Musicians* (1927) two pages were deemed sufficient for a discussion of his work whereas by the fifth edition (1953) the allowance had been doubled. Though a late entrant to the arena of public esteem he can no longer be denied recognition alongside the old war-horses.

Like his compatriot Franz Schubert (whose page-allocation in *Grove*, by the way, has dropped from fifty-five to thirty-five) ANTON BRUCKNER (1824–96) was the son of a schoolmaster and became one himself at seventeen. There the biographical similarity ends, for Schubert abandoned the drudgery at eighteen and Bruckner supported it till he was thirty-two (an age which Schubert never attained). Born at the pretty hillside village of Ansfelden, seven miles south of Linz and now lying alongside the Vienna–Salzburg *Autobahn*, he stayed in that region of Upper Austria (except for occasional visits to Vienna) until he was forty-four: he was schoolmaster-cum-organist at the villages of Windhaag (two years), Kronstorf (two years) and St Florian (eleven years) in turn, and from 1856 to 1868 organist (without school-teaching) at Linz Cathedral. During his twenties and early thirties he wrote some mediocre choral music and a handful of organ and piano pieces but his creative powers were slow to develop. (Compare his fellow organist and close contemporary César Franck, chapter 26.) St Florian, to this day a picturesque centre of monasticism, might be regarded as the spiritual home of Bruckner the organist, but it was not until he settled in Linz that Bruckner the composer began a meticulous study of harmony, counterpoint, fugue, form and orchestration; by 1862 he was armed with a portfolio of academic certificates which gave him greater confidence. The first few works of his maturity – three Masses and three symphonies (the third of which is that now known as no. 1) – were completed before he left Linz in 1868 on being appointed professor of counterpoint and fugue at the Vienna Conservatoire. The remainder – notably eight more symphonies (nos. 2 to 9) – all belong to Vienna, where he lived for the rest of his life. Meanwhile he made several trips abroad: he visited Nancy and Paris in 1869 and London in 1871 as a practising organist; Bayreuth in 1876, 1882, 1886 and 1892 as a devoted Wagnerite; Berlin in 1891 and 1894 as a distinguished composer. During his late sixties he suffered from ill-health and was obliged to resign his professorship, but he went on composing until his death at the age of seventy-two.

From the writings of friends and foes – and he had plenty of both – Bruckner emerges as a simple-minded countryman, clean-living and devout; he cuts an incongruous figure beside Schubert the engaging bohemian, Mendelssohn the spoilt darling of society, Liszt the cosmopolitan man-of-the-world, Wagner the turbulent rebel and Verdi the earnest freethinker. From his forties onward he was continually offering marriage to young girls and being refused; the nearest he came to matrimony was when a chambermaid at a Berlin hotel proposed to *him* and was accepted – but her Lutheran father put his foot down when he realized that she would have to become a Catholic.

Anecdotes abound of Bruckner's rustic gaucherie and some of them are well authenticated: it is a fact that after the successful first performance of his so-called 'Romantic' symphony (no. 4) he pressed a small coin into the hand of the conductor – Hans Richter – with the words 'that was splendid, my man; go and buy yourself a glass of beer'. One of his most ardent admirers, Franz Brunner, in a monograph published during Bruckner's lifetime and paying high tribute to his artistic idealism, recognized – and excused – his social imperfections.

Regarded by his colleagues as a shy simpleton and by the leaders of society as a boor, he is in truth a typical Austrian: warm-blooded, excitable, kindhearted, generous to a fault – and altogether a most worthy fellow.

Ill-wishers chose to make out that this most worthy fellow was little better than a village idiot, but village idiots do not write symphonies which posterity acclaims as master-pieces, and so the unworldly Bruckner has the last laugh over spiteful sniggerers.

A turning-point in his career came in 1863 when he heard *Tannhäuser* for the first time; he promptly conceived an intense admiration for its composer and thereafter sought him out on every possible occasion. (Wagner treated him no better and no worse than one might treat an embarrassingly affectionate spaniel.) But he did himself more harm than good by naïvely glorifying his idol in Vienna at a time when Viennese musicians and music critics were predomin-antly anti-Wagner: for instance Wagner's arch-enemy Eduard Hanslick of the *Neue freie Presse*, having been lampooned as Beckmesser in *The Mastersingers*, revenged himself on poor unsophisticated Bruckner.

He seems to have accepted certain Wagnerian pieces as models for symphonic construction ... Tossed about be-tween intoxication and desolation, we arrive at no definite impression and enjoy no artistic pleasure. It is not out of the question that the future belongs to this muddled hang-over style – which is no reason to regard the future with envy. Wagnerian orchestral effects are met on every hand; one would prefer that symphonic music remain undefiled by a style only relatively justified as an illustrative device for certain dramatic situations ... The finale, with its baroque themes, its confused structures and inhuman din, strikes us only as a model of tastelessness.

Bruckner was very sensitive to criticism and this sort of thing sapped his self-assurance, driving him to spend much time on revision: several of his symphonies were played during his lifetime in two or three distinct versions, added to which he never ceased making minor corrections and even allowed well-meaning friends to tamper with nos. 5

and 6. During the 1930s and 1940s a measure of order was brought to the chaotic pile of issues and re-issues by the Austrian musicologist Robert Haas, whose knowledge and understanding of his subject enabled him to disentangle spontaneous alterations from those which were made, as it were, under duress – or by colleagues. It would be going too far to say that Haas's editions are definitive, but they are as near to true Bruckner as we are likely to get.

His symphonies – each one of which holds its moments of loveliness – are cast in the classic mould of late Beethoven and late Schubert, carrying the style of their famous no. 9s to a logical conclusion, but they are laid out on an even larger scale: no vocalists are required but playing-time is anything from an hour to an hour and a half. Moreover the quick movements (leaving aside the scherzos which usually rely on wild energy) seem to adhere to the *festina lente* principle; this is partly because of Bruckner's habit of introducing solemn chorales or other ecclesiastical strains (including orchestral transcriptions of passages from his own Masses); partly because of their constructional disjointedness – typified by frequent pauses for breath (or, if you prefer, pregnant silences); partly because of the prevailing squareness of the rhythm. (Only in the scherzos – and in the middle sections of the slow movements of nos. 1 and 3 – does he escape from 2/2 or 4/4 time, and the tyranny of the four-bar phrase is almost everywhere apparent.) Perhaps the slow movements make the strongest appeal, particularly those of nos. 7, 8 and 9 which display a resource of rhapsodic eloquence hitherto shrouded by a veil of formality. (No. 9 has no finale; Bruckner sketched one but did not live to finish it.) Although his three Masses (all originally completed before he left Linz but later revised) contain fine individual sections – especially the first, in D minor – and the *Te Deum* (1881) is almost suggestive of Berlioz in its emancipation from convention, Anton Bruckner's Church music has justly been put in the shade by the hefty and beautiful symphonies (religious symphonies as Alfred

Einstein called them) to which he devoted himself during the last thirty years of his life as whole-heartedly and exclusively as his adored Richard Wagner did to his hefty and beautiful (but not always religious) music dramas.

CHAPTER TWENTY-NINE

Brahms

It was unfortunate for Bruckner that during the twenty-eight years which he spent in Vienna the city also housed another master-musician. There is no need to recount here the activities of the rival Brucknerite and 'Brahmin' factions; the principals (like Gluck and Piccinni in Paris a century earlier – see page 44) tried to stand aloof from the warring of their partisans but were inevitably involved from time to time. Their profound differences of approach have been analysed by many historians; Bruckner and Brahms themselves, when dragged willy-nilly into the fray, put the matter in two small nutshells with their pithy and unconsciously self-revealing comments.

Bruckner:

> He is Brahms – my profound respect. But I am Bruckner and I prefer my own stuff.

Brahms:

> Bruckner writes only for effect; his symphonies are a colossal swindle.

It should be stressed that both were good-natured individuals and that neither cherished personal animosity, but Bruckner, with his limited intellectual capacity, understood no musical idiom but his own, while his high-minded adversary might have been an even greater composer than he was had he not regarded it as dishonest to write for effect.

JOHANNES BRAHMS (1833-97) was born at Hamburg, to be precise at 24 Schlüterhof just off the Speckgang, a narrow slum midway between the Alster and the Lower Port. (The tenement was destroyed by bombing in 1944, and the site is now occupied by a new building – 60 Speckstrasse.) His father was a double-bass player and though far from affluent somehow managed to ensure that Johannes received a sound musical education. At first he had to be content with entertaining the sailors who frequented the neighbouring brothels, but between the ages of fourteen and nineteen he made several public appearances as a pianist in more respectable surroundings and composed a handful of songs and piano pieces – including three sonatas. In 1853 he travelled Germany with the young Hungarian violinist Eduard Reményi, giving recitals at Hanover, Göttingen, Weimar and elsewhere. When the tour ended they parted company and Brahms made his way to Düsseldorf, armed with a letter of introduction to Robert Schumann. Schumann promptly formed a high opinion of his talent and suggested that he should write a symphony, whereupon Brahms started work on one but only completed two movements. Over the next year or so he repaid kindness and hospitality by befriending Clara Schumann during her husband's distressing last illness (see page 112), and subsequently she helped him to find part-time employment as piano-teacher at the court of Lippe-Detmold (a small principality lying in the north-eastern corner of what is today the province of North-Rhine Westphalia) which remained his headquarters until 1860. Further concert tours followed, one of which took him to Vienna; like Beethoven before him he found the atmosphere so congenial that he settled there permanently.

Brahms the man was as level-headed as Brahms the composer (which is saying a lot) – and never married. Not that he was unattracted by women: since his mother was seventeen years older than his father it may have been a hereditary kink that drove him as a youngster to nourish a hopeless passion for Clara Schumann, a mere fourteen years his senior, but it is known, too, that in later life he had three less calf-like (though probably equally innocent) love affairs. It may be significant that in each case the object of his affection was a mezzo-soprano, for moderation in all things was his motto. It is impossible to imagine such a steady middle-of-the-road character becoming involved (like Liszt) with a princess or (like Bruckner) with a chambermaid, and by the same token much of his music achieves its desired effect at somewhere between *mezzo piano* and *mezzo forte*. (How different from his rival's! When listening to a Bruckner symphony on the radio one has to tune up the quiet passages in order to hear them at all and tune down the Wagnerian climaxes in order to avoid complaints from the neighbours.)

During the six years that elapsed between his departure from Düsseldorf and his arrival in Vienna Brahms steadily added to his reputation as a composer – not only with more songs and piano pieces but also with chamber and orchestral works. Among them were a piano trio, two piano quartets, a string sextet, two (lengthy) orchestral serenades and – most important of all – a fine piano concerto in D minor, largely based on the uncompleted symphony of Düsseldorf days and dedicated in effect though not in superscripture to Schumann's memory. Like Berlioz in the *Symphony fantastique* (written at the same age, twenty-six), Brahms in this concerto established once and for all his true quality, since it displayed many of the features which one associates with nearly all the music of his full maturity: sincerity of expression; earnest striving after absolute beauty with consequent deliberate avoidance of anything approaching facile charm; a mastery of symphonic form; forthright theme-presentation *à la* Beethoven (*pianissimo* openings, much favoured by Bruckner, are rare in Brahms); a strongly developed sense of harmonic contrast (coupled with an irritating predilection for consecutive sixths, a German characteristic); complete freedom from the four-square rigidity which afflicted Wagner until middle-age and Bruckner throughout his life; an astonishing flair for effective off-beat rhythmic accentuations, often of complex pattern; workmanlike but somewhat thick orchestration – more skilful than Schumann's but not to be compared with Mendelssohn's or Wagner's.

During his first five years in Vienna Brahms was still active as a concert pianist, in which capacity he paid several visits to his native Germany, to Switzerland and to Hungary. From about 1868, however, he devoted himself almost entirely to composition and presently produced four big choral works – the Requiem (with solo parts for soprano and baritone), *Harz Journey in Winter* (with contralto solo, and commonly known as the alto rhapsody), *Song of Destiny* and *Song of Triumph* (i.e. the triumph of Prussia in the Franco-Prussian war of 1870–71). With all respect to admirers of these works and especially of the Requiem – which was a setting not of the liturgy but of a biblical text – this was a field in which he was never quite at home, despite the fact that his vocal writing was extremely competent. 'Bach brought up to date' it was said, but 'Handel brought up to date' would have been a more accurate parallel, since Brahms relied more on harmony than on counterpoint and the contrapuntal passages, when they came, were more noteworthy for solidity than for virtuosity. (One is glad to point out that he was a *rara avis* among the German musicians of his day in showing a proper appreciation of Handel's quality.)

To the next period, 1873-86, belong Brahms' eight orchestral masterpieces – the 'St Anthony' variations on a theme of Haydn, the four symphonies, the violin concerto, the piano concerto in B flat major and the double concerto for violin and cello. In these works the strengths and weaknesses noted in the earlier D minor piano concerto (see previous page) are still apparent; bearing them in mind, only a few further remarks are necessary.

(1) It is an apt if cruel comment on his orchestration that the Haydn variations are even more effective in their original form – a duet for two pianos.

(2) The first movement of symphony no. 1 displays genius, for although there is hardly a vestige of a tune it is nevertheless a highly organized entity and far from boring.

(3) The cyclic key-sequence of the four movements of this same symphony – each up-grading by a major third (C

minor, E major, A flat major, C major) – is unconventional but logical.

(4) The tremendous opening of no. 3, while unmistakably Brahmsian when it throws into relief the significance of a chromatic A flat in the key of F major, clearly derives from the opening of Schumann's no. 3 in its melody – and even more so in its almost identical rhythm.

(5) The finale of no. 4 is unique: it is an extended passacaglia (i.e. variations on a continually repeated 'ground bass') – and possibly the most satisfying last movement in eighteenth- and nineteenth-century symphony.

(6) In his second piano concerto Brahms broke new ground by writing four movements instead of the customary three; the extra one, an *allegro appassionato* placed second and not third, is in parts excitingly tempestuous.

(7) Even when in light-hearted mood he was rarely light-handed and as a rule only qualified praise can be given to his attempts at sprightliness – e.g. in the third movements of symphonies 1, 2 and 4, and in the finales of all three concertos. (For the same reason one prefers the characteristic *Tragic* overture to its companion the *Academic Festival*, which is based on German student-songs of ponderous jollity.)

(8) Possible exceptions to the generalization implied in (7) are the lovely second movement of the violin concerto (a gift to the oboist) and the suave third movement of symphony no. 3; they are not exactly light-handed, but here Brahms did achieve a high measure of lyrical charm. (This *poco allegretto* from no. 3, incidentally, provides a straightforward example of the composer's *penchant* for ambiguous rhythmic accentuation.)

Brahms was last in the line of illustrious Viennese musicians who composed string quartets in the classical manner. He produced only three – as against eighty-two by Haydn, twenty-three by Mozart, sixteen by Beethoven and fifteen by Schubert; they were all written in his late thirties or early forties and were noteworthy for the prominence given to the viola – often regarded as the ugly duckling of the ensemble. Brahms added a second viola for two string quintets and a second cello (as well) for two sextets; in all these works he demonstrated a sure instinct for the medium. Two piano trios (ops. 87 and 101) were better still, showing him to greater advantage than the early piano quartets (see page 165); but his piano quintet cannot quite hold its own beside those of Schumann (page 113), Franck (page 148) and Dvořák (page 197). On the other hand, in his violin sonatas (ops. 78, 100, 108) Brahms was on top form; I am surprised to find myself in a minority when rating op. 100 (in A major) the best of the three: this sonata and the admirable clarinet quintet op. 115 are to my mind the composer's finest achievements in chamber music, for they exhibit most of the typical strengths and few of the typical weaknesses which have already been enumerated. Outstanding among his piano pieces are the rhapsodies, capriccios and *intermezzi* comprised in ops. 79, 116 and 119 and the deservedly popular waltzes op. 39 – which were originally written for piano duet. So too were the *Hungarian Dances*, skilful arrangements of traditional or contemporarily popular Magyar tunes; these are often played nowadays in orchestral transcriptions which his friend Antonín Dvořák provided.

There are those to whom Brahms' music, taken by and large, makes little appeal; they are often the very people who tend to overrate the worth of his songs and vocal duets, maintaining that here alone did he prove himself capable of expressing human emotion or achieve any delicacy of touch. Others aver that his genius was more fully conveyed in the symphonies, concertos and chamber music, and are not prepared to concede that as a song-writer he came into the same category as Schubert. If Brahms' idea of human emotion was the *Wiegenlied* ('Guten Abend, gut' Nacht'), they feel, so much the worse for him; as for delicacy of touch, it is understandable that fastidious listeners should find themselves embarrassed by the archness of *Vergebliches Ständchen*, the *Liebeslieder* waltzes, and some of the folk-song arrangements. Fortunately this is not the whole story: out of Brahms' two hundred or so songs there are many which defy such criticism and a round dozen at least which deserve to rank with the finest *Lieder* ever written: the love songs *Wie bist du, meine Königin*; *Von ewiger Liebe*; *Meine Liebe ist grün*; *Wir wandelten*; in more sombre mood *Die Mainacht, Feldeinsamkeit, In Waldeseinsamkeit* and *Der Tod, das ist die kühle Nacht*; above all the *Four Serious Songs*, with scriptural words, composed during the last year of his life when he knew that he was dying of cancer. Although Johannes Brahms belonged to no religious denomination, refusing to accept *in toto* the doctrines of either Catholicism or Protestantism, he was a Christian in the broadest sense of the term and in the *Four Serious Songs* gave expression to his deepest personal convictions.

CHAPTER THIRTY

Borodin

That national or regional characteristics in music must in and of themselves be worthy of admiration is a fallacy. Of the folk songs, for instance, that have sprung from Somerset, the Hebrides, Ireland, Spain, Yugoslavia and – at second-hand, as it were – from the deep south of the United States of America, some are truly beautiful by any standard, but many others if judged objectively are not: their sole interest lies in the national or regional characteristic itself. Sometimes the vicarious nostalgia of xenophile enthusiasts is tinged with misapprehension, misapprehension particularly noticeable in the attitude of a certain school of music lovers in western Europe towards Russian composers. There are those who incline to shrug Tchaikovsky aside as a cosmopolitan (which he was) and as an artistic renegade (which he wasn't), who acclaim Mikhail Glinka (1803–57) as the father of modern Russian music for the wrong reason. He was just that, but he only became so because during the course of his career he travelled and studied in the west; while never forsaking his native idiom he was as much influenced by the popular music of Spain (where he lived for two years) as by Russian folk song – and certainly owed more to his familiarity with Mozart, Weber and Schubert than to the inheritance of obscure eighteenth-century compatriots like Mikhail Matinsky, Dimitri Bortniansky and Vassily Paskevitch. Glinka's lineal successor ALEXANDER BORODIN (1833–87) was also endowed both with a wanderlust and with an artistic probity which took little heed of national or regional frontiers – and he steadfastly if unconsciously pursued Glinka's healthy policy of integration.

Borodin was born at St Petersburg (now Leningrad); he was the illegitimate son of the ageing Prince Luka Gedeanov by the youthful Avdotya Kleinecke, daughter of a soldier.

As was usual in such cases the baby was registered as the child of one of his father's serfs (Porphyri Borodin), but since his mother was well-provided-for there was nothing serf-like about his upbringing: he was treated with every consideration and instead of being sent to school was educated by a succession of private tutors. It was at the age of about ten that he first began to develop side by side the two great interests of his life – chemistry and music. At seventeen he entered the St Petersburg Academy of Medicine and Surgery, and six years later (having passed all examinations with distinction and thereafter attended a conference of scientists at Brussels) was practising at an army hospital. Next came a period abroad, 1859–62, much of which was spent at the university of Heidelberg but which also included an extended tour of France, Switzerland, Italy and Austria. On returning home he married a Moscow girl of gentle birth named Ekaterina Protopopova whom he had met while on his travels; she was a very good pianist and during a somewhat protracted courtship had introduced her future husband to the music of Chopin, Schumann and Liszt. In 1864 Borodin was appointed professor of organic chemistry at the Academy and as a respected and valued member of the teaching staff (he spoke German and Italian fluently and had a good working knowledge of French and English) was accommodated rent-free in a flat on the premises – which was to be his home for the rest of his life.

Thus far he had devoted more time to listening to music than to making it, although he played both cello and organ with great enthusiasm and had written some chamber works – of which only a piano quintet is preserved complete (in manuscript). About the time that he became a professor of chemistry, he also became the junior member – junior by date of admission that is, not by age – of the *kutchka*, a select company of musicians who met under the leadership of Mily Balakirev (1837–1910) – the uncompromisingly nationalistic composer of the symphonic poem *Tamara* and the piano fantasy *Islamey*. The other three members of the group (sometimes referred to as 'the five') were all, like Borodin himself, amateurs: César Cui (see page 181) was by profession a military engineer, Mussorgsky (chapter 32) a clerk in the civil service, Rimsky-Korsakov (chapter 36) a naval officer. Thenceforth Borodin, encouraged by Balakirev, became a weekend composer; in view of his other commitments it is not altogether surprising that his first symphony took five years to complete, his second seven years and the two string quartets four years each; the opera *Prince Igor*, on which he began work in 1869, was still unfinished when he died – eighteen years later. The wonder is that he was ever able to compose at all, for the easy-going and ill-managed Borodin household – where the tables were always littered with retorts and test-tubes, the floors strewn with half-unpacked suitcases and piles of music manuscript, the corners cluttered with the rubbish of months – was regarded as a home from home by innumerable friends and relations (all impoverished), by absent-minded scholars, by penniless students and by all manner of stray cats (animal and human); it was rarely that Borodin himself, hoping for a good night's rest, found his own bed unoccupied when at last he reached it. This was *la vie de bohème* on a scale never envisaged by Henri Murger (although sometimes portrayed by Tchekhov), and Mrs Borodin, driven nearly out of her mind by the constant succession of unwelcome guests, came to spend more and more of her time with her parents in Moscow. Presently her husband fell ill with cholera and although he recovered sufficiently to make two more trips abroad (to Belgium) he was thereafter obliged to restrict his activities – both scientific and musical. A few years later, at the age of fifty-three, he fell dead of a sudden heart attack while attending a fancy-dress ball.

For reasons already made clear Borodin's musical output was not large, and little more than a line will suffice to catalogue the mature works upon which his reputation depends: one unfinished opera, two symphonies (plus a third, barely half-finished), one tone-poem for orchestra, two string quartets and eleven songs. Of the songs *The Sleeping Princess* (where like Glinka before him in the opera *Russlan and Ludmila* he anticipated Debussy's use of a whole-tone scale – see page 241), *Dissonance* and *The Sea* (all with words by Borodin himself) were perhaps the best; the three completed orchestral works, the two quartets and the opera call for rather more detailed comment.

Borodin's symphony no. 1 in E flat major has been described as immature, but the adjective can be applied only in a relative sense. The first movement, indeed, is in one respect ahead of its time, for it develops vigorously out of strands of theme in the manner which Sibelius later made his own (see page 260) and ends, most originally and effectively, with a very tranquil summing-up. The second movement is a scherzo of Mendelssohnian lightness, contrast being provided by a middle section which is the most characteristically Russian part of the whole work. The rhapsodic third movement firmly stresses throughout the extremely unconventional key (in the E flat context) of D major, and the finale is full of uninhibited vitality.

During one of his visits to the west Borodin met Liszt and showed him the manuscript of his recently completed symphony no. 2 in B minor. The old man was fulsome in his praise; one wonders whether he noticed that the first ten bars recalled the opening of his own piano concerto in E flat major (see page 118). Borodin's arresting motto-theme, whether presented in 2/2 or 3/2 time, in diminution or augmentation, whether marked *allegro, poco meno mosso, animato assai* or (as at the finish) *poco a poco allargando e pesante*, formed the basis of a wonderfully exciting movement. As in the first symphony the scherzo came next, a *prestissimo* one-beat-to-the-bar (four crotchets) affair in the remote key of F major; the slow third movement, extraordinarily impressive in its sombre solemnity, was one of the composer's finest achievements, and a truly great work was rounded off with a finale which – with its frequent changes of time-signature (2/4, 3/4, 4/4) – was a lively and stirring evocation of Slavonic dance rhythms. (The incomplete symphony no. 3 in A minor included a scherzo in quick 5/4.)

Borodin's tone-poem *In the Steppes of Central Asia* gave him a chance to prove that when he wished he could be as 'national' as Balakirev or anyone else. Here is his own programme-note in which I have inserted, parenthetically, the instrumental means by which he evoked the appropriate atmosphere.

In the silence of the monotonous steppes of central Asia [two solo violins in the highest register] is heard the unfamiliar sound of a peaceful Russian song [clarinet, then horn, virtually unaccompanied]. From the distance we hear the approach of horses and camels [*pizzicato* cellos and double basses] and the bizarre and melancholy notes of an oriental melody [cor anglais]. A caravan approaches, escorted by Russian soldiers [opening theme repeated with full orchestra], and continues on its long way through the immense desert. The notes of the Russian and Asiatic melodies join in a common harmony [alternating instrumental combinations], which dies away as the caravan disappears in the distance [flute and four solo, muted, violins].

Besides being straightforward in construction this poetic little work is admirably concise; it lasts only about six minutes.

By comparison Borodin's first string quartet (in A major) – although not completed until 1879, by which time he was already planning *The Steppes* – is almost *un*-Russian, being in some places reminiscent of Beethoven and in others of Mendelssohn once again. Perhaps its most interesting feature is the up-to-date exploitation of improved string practice to obtain modern effects, e.g. the sweeping-back-and-forth arpeggios in the first movement (between letters F and G) and the extensive use of artificial harmonics in the trio of the scherzo. In the second quartet (D major), on the other hand, Borodin, as in his second symphony, successfully combined native inspiration with western technique: except perhaps in the charming waltz-like scherzo (cf. Tchaikovsky, page 191) the mood was as Russian as anyone could wish for, but the delicately adjusted instrumental balance displayed an understanding of the medium more often associated with the Viennese masters. The wonderfully expressive melody of the nocturne has brought this movement a large measure of popular recognition outside its context and it cannot be denied that it represents Borodin, in romantic frame of mind, to perfection.

At times Borodin showed less assurance in his handling of an orchestra and his friendly colleague Rimsky-Korsakov (see chapter 36) along with the younger Alexander Glazunov (a talented composer of the next generation who never quite fulfilled early promise) 'revised' the two symphonies. Both were expert orchestrators and if they had confined themselves to surface matters there might be little cause for complaint (although I maintain private doubts about certain passages); unfortunately they also took it upon themselves to 'improve the harmony' where they judged that Borodin's progressions were too harsh to suit contemporary taste. However well meant at the time, such editing can be seen in retrospect to have been misguided. Nevertheless praise should not be grudged the same pair for having evolved *Prince Igor* from the tangled collection of shreds and patches which Borodin left behind at his death, a task which occupied them for three years. As presented to the public in 1890 the constructional basis of the opera was the responsibility of the composer and his associate-librettist (Vladimir Stassov) only to a very small degree. So far as the music is concerned the melodic content was probably about 90 per cent Borodin (it was often reminiscent of his second symphony), 10 per cent Rimsky or Glazunov; the harmonization 60 per cent Borodin, 40 per cent Rimsky or Glazunov; the orchestration 10 per cent Borodin, 20 per cent Glazunov (which included the overture) and 70 per cent Rimsky. Borodin's spontaneous melodies (spirited, tender, voluptuous) were often embellished by appropriate oriental touches – in Konstchakovna's cavatina at the opening of Act II for instance; Rimsky-Korsakov's flair for orchestration was never better demonstrated than in the superb sequence known to concertgoers as the 'Polovtsian Dances'. Indeed *Prince Igor*, rather than turning out to be the amorphous pasticcio which might have been expected, soon became recognized as one of the finest operas of the late nineteenth century. To admit that this was partly due to the able abetting of the junior collaborators need imply no diminution of respect or admiration for the achievements of Alexander Borodin himself – both here and elsewhere. Although he may not have been the greatest and was certainly not the most prolific composer ever to emerge from Russia, he was eminently successful in forging a strong musical link between his own country and the rest of Europe.

CHAPTER THIRTY-ONE

Saint-Saëns

Chronologically speaking CAMILLE SAINT-SAËNS (1835–1921)
was a 'bridge figure': he began to compose music during the
lifetime of Luigi Cherubini – who was only five years
younger than Mozart – and was still hard at it after the
death of Claude Debussy in 1918. In no other sense, however,
did he build a bridge or even venture to cross one, pre-
ferring to remain in a comfortable tent on his own side
of the stream; he took careful note of the activities on
the opposite bank of such eminent contemporaries as
Hector Berlioz, Richard Wagner, César Franck and Gabriel
Fauré (one of his own pupils), but he felt no inclination
to join in them. It is true that in youth he was a great
admirer of Wagner, entertaining him in Paris – and paying
several visits to Germany for the sole purpose of hearing his
operas, but after the Franco-Prussian war of 1870–71 his
enthusiasm slipped from top to bottom gear and indeed
eventually went into reverse: patriotic sentiment clouded
aesthetic judgement. As the French music critic Henry Prunières later wrote, 'Debussy fought against Wagner's influence
because he considered it detrimental to French art, but
Saint-Saëns attacked him merely because he was a German'.*
Although at one stage Saint-Saëns crossed swords with
Franck, this had nothing to do with either music or politics
and they only quarrelled because at one time both were in
love with the same woman; Berlioz and Fauré he always held
in the highest esteem. Nevertheless he preferred to go his
own way so far as composition was concerned. A brilliant
all-round musician, a skilled professional who knew all the

* After the outbreak of the 1914–18 war Saint-Saëns went so far as
to declare that 'it is now as impossible for a Frenchman to listen
to Wagner's operas as it would be for him to applaud a singer who
had raped his mother'.

tricks of the trade and was adept at cloaking trivialities in attractive garb, he adopted early in life a pleasant and conventionally cultured manner which combined acceptable features of both classicism and romanticism (and met with widespread public approval); he could see no valid reason for varying it – and never did. His output was considerable, although not prodigious when the length of his career is taken into account: fourteen operas or operettas, incidental music for six plays, forty-odd choral works and eighty-odd for various orchestral and instrumental combinations, nearly a hundred piano and organ pieces and over a hundred songs. A small pick from this substantial bunch retains popularity to this day, for he had a happy knack of contriving agreeable if somewhat undistinguished tunes and was a pastmaster at producing a tasty omelette out of one small egg. Those works with which readers are likely to become familiar will be referred to in the course of the brief biographical survey which follows.

Saint-Saëns was born in Paris; his father, a civil servant, died less than two months later, and he was brought up by his mother and a great-aunt (also widowed). He was an infant prodigy who before he was three years old could strike and name the different notes on the piano and soon afterwards wrote a waltz; at six he began to study orchestral scores, and by the time he was ten he had already enjoyed success as a concert pianist. At the age of thirteen he won an organ scholarship to the Conservatoire where he studied composition with Fromental Halévy, and in 1853, having ensured his livelihood by securing a post as a church organist, he began to compose in earnest: during the next seven or eight years he completed two symphonies (in E flat major and A minor), a piano quintet (in A minor), a Mass, a piano concerto (in D major) and two violin concertos (in A major and C major).* Meanwhile he had fallen in love with the voluptuous Augusta Holmès, a talented amateur musician who (to quote Saint-Saëns' biographer James Harding) 'had bold, beautiful features, abundant golden hair, and hand-

* Several of these works were not published until much later.

some breasts of which she was justifiably proud', but he does not seem to have been unduly perturbed when she turned down his offer of marriage. (His rival in love, César Franck, was already married.)

In 1854 the Swiss-born Louis Niedermeyer, who had studied in Austria, produced operas in Italy and taught music in Belgium, came to Paris to compose Masses and anthems and take charge of the half-moribund Ecole de Musique Religieuse Classique, which under his energetic sway, and renamed Ecole Niedermeyer, soon widened its scope; Saint-Saëns was appointed professor of composition there in 1861. Having by now really found his feet, he presently completed two works which were destined to achieve lasting popularity: *Introduction et rondo capriccioso* for violin and orchestra, and a second piano concerto (in G minor) – aptly described as an appetizing mixture of Bach and Offen-Bach. The cantata *Les Noces Prométhée* and a third piano concerto (in E flat major) also belong to the 1860s.

When war broke out between France and Prussia in 1870 many Paris musicians did themselves little credit as citizens: there seems to have been a scramble to get on board the next train for Bordeaux or the next *paquebot* from Calais to Dover as quickly as possible. All credit therefore to Saint-Saëns who – like Bizet (see page 141) – promptly enlisted in the National Guard.* After the war he turned his attention to the stage, producing the accomplished but little-known operetta *La Princesse jaune* and the accomplished and far better-known 'biblical' opera *Samson et Dalila* (with 'Fair spring is returning' and 'Softly awakes my heart'). Among other compositions dating from this period are the remarkably effective tone-poems *Le Rouet d'Omphale, Phaëton* and *Danse macabre*, a cello concerto (in A minor), a fourth piano concerto (in C minor) and an 'Allegro appassionata' for cello and piano. Saint-Saëns' fame as a composer had reached its apex when, in 1875, at the age of thirty-nine, he married a girl twenty years younger than himself; six years later they separated.

* Another honourable patriot was Gabriel Fauré (see page 207).

Although Saint-Saëns continued to compose with enthusiasm to the very end of his life and many of his later works enjoyed contemporary success, it can be seen in retrospect that by the time his marriage broke up he was already past his best. The operas which followed *Samson et Dalila* are today quite unknown (although one suspects that the operetta *Phryné*, of which the composer was very proud, might bear revival); the somewhat turgid third symphony (in C minor) and the flashy fifth piano concerto (in F major) are still heard occasionally, but the only works belonging to the last two decades of the nineteenth century that remain deservedly familiar are the *Suite algérienne*, the third violin concerto (in B minor) and – of course – *Le Carnaval des animaux* (incorporating 'Le Cygne'). The twentieth century? Well, during the last year of his life the eighty-five-year-old Camille Saint-Saëns had the initiative to provide welcome additions to the sparse repertories of solo woodwind players with an oboe sonata, a clarinet sonata and a bassoon sonata; all three were truly representative of that slick professional expertise which he had consistently exploited to good purpose and which was perhaps his most engaging characteristic.

CHAPTER THIRTY-TWO

Mussorgsky

MODEST MUSSORGSKY (1839–81) was born at Kareva, a village lying roughly two hundred and fifty miles south of St Petersburg, two hundred and fifty miles west of Moscow, two hundred and fifty miles east of Riga and a hundred miles north of Smolensk. Apart from the fact that his paternal grandmother had been a common serf the family escutcheon was untarnished, many of his ancestors having been army officers loyally serving a succession of imperial Czars and his father being a socially acceptable landowner. At the age of ten Modest accompanied his parents when they moved to St Petersburg – and it was there that he spent the rest of his life. Unlike Borodin (who knew his way round Brussels, Paris, Rome and Vienna), let alone Tchaikovsky and Rimsky-Korsakov (who, as we shall see presently, penetrated as far afield as London and New York), Mussorgsky never left Russia and indeed only once left the surroundings of St Petersburg – when in 1879 he undertook a joint concert tour of the Ukraine and the Crimea with the contralto singer Daria Leonova. It is therefore not surprising that he ultimately proved to be more aggressively nationalistic than the other members of Balakirev's *kutchka* – Borodin, Rimsky-Korsakov and Cui. (Cui, of French descent, never quite kept up with the rest; but he was by no means a negligible figure in the history of Russian music, for although his operas were failures he remained an ardent propagandist of Borodin and up to a point of Mussorgsky. Furthermore he wrote some pleasant chamber music and even those who normally appreciate the punster's art may be inclined to regret that Ernest Newman, whose critical erudition was matched only by his fondness for a joke, yielded to the temptation of prefacing his notice of a recital of Cui's compositions with the headline *'Cui bono?'*.)

As a boy Mussorgsky learnt to play the piano remarkably well, but at seventeen – in accordance with family tradition – he enlisted as a cadet in a famous regiment known as the Preobrazhensky Guards where he acquired the habit of hard drinking that was later to cause his downfall. He maintained an interest in music however, sought acquaintance with Balakirev, prevailed upon that enthusiast to give him lessons and was so satisfied with the results that he soon left the army and set out confidently to earn fame as a composer. But some of the ground was cut from under his feet when in 1861, by decree of the reigning Czar Alexander II, the hitherto knout-bound serfs of Russia were emancipated, while the idle and wealthy land-owning class, to which Mussorgsky belonged, was largely dispossessed of its vested interest in property. Thereafter he was obliged to earn his living in the ill-paid though not overworked clerical grade of the civil service, first in the Ministry of Transport and later in the Ministry of Agriculture. Meanwhile he composed about eighty songs, a collection of piano pieces entitled *Pictures at an Exhibition* and the tone-poem *Night on the Bare Mountain*. He also planned half a dozen or so operas; he made fair progress with *Salammbô*, *The Marriage*, *Khovanshtchina* and *Sorochintsky Fair*, but the only one he ever finished was *Boris Godunov*. The pity was that he drowned himself in drink: although he pulled round during the early 1870s when he was engrossed in *Boris*, he soon relapsed once more into chronic alcoholism. The last six years of his life have been described as a protracted debauch; this is an exaggeration, since he behaved well enough on the Ukrainian tour which has already been referred to, but in the long run nothing could check the miserable sequence: *delirium tremens* – epilepsy – premature death at the age of forty-two.

So much for the *personal* tragedy of Mussorgsky. It was an *artistic* tragedy that he was born when he was, rather than fifty years later, for he was an intrusive realist in a predominantly romantic age. No previous composer had adopted such a stark approach to the problems of aesthetic interpretation; there was very rarely any appeal to sentiment – even in his songs. Admittedly a lyric strain was noticeable in *The Garden by the Don*, *The Hebrew Song* and the song-cycle *Sunless*, but Mussorgsky's real *forte* lay in his ability to paint a scene or an incident with a few deft strokes of impressionism – often pointing a satirical contrast. Some of his songs ran into trouble with ecclesiastical or military censors: *The Seminarist* for instance (in which the priestly devotions of a divinity student are interrupted by erotic visions), and *Forgotten* (a soldier's rotting corpse is pecked by vultures while far away his wife croons their baby to sleep with a lullaby of which the burden is 'Daddy will soon be home'). Less extravagant in conception – and therefore more genuinely moving – are *Darling Savishna* (in which the village idiot stammers out his love to the village beauty) and *Kalistratuschk* (a poverty-stricken peasant compares the happy sort of life envisaged for him by his mother with the wretched existence he now has to endure). When humour emerges it is nearly always bitter: in *Hopak* a lively young woman dances away from her elderly husband and abandons herself to a 'handsome lad'; in *The He-Goat* a girl eludes a lecherous old goat and then marries a lecherous old man with a goatee-beard. Mussorgsky's last and most familiar song, *The Flea*, can perhaps be taken to typify his approach to this branch of composition. He tried to exploit the tone-quality and dynamic potentialities of a solo piano to the same end in *Pictures at an Exhibition* (inspired by the paintings of his artist friend Victor Hartmann) and although he was not completely successful there can be no denying the forceful realism of picture no. 1 (a misshapen gnome) and the sardonic intent of picture no. 6 (a rich Jew and a poor Jew).*

The tone-poem *Night on the Bare Mountain* (1867) depicted the Witches' Sabbath popularly supposed to take place each midsummer's eve on Mount Triglav near Kiev in the Ukraine. Not even Balakirev, though he praised its power

* *Pictures at an Exhibition* was orchestrated by Maurice Ravel (see chapter 49), a great admirer of Mussorgsky.

and originality, was sufficiently advanced to stomach its harsh dissonances and what he found its 'barbaric disorder'; when several years later Mussorgsky revised the score with a ballet production in view nothing came of it, and the work was never performed complete during his lifetime. After his death, however, Rimsky-Korsakov fashioned a new tone-poem built on the same thematic material, and it is this crafty version of *Night on the Bare Mountain* which is known to present-day listeners. (Rimsky's night was not so dark as Mussorgsky's, his mountain not so bare, his witches not so obscene in their orgies.)

It was not long before Mussorgsky abandoned his first serious operatic venture *Salammbô* (after Gustave Flaubert), for which he had written only a few short scenes. In 1868 he completed a piano score of the first act of *The Marriage* (after Nikolai Gogol) but he laid this aside too when his imagination was inflamed with the idea of transmuting Alexander Pushkin's forty-five-year-old historical drama *Boris Godunov* into an opera. The huge task occupied him little more than a year (despite civil service distractions); in 1870 he submitted the score to the directors of the St Petersburg Imperial Theatre who, to do them justice, seem to have given it careful consideration but in the event turned it down – (*a*) because the subject was too sombre and there was no love interest and (*b*) because the music was too 'modernistic'. The composer accepted their decision in good part; his heart and soul were in *Boris* and in order to secure a production he now substituted lighter scenes for some of the more sombre, augmenting the feminine interest by the introduction of a totally new character – the Polish princess Marina Minschek. This second version of *Boris* – modernism and all – was accepted by the theatre's directorate and the first performance took place in 1874. Not surprisingly it had a mixed reception: *kutchka* members (bar one) were enthusiastic, none more so than Rimsky-Korsakov, but the opera-going public was puzzled and suspicious. *Boris* was not an utter failure and was played now and again during the next few years, but by the time its composer was dead and buried it too had sunk into a half-forgotten limbo. The excitement lay ahead.

In 1896, fifteen years after Mussorgsky's death, the indefatigable Rimsky-Korsakov rescued *Boris Godunov* from oblivion. Without such an experienced public-relations officer this fine opera might never have attained recognition, its composer's name today mean nothing to many music-lovers – and little to most students. But the other side of the medal is inescapable: Rimsky-Korsakov, like the rest, ascribed Mussorgsky's unorthodox approach to the problems of harmony, orchestration and technique in general to lack of musical education rather than to inborn genius subconsciously striving to burst conventional bonds. As a musician of impeccable taste he found it inconceivable that Mussorgsky really meant everything that he put down on paper; he was doing a favour, he thought, when for the sake of his old friend's posthumous reputation he replaced so-and-so with such-and-such. His authority to tamper with the 1874 edition was almost immediately challenged by the French musicologist Pierre d'Alheim, and other critics followed suit about fifteen years later; since then the controversy has raged furiously, fuel being added to the fire when in 1928 it was discovered that some of Rimsky's tamperings with the 1874 edition had in fact been reversions to the original of 1870. Most of us prefer to take no active part in this dispute; we freely concede that the 1896 *Boris Godunov* differs in many details (constructional, stylistic, orchestral) from both the 1870 and 1874 versions, yet we feel we can acclaim Mussorgsky for a supreme achievement and at the same time spare a word of thanks for the well-meaning adaptor who gave us the opportunity to acquaint ourselves with such a masterwork.

It was Rimsky-Korsakov again who completed and otherwise ministered to Mussorgsky's second historical opera *Khovanshtchina,* based on a libretto of his own contriving and but a pale reflection of *Boris* – although the scene where the drunken Khovanshky meets his doom (while being carried off the stage after clumsily cavorting with a bevy of dancing-girls) is extraordinarily effective in its restraint. In the unfinished comic opera *Sorochintsky Fair* (after Gogol) Mussorgsky struck an unwonted lyrical vein, but Rimsky-Korsakov never bothered with it and of the half-dozen or so completions by less accomplished craftsmen none has done much credit either to the composer or to the craftsmen.

In a prefatory note to this book it was hinted that posterity cannot normally form a reasoned judgement on the ultimate worth of a composer's contribution to music until perhaps fifty years or so after his death. Modest Mussorgsky was so far ahead of his time that in his case the margin should be doubled at least; perhaps only when the world is old enough to assess the achievements of Aram Khatchaturian and Dmitri Shostakovitch will it be prudent to assert (or deny) with confidence that the genius of their predecessor was both rare and prophetic.

CHAPTER THIRTY-THREE

Tchaikovsky

Whereas Borodin was born in St Petersburg itself and Mussorgsky within its orbit, PETER TCHAIKOVSKY first saw the light a thousand miles away to the east at Votinsk, an iron-and-steel centre in the basin of the river Kama which winds its way through the Ural foothills to join the Volga some fifty miles south of Kazan. His father Ilya Tchaikovsky, a mining engineer, was thrice married – in 1827, 1833 and 1865; the composer, born in 1840, was the second of six children by his second wife Alexandra, who was French by ancestry. In 1849 the family moved to Alaparev near Nizhny-Novgorod and the following year Peter, a gifted child already showing signs of musical ability, was sent to St Petersburg where he stayed with friends and continued his education with a view to becoming a lawyer. Morbidly sensitive, his regard for his mother as an ideal woman surpassed the bounds of normal filial affection and suggested an Oedipus complex; her death in 1854, he later confessed, might have driven him literally mad had he not been able to immerse himself in music – rather than in legal studies. (A few immature compositions date from this adolescent period.) Nevertheless he stuck to his allotted task, passed his law examinations and shortly after his nineteenth birthday secured a clerical post in the Ministry of Justice. But like other minor bureaucrats he seems to have spent most of his office hours playing darts and drinking tea, and in 1861 he took a long holiday abroad during the course of which he visited Berlin, Brussels and Paris. On his return he entered the St Petersburg Conservatoire, recently founded by Anton Rubinstein, applied himself seriously to music – and formally resigned from the civil service. By 1866 he was sufficiently established as an oncoming musician to be appointed to the teaching staff of the Moscow Conservatoire under the direction of Anton Rubinstein's brother Nikolai. (The Rubinsteins were of German-Polish descent and their outlook on music differed radically from that of Balakirev or Mussorgsky; both were distinguished pianists and in addition Anton was a prolific composer whose piano concertos were long favoured by *virtuosi*.) Moscow remained Tchaikovsky's headquarters for the rest of his life, but from 1873 onwards he travelled much abroad – to Germany, Switzerland, Italy, France and Britain on several occasions and to the United States once; meanwhile (except for a period of comparative stagnation in the early 1880s) compositions flowed fast from his pen. Thanks to this extensive travel he was even more influenced than Borodin by western music; for all their individuality his symphonies, taken as a whole, owed much to the classic Viennese models, his operas to the Italian, his ballets to the French; he was not a member of the *kutchka* and maintained little contact with his St Petersburg colleagues.

Perhaps it was Tchaikovsky's idolization of his mother – and to a lesser extent of his sister, also christened Alexandra – which rendered him immune to feminine blandishment outside the family circle and led him to homosexuality. Unfortunately he was indiscreet in his *amours* and presently realized that he would have to take drastic action if he wished to avoid being involved in a first-class scandal. In 1877, therefore, he put up a smoke-screen by marrying Antonina Milyukova, a vain and importunate young lady who had persistently been setting her cap at him. Three days after the wedding he wrote a distressing and distasteful letter to his younger brother Anatole.

I have taken no advantage of her, for I warned her from the outset to expect no more than brotherly affection. Physically, she revolts me.

Brotherly affection was not what Antonina had been looking for, and the whole deplorable episode ended in utter and near-tragic fiasco: the remorseful husband had a mental breakdown and tried to commit suicide by immersing himself in an ice-cold river – but only succeeded in catching pneumonia (from which he duly recovered). Meanwhile he had already embarked upon intimate pen-friend intercourse with Nadezhda von Meck – whom he never met face to face although she was often present in the audience when his works were played in public. She was the rich widow of a railway tycoon and the mother of twelve children, but her outlook on life was one more usually associated with a frustrated old maid: she was very much in love – at a safe distance.

> I want you to speak to me, and to no one else, of nature and destiny, of heart-break, trampled faith, wounded pride, of happiness irretrievably lost, of self-abandonment to despair. No art can express all this like music can, and no one understands *me* better than you do.

How right she was! Tchaikovsky understood her perfectly and for fourteen years fed her starved emotions with pseudo-passionate songs and piano pieces – in return for substantial financial patronage. Eventually, as might have been foreseen, Nadezhda's descendants, resentful that their inheritance was being frittered away on a composer with a dubious moral character, opened her eyes to the more unromantic aspects of her protégé's private life; the love letters and the generous pension ceased forthwith – and the toucher was deeply touched.

> My faith in my fellow-humans and my confidence in the world itself are undermined. I have lost my tranquillity, and the happiness that fate might yet have held in store for me is gone for ever.

Tchaikovsky was always subject to moods of extreme depression and it could have been with deliberate intent that while on a visit to St Petersburg in 1893 (three years after his break with Nadezhda von Meck) he drank a glass of unboiled tap-water; a few days later he was dead from cholera.

Beside Beethoven's 'Emperor' concerto, seventh symphony, 'Waldstein' sonata and *Adelaide*, Tchaikovsky's piano concerto in B flat minor, his fifth symphony, *Chant sans paroles* and *None but the Weary Heart* cannot be accounted masterpieces, but judged by any other standard they are admirable compositions and need not be disparaged because they are popular. His fourth, fifth and sixth symphonies, whatever their other shortcomings, are very well constructed and in parts powerfully dramatic. Moreover Tchaikovsky lovers are at liberty to point out that *Eugen Onegin* is a better opera, *qua* opera, than *Fidelio*; particular attention should be drawn to the charming and accomplished vocal quartet in Act I scene 1 and to Lensky's fine dramatic aria in Act II scene 2. But there has rarely been a composer whose temperament was more closely reflected in his music, much of which was redolent of self-pity – self-pity finding expression as early as the *Romance in F minor* for piano (1868) and the song *E'en Though my Heart should Break* (1869). Later it reared its head in the third movement of the otherwise light-hearted symphony no. 3, in two movements of the string quartet in E flat minor op. 30, in the technically accomplished concert overture *Francesca da Rimini* and in the tear-away treatment of the motto-themes of symphonies 4 and 5. It reached a climax in the elegiac gloom of the first movement of symphony no. 6 (the 'Pathetic') and in the almost unrelieved pessimism of its finale. (Tchaikovsky deserves credit, however, for having thus ventured to conclude a symphony with a slow movement, a precedent of which Gustav Mahler and Ralph Vaughan Williams showed themselves fully conscious.) On the other hand the violin concerto was innocent of such trends, and it would be a very squeamish critic who failed to appreciate the altogether healthier sentiment of the *Serenade for Strings*, the orchestral suite in G major op. 55, the concert overture *Romeo and Juliet*, parts at least of the symphonic poem *Manfred*, the unaccountably neglected piano concerto in G major, a handful of the hundred or so songs – *The Corals*, for instance, and *Does the Day Reign?*. And although, as we have seen, Tchaikovsky was not a strongly nationalistic composer he often made effective use of Russian folk idiom: notably almost throughout symphonies nos. 1 and 2, the string sextet curiously entitled *Souvenir de Florence* and the opera *Vakula the Smith*; as well as in the favourite *andante cantabile* from the string quartet in D major op. 11, the finale of the violin concerto, and several scenes from two other little-known operas, *The Oprichnik* and *Mazeppa*.

In some respects Tchaikovsky's main hold on one's affections may depend upon his ballet music, where delicacy of touch and superb orchestral technique combined to make him a master. I am thinking not only of *Swan Lake*, *The Sleeping Beauty* and *Casse-noisette* (which are *hors concours* in that field), but also of the unconventional ballet-like intrusions on other media – e.g. the waltzes of the *Serenade for Strings* and symphonies nos. 2 and 5, the so-called scherzos of the piano sonata op. 37 and of symphony no. 4. For simultaneous exposure of nearly all his qualities, good and bad, one might turn to the first movement of this same symphony (no. 4), where echoes of the bleak Russian countryside and the gilded Russian ballroom are heard against a background of barely repressed hysteria; yet all these elements are incorporated in a framework of classical sonata form skilfully adapted to the needs of the moment.

Peter Tchaikovsky's approach to his art was in almost every respect the exact antithesis to that of his German contemporary Johannes Brahms, but his music has given pleasure to countless thousands and only highbrows will complain if it continues to do so.

CHAPTER THIRTY-FOUR

Dvořák

Observant tourists with a bent for sociology may have noticed that in many continental countries the village pub is often combined with a retail shop of some sort: in Italy one finds perhaps an *osteria/alimentari*, in central Europe more likely a *Gasthaus/Metzgerei* – or a *hostinec/řeznický*. Giuseppe Verdi was the son of the innkeeper-grocer of Roncole; ANTONÍN DVOŘÁK was born on 8th September 1841 to the innkeeper-butcher of Nelahozeves on the banks of the river Vltava – by trunk road no. 8 about eighteen miles north of Prague. He showed early promise in music but when the family moved to Zlonice, a nearby mining village, he was obliged to work as assistant butcher-cum-bartender, since his father (despite musical inclinations) did not take his artistic aspirations very seriously. But slicing carcasses and serving beer did not satisfy Dvořák's inner urge, and at the age of sixteen he made his way to Prague, where after studying for a few years at the Organ School he secured a position as viola-player in the orchestra of the newly-founded Czech National Theatre not long before Smetana was appointed its conductor (see page 154).

Dvořák remained at the theatre for ten years; meanwhile he established himself as a sought-after music teacher – and fell in love with Anna Čermáková, a professional singer, whom he married in 1873. (They had nine children all told, but the first three died in infancy.) The compositions of this period – his twenties – were strongly influenced by Wagner; many were subsequently thrown on the fire by the composer himself and those which survive are unrepresentative of the Dvořák who has achieved immortality. In the early 1870s, however, he turned over a new leaf with the cantata *The Heirs of the White Mountain* and the operetta *King and Collier* (a complete re-setting of an earlier and pseudo-Wagnerian essay) where the approach was more spontaneous. Indeed only a Slav idiom (such as Smetana favoured in his most characteristic works) would here have been acceptable, for the White Mountain was the scene of a crucial battle in the Thirty Years' War and symbolized Bohemia's loss of her treasured independence, and the libretto of *King and Collier* also had a nationalistic slant. This was followed by two even better operettas – *The Pigheaded Peasants* and *The Peasant a Rogue* (sometimes dubbed, not ineptly, the Czech *Figaro*) – and the *Stabat Mater*, which brought its composer recognition far beyond the boundaries of Bohemia; thereafter he never looked back.

In 1884 Dvořák and his growing family established a permanent home at Vysoká near Příbrom, some thirty miles south of Prague, but from then onward he travelled much abroad. Like Mendelssohn he was a great favourite in Britain, which he visited on nine separate occasions: the cantata *The Spectre's Bride* was specially written for the Birmingham Festival of 1885, the oratorio *Saint Ludmila* for the Leeds Festival of 1886; the Requiem had its world première at Birmingham in 1891. The following year he was appointed Director of the National Conservatory of Music in New York, but he never settled down in America and in 1895 returned home: humble in origin and pious in (Catholic) religious observance, he was never truly happy when parted from his ain folk. He belonged too to that select community of musicians – and writers on music – who, while in other respects staid and responsible members of society, cherish an unbridled passion for railways: early in April 1904 an orgy of engine-spotting in cold weather brought on a bad chill which aggravated chronic uraemia; he died on May Day. His widow survived him by twenty-seven years; she and their son-in-law composer Josef Suk carried the family tradition into the 1930s, and their great-grandson – another Josef Suk (a professional violinist) – has carried it into the 1970s.

Dvořák's music here and there displayed a Brahmsian depth of feeling, but whereas Brahms appealed to the emotions through the intellect, with Dvořák it was the other way round. One can trace affinity with his German contemporary in the straightforward expositions of thematic material and the strong sense of harmonic contrast, but on the whole he had more in common with Schubert: notably an unquenchable flow of melody, a natural genius for modulation, an instinct for the right medium of expression – and a tendency to uncontrolled repetition (which to Brahms was anathema). Although much of his music, leaving aside the early attempts to emulate Wagner, was typically national, he rarely, if ever, made use of actual folk or gipsy tunes as did Brahms in his German folk-song settings and *Hungarian Dances*. For instance, the admirable *Moravian* (vocal) *Duets* – the first of his compositions to attract attention in Vienna – and the even more admirable *Slavonic Dances* – originally written as piano duets and the first to attract attention in London – conformed with Slav tradition in mood and rhythm but were one hundred per cent his own work. So were the songs and piano pieces, most of which, however, provided little more than an excuse for pleasant relaxation: unlike both Schubert and Brahms, Dvořák showed strength, rather, in large-scale choral works. The British press over-praised *The Spectre's Bride* and *Saint Ludmila*, but there can be no gainsaying the quality of the *Stabat Mater*; of the unassuming Mass in D major to which one is tempted to apply the irreverent epithet charming; of the Requiem with its constantly recurring five-note *idée fixe* which achieves apotheosis in the concluding 'Agnus Dei' section; of the stirring *Te Deum*, Handelian in its sturdy optimism. Of these four works the *Stabat Mater* and the Requiem, at least, have retained a hold on the public allegiance; the wholesale neglect of Dvořák's operas I find unaccountable. Ten years in a theatre orchestra gave him a good sense of stage requirements, and only when the libretto was hopeless – as in *Vanda* and *Armida* – did he fail to do it justice. *King and Collier* and *The Peasant a Rogue* have already been briefly noticed; *Dimitri* (1882) was my way of being a sequel to Mussorgsky's *Boris Godunov* and in retrospect is subject to unfavourable

comparison, but in *The Jacobin* (1888) – an agreeably senti-
mental evocation of rural Bohemia – Dvořák was on firmer
ground and much of the music showed him at his best.
Around the turn of the century he touched still higher
peaks with the rustic comedy *The Devil and Kate* and the
fairy tragedy *Rusalka* – in which initiative was matched by
long experience.

By the time he was thirty-five Dvořák had completed five
symphonies. For many years only one of these – no. 5 in
F major – held a place in the standard repertory, but the
first four, also, have recently been recorded. These five symphonies were overshadowed by the magnificent *Symphonic
Variations*, the sparkling *Scherzo capriccioso* and the sixth
and seventh symphonies, all composed between 1877 and
1885. Symphony no. 6 in D major, as Donald Tovey rightly
said, shows Dvořák at the height of his powers; I would
add that in the third and fourth movements at least it
gains rather than loses by comparison with Brahms' no. 2
in the same key, which is often thought to have provided
the stimulus. The seventh symphony is also a masterpiece
– its slow movement is deeply expressive and in the scherzo
one notes the characteristically contrasted 3/2 and 6/4 *furiant* rhythms – but there are occasional signs that the composer's grip on the underlying principles of sonata form is
insecure. (To particularize: the sombre yet passionately
masculine opening theme of the first movement, after firmly
establishing D minor, prepares the way for a disarmingly
feminine dialogue between horn and oboe in the remote
key of E flat major. Any first-time listener – bearing in mind
the precedent of Schubert's 'Unfinished' – might be excused
for assuming that the exposition of the first subject, however
terse, was already completed and that the second group of
subjects was by now under way in an unconventional key;
Dvořák shatters the illusion by scuttling back to D minor
and repeating the opening all over again with heavier scoring. Those captivating horn and oboe phrases are therefore
no more than an inconsequent episode – never to be heard
again and only momentarily to be referred to.) Structural

deficiencies are even more noticeable in symphony no. 8 in G major (1889) and no. 9 in E minor (1893, 'From the New World'). The first and third movements of the G major are close-knit and attractive, but the second is long-winded and the finale, which sets forth confidently as though it were to be a theme with variations, ends by chasing its own tail. The 'New World' is justly beloved as a storehouse of memorable tunes (none of them specifically negroid, by the way, although some might be regarded as based on the highest common factor of Negro and Slav elements), but once again they tend to run round in circles without getting anywhere; here Dvořák seems to have followed Robert Louis Stevenson's maxim that to travel hopefully is better than to arrive. By this time, perhaps, he himself realized that he was a romantic rather than a classical composer, for in 1896 he entered the field of programme music. The four symphonic poems *The Water Goblin*, *The Noonday Witch*, *The Golden Spinning-wheel* and *The Wild Dove* were inspired by the folk ballads of the Czech poet Karel Erben; a fifth, *The Hero's Song*, was neither inspired nor inspiring. Those who are unfamiliar with Erben's fairy-tales may find *The Water Goblin* and company somewhat frustrating. The orchestration is as brilliant as usual (Dvořák was a master in that respect), there are many passages of charm and a few of real beauty; for the uninitiated, however, constant repetition is poor compensation for the lack of coherent musical development which one has a right to expect in a symphonic poem.

Dvořák's splendid cello concerto of 1895 ('Why didn't I know that one could write a cello concerto like this?' asked Brahms) surpassed in artistry the earlier piano and violin concertos, and much of his chamber music, too, was truly representative of his genius. He wrote fifteen string quartets all told, about half of which belong to his maturity; one would not expect to find the same depth of expression as in Beethoven's 'Rasumovsky' quartets (see page 66) or the last four of Schubert (page 85), but ops. 51, 105 and 106, at least, are nevertheless admirable specimens of the genre. In their different ways the comparatively early *String Ser-*

enade and string quintet (with double bass), the later piano trios ops. 65 and 90 and the piano quintet op. 81 are also most polished works of art; the last-named is especially worthy of close study. The smooth-flowing first movement, where the long opening melody is characteristically allotted to the cello; the *dumka* (elegy) with its alternating moods of resignation and resentment; the scherzo, which is something like a quick waltz; the gay and uninhibited finale: here is a symposium of the methods and style of Antonín Dvořák, one of the most human and most lovable of famous composers.

CHAPTER THIRTY-FIVE

Grieg

The gifted Niels Gade (eight symphonies), Ivar Hallström (six operas), Johan Svendsen (*Carnival in Paris*) and Christian Sinding (*Rustle of Spring*) all reached maturity during the second half of the nineteenth century; their names are not entirely forgotten, but the only Scandinavian composer of that period who could reasonably claim to qualify as famous was EDVARD GRIEG, born 15th June 1843 at the important commercial seaport of Bergen on the west coast of Norway where his father, Alexander Grieg, of partly Scottish descent (his name having been originally spelt Greig), was the acting British Consul. Edvard's mother Gesine, *née* Hagerup and one hundred per cent Norwegian, gave him his first piano lessons at the age of six. At fifteen, on the advice of the eminent violinist Ole Bull (an old friend of the family), he was sent to the Leipzig Conservatoire of Music where he remained for the best part of four years and, like many another confident youngster before and since, was inclined to be critical of his preceptors: to quote his own comment, 'what they failed to teach me I sought to learn from Mozart and Beethoven'. Subsequently he studied for a year or so at the conservatoire in Copenhagen under J. P. E. Hartmann (the director) and Niels Gade (see above), with whom he found himself more *en rapport* than with his Leipzig mentors; but since Gade's great ambition was to be recognized as the Danish Mendelssohn and he gave instruction to his pupils on the assumption that they too held aspirations of a similar nature, the turning-point in Grieg's career did not come until 1864, when at the age of twenty-one he became acquainted with Rikard Nordraak (twenty-two), an enthusiast for Norwegian folk music. Nordraak died two years later, but during those two years stimulated his new friend to aim at becoming a 'national' composer rather than merely a Norwegian imitator of Mendelssohn or Schumann.

When Nordraak met his tragically early death Grieg, thanks largely to the generosity of his parents, was enjoying a working holiday in Rome.* On his return to Norway he applied unsuccessfully for the post of conductor at the National Theatre in Christiania (now Oslo), but settled there for the time being when in 1867 he married his first cousin Nina Hagerup, a professional singer who introduced many of his songs to the public; in 1874 they left Christiania and made their home in the small village of Lofthus on the Hardanger Fjord, not far to the south of Bergen, his birthplace. Having meanwhile composed a piano sonata, two violin sonatas and an immediately successful piano concerto, as well as numerous attractive songs and piano pieces, Grieg was by now recognized as an outstanding musician and was granted a pension by the Norwegian Government, which enabled him to indulge in fairly frequent travel abroad. During the course of the next twenty years, usually accompanied by his wife, he attended the first Bayreuth Festival (1876), made two comprehensive tours of Germany and Holland (1883 and 1886), paid three visits to London (two in 1888 and one in 1894) and one each to Paris and Vienna (1889). Subsequently he suffered from his share of ill-health and was obliged to restrict his activities somewhat, but his sudden death on 4th September 1907 at the age of sixty-four came as an unexpected shock to his relatives and friends. (His widow survived him by twenty-eight years.)

New ideas concerning folk song and the like were certainly put into Grieg's head by Rikard Nordraak (and later, too, by Frants Beyer), but some historians have tended to over-emphasize the significance of their impact on his music as a whole, for his methods, if not his manner, remained as firmly based on classical tradition as did those of another 'national' composer, his close contemporary Antonín Dvořák; his music has therefore, like Dvořák's, been greatly

* It was on a *second* visit to Rome, in 1869, that he met Liszt, as recorded on page 115.

appreciated far beyond the land of its origin.* Grieg subconsciously realized his limitations and never completed an opera, an oratorio, a cantata or even a symphony, nor was he altogether at ease in his string quartet, his three violin sonatas and his single cello sonata: his only really successful large-scale achievement was the piano concerto (1868), and anyone who disparages that work because it is tuneful and popular should for the same reason disparage Schubert's *Rosamunde*, Wagner's *Tannhäuser* overture and Brahms' *Hungarian Dances*. The fact remains that although Grieg provided some admirable incidental music for Bjørnson's *Sigurd Jorsalfar* (1872) and Ibsen's *Peer Gynt* (1876, with 'Morning', 'In the Hall of the Mountain King' and 'Solveig's Song') he was happiest when exploiting a purely lyrical rather than dramatic vein: witness the uninhibitedly invigorating *Holberg Suite* for piano (1884) and arranged for string orchestra (1885); the ten volumes of *Lyric Pieces* for piano, spread over the period 1867–1901 and incorporating the familiar *Bridal Procession*, *Erotik* and *March of the Dwarfs*; the many songs, ranging from *I love thee* (1864, words by Hans Christian Andersen) to the *Haugtussa* cycle (1898, Arne Garborg).

If Edvard Grieg never quite topped the summit peaks of true greatness, neither did he ever descend to the depths of triviality: he was *par excellence* a composer for middlebrows.

---

* Dvořák and Grieg were mutual admirers, but only once did they meet face to face – when in 1903 Grieg, although ailing, travelled to Bohemia to conduct a concert of his own works in Prague and Dvořák's daughter Magda, a promising young soprano, took part in it.

CHAPTER THIRTY-SIX

Rimsky-Korsakov

My dictionary defines an amateur as 'one who cultivates a particular study or art for the love of it, and not professionally'; a professional as 'one who makes his living by an art, game, etc., as opposed to an amateur who practises it merely for pastime'. There is no need to cavil at these admirably concise definitions, although so far as composers go the terms are sometimes used with a slightly different nuance, an amateur being one who has never really learnt the job and relies mainly on inborn flair, a professional being one who knows the job from A to Z even though he may not necessarily earn his living by it. Whether Borodin, in that sense an amateur, was a greater or lesser composer than Mendelssohn, in that sense a professional, I do not propose to argue; but I must record how it came about that at one stage of his career NIKOLAI RIMSKY-KORSAKOV (1844–1908) changed almost overnight not just from amateur to professional but from clumsy amateur to expert professional.

Born at Tikhvin, not far from Nizhny-Novgorod, he belonged to an aristocratic family with the sea in its blood and at the age of twelve became a naval cadet. For the next five years or so he was stationed at St Petersburg and spent all his spare time indulging a love of music at concerts and operatic performances; presently he made contact with Balakirev, who quickly sensed that here was a likely disciple, gave him a few perfunctory lessons in composition, admitted him to the *kutchka* and encouraged him to embark on a symphony. Almost simultaneously, however, his admiral summoned him to embark on a warship for a cruise in Atlantic waters; this lasted nearly three years and took in London, New York and Rio de Janiero. When eventually allocated to a further spell of shore duty at St Petersburg, the young hopeful (his outlook now broadened by travel) was able to turn his attention more seriously towards music, and between 1865 and 1870 he produced a fair quantity of vocal and orchestral works which were sufficiently Russian in character to satisfy his mentor Balakirev. They included a few charming miniatures like the song *The Rose enslaves the Nightingale*, but taken by and large owed more to enthusiasm than to ability, being mostly diffuse and ill-constructed – in a word, amateurish. Rimsky-Korsakov himself realized that something was lacking and was unhappy about it; fortunately it was not long before he was given an opportunity to alter his course and by so doing become a professional, a professional – as in the event it turned out – in the Mendelssohn category. The *volte-face* took place in 1871, when he was surprisingly offered the post of professor of composition at the St Petersburg Conservatoire, which he accepted forthwith although he knew perfectly well that his qualifications were inadequate. He had never thoroughly studied harmony, counterpoint and such-like, and it was now suddenly borne upon him that his failure to have done so might be the root cause of his prevailing insufficiency. So he promptly resigned his commission in the Navy, shut himself up with a pile of text-books and in an incredibly short space of time (at the age of twenty-seven there was never a quicker or more industrious student) emerged well equipped as a budding professor of composition – and revivified as a composer. (About the same time he married Nadezhda Purgold, a professional pianist; their son Andrey, when he reached his thirties, became a music critic.)

After the transformation it was above all in the field of opera that Rimsky distinguished himself. He produced fourteen, ranging from *Ivan the Terrible* (1872) to *The Golden Cockerel* (1907); in between came *A Night in May*, *The Snow Maiden*, *Sadko*, *The Legend of Czar Saltan* and eight others of less significance. Of the six here named *Ivan the Terrible*, roughly contemporaneous with Mussorgsky's *Boris Godunov*, took a more romanticized view of a rather similar episode in Russian history; *A Night in May* (after Gogol) was in essence a peasant opera which might almost remind

202

one of Smetana's *Bartered Bride* or Dvořák's *Jacobin* (see pages 153 and 195) had not the composer also attempted to depict (I quote his own words) 'the ceremonial side of folk life which gives expression to the survivals of ancient paganism'. The other four all belonged to that half-world which Rimsky-Korsakov made peculiarly his own – a blend of fairy-tale with folk-legend, of extravagant fantasy with bucolic humour. They are still played regularly in Russia and occasionally, one is glad to say, in Britain, where however *The Snow Maiden* is mainly remembered for the 'Dance of the Tumblers', *Sadko* for the 'Hindu Song', *Czar Saltan* for the 'Flight of the Bumble Bee' and *The Golden Cockerel* for the 'Hymn to the Sun'. (The libretti of the two last were both after Pushkin – some way after.)

Even after his 1871 regeneration Rimsky-Korsakov found 'absolute' music rather hard going. During the next few years he completed a symphony in C minor, a string quartet in F major, a string sextet in A major and a quintet in B flat major for the unusual combination of flute, clarinet, bassoon, horn and piano, but they aroused little interest and today are almost forgotten. He was far more at home in the programmatic symphony *Antar* (1875), based on an Arabian fairy-tale by Brambeus Sankovsky, where he could indulge to the full his love of oriental colour and decoration. (*Antar* was the wholesale revision of an earlier work of amateur days and it is indicative of the composer's praiseworthy addiction to self-criticism that even the 1875 version failed to satisfy him: he revised it again in 1897.) Still more successful was the symphonic suite *Scheherazade* (1888), inspired by *The Thousand and One Nights*: in this gorgeous evocation of eastern splendour, barbarity, passion and langour, Rimsky-Korsakov reached a zenith; it was, one might say, the apotheosis of all he had striven for in *Antar*.

Whereas *Scheherazade* showed him on top form the same could not be said of the *Russian Easter* overture (also 1888). The *Spanish Capriccio* (belonging to the previous year) demands more positive comment and I shall leave it to the composer himself (as detached as ever) to supply it.

The opinion formed by both critics and the public, that the capriccio is a *magnificently orchestrated piece*, is wrong. It is a brilliant *composition for orchestra*. The change of timbres, the felicitous choice of melodic designs and figuration patterns, exactly suiting each kind of instrument, brief virtuoso cadenzas for instruments solo, the rhythm of the percussion instruments, and so on, constitute here the very *essence* of the composition and not its garb or orchestration. The Spanish themes, of dance character, furnished me with rich material for putting in use multiform orchestral effects. All in all the capriccio is undoubtedly a purely external piece, but vividly brilliant for all that.

Here Rimsky-Korsakov laid a finger on his own most serious shortcoming: it is not in the *Spanish Capriccio* alone that one is disturbingly aware of this tendency to make orchestration the very essence of composition. More often than not, one feels, acquired technique was unmatched by spontaneous inspiration (a common enough failing among professionals); it was only when he partially relaxed control of latter-day inhibitions (thereby giving rein, perhaps, to a resurgence of the spirit of amateurism at its best) that his music reached the heights. What raised *Scheherazade* above *Antar* – and indeed to the level of a masterpiece – was not any added brilliance of treatment but the greater point and attraction of the melodies themselves. For the same reason one is inclined to rank *The Golden Cockerel* (which is full of good tunes) as the best of his operas, although nearly all have passages of beauty and charm – e.g. the lovely duet between the Princess of the Sea and the King of the Sea which concludes the second act of *Sadko*.

Nikolai Rimsky-Korsakov died of angina pectoris at the age of sixty-four. There are three counts on which he should be remembered: first, as a composer who by taking thought or being anxious added cubits to his stature and at times touched greatness (even if he never rose quite high enough to maintain a firm grip on it); secondly, as the untiring and effective – if controversial – propagandist of the two illustrious composers whose achievements were recorded in chapters 30 and 32; thirdly, as a professor of composition who earned the heart-felt gratitude of a long line of distinguished pupils, none of whom was more directly influenced by his teaching than Igor Stravinsky (1882–1971).

CHAPTER THIRTY-SEVEN

Fauré

The river Ariège has its source on the high plateau of Font
Nègre (8,000 feet above sea-level) where stands a three-
country stone of France, Spain and Andorra; ninety miles
away to the north it joins the mightier river Garonne just
above Toulouse; meanwhile its initial torrential down-flow
and its subsequent meandering lend interest to one of the
most unspoilt regions of southern France. It was in this
Pyrenean valley that GABRIEL FAURÉ spent his early boyhood;
born 12th May 1845, he was the sixth child of an assistant
schoolmaster at Pamiers, the largest town in the *département*
of Ariège (although Foix, twelve miles upstream, is its
capital). Until four years old he was farmed out to foster-
parents at the nearby village of Verniolle, but he rejoined
the family in 1849 when his father, Toussaint Honoré Fauré,
hitherto very impecunious, was appointed head of a teachers'
training college at Foix. In a district more noteworthy for
scenic attraction than for cultured sophistication a child's
talent for music was recognizable by only the veriest few
among the neighbours, but it so happened that in 1854
Louis Niedermeyer, who (see page 179) had just taken charge
of a musical academy in Paris, made an extensive explora-
tory tour in search of promising students; he penetrated as
far as Foix, and was so much impressed with the potential
talent of young Gabriel that he immediately proffered free
board, lodging and tuition. So Fauré, rescued from the
Pyrenean foothills at the age of nine, became a pupil at the
Ecole Niedermeyer; his principal studies were piano, organ
and composition. Six years later, as recorded in chapter 31,
Camille Saint-Saëns joined the teaching staff; he was only
twenty-five years old at the time and, being of a friendly
disposition, was soon on *tutoyer* terms with his most promising pupil and drew his attention to the works of Beethoven

and Schumann – still regarded with grave suspicion by many conventional French musicians.

After leaving the Ecole Niedermeyer in 1865 Fauré was organist at the church of St Sauveur at Rennes in Brittany for four years; for the next forty-five he earned his living in Paris – except during the Franco-Prussian war, when he served in the field. He was organist at Notre Dame de Clignancourt and at St Honoré d'Eylau before becoming C. M. Widor's assistant at St Sulpice, but from 1877 onwards his headquarters were at the Madeleine where he was choirmaster for seventeen years and was appointed head organist in 1896. Other important posts which he held simultaneously were those of inspector of music to state-aided schools (from 1892), professor of composition at the Paris Conservatoire (1896–1905), director there (from 1905) and music critic of *Le Figaro* (from 1903).

In character Fauré was unassuming to the point of diffidence, and his career was correspondingly uneventful in the sense that there were few dramatic incidents. In his late twenties he (*a*) went to Weimar with Saint-Saëns, who there introduced him to Liszt, and (*b*) began a long courtship of Marianne Viardot, daughter of the famous singer Pauline Viardot-Garcia. In his early thirties he (*a*) paid three more visits to Germany, where he heard at least one complete cycle of Wagner's *Ring of the Nibelung*, and (*b*) at last became betrothed to Marianne, who however broke the engagement a few months later. In 1883, at the age of thirty-eight, he married Marie Fremiet, daughter of the sculptor Emmanuel Fremiet. This was a marriage of convenience in the best sense of the term: no one suggested that the bridal pair were passionately devoted to one another, but they lived amicably together until Fauré's death forty-one years later; the tragedy of his life was that from about 1905 onwards he was afflicted by deafness. During the latter part of the 1914-18 war he and his wife stayed with one of his brothers at Pau in Gascony (which was a hundred miles away from his birthplace but where nevertheless he was within sight of the Pyrenees). Soon after the armistice, being now well on in his seventies and almost completely deaf, he resigned all his official appointments and went into semi-retirement at Annecy in Haute-Savoie, but later he returned to Paris and it was there that he died on 4th November 1924.

Fauré, one of the most distinctively French of all French composers in an age when Teutonic hegemony in the world of music was still taken for granted, never joined the ranks of the *avant-garde* (although several of his pupils were numbered among them): admittedly he had more sense of style and eventually developed far greater harmonic initiative than his more prolific colleagues Saint-Saëns and Jules Massenet (1842–1912) but his roots, like theirs, lay in classical tradition. Although a professional organist, he wrote nothing for organ alone, and indeed his only important contribution to Church music was a Requiem (1887). In extreme contrast to that of his compatriot Berlioz (see page 103) this was a very reticent setting (for soprano, baritone, small chorus, small orchestra and organ), possibly owing something to the modal training which was part of the Ecole Niedermeyer curriculum; admirably suited for liturgical purposes, it is less satisfying in the concert hall. The same restraint, almost asceticism, is noticeable in the incidental music for Shakespeare's *Merchant of Venice* (1889, entitled *Shylock*) and Maeterlinck's *Pelléas et Mélisande* (1898)* as well as in two operas which came soon afterwards, *Prometheus* and *Pénélope* (though here it derived from a different source – a deep admiration for the cultural ideals of ancient Greece). None of Fauré's stage-works made much lasting impression: his genius was lyrical rather than dramatic and inevitably found fuller expression in his piano pieces and songs. Of the former the most ambitious, structurally, was the rather Schumannesque *Theme with variations* op. 73, but his quintessence lay in the better-known nocturnes and barcarolles (thirteen of each); the earlier specimens, as might have been expected, were reminiscent of Chopin, but in due course – and notably perhaps in nocturnes nos. 6, 7 and 13 and

* For the opera *Pelléas et Mélisande* by Debussy see pages 240–41.

barcarolles nos. 5 and 9 – he came to combine a Chopin-like melodic fluency with subtle harmonic devices which as a rule were individual and unmistakable. ('As a rule', because now and again there was a tiny echo of Wagner.)

Fauré was France's greatest song-writer. Although he left only sixty, as against the six hundred left by the greatest song-writer the world has ever known, I am tempted to repeat a phrase I used on pages 86–7 and say that although they were not all masterpieces it is astonishing how many of them were. Most – and perhaps all the very best – were quiet and contemplative: Fauré usually preferred to set verses fitting that mood and proved himself, in particular, a perfect interpreter of Paul Verlaine in nine songs from *La Bonne chanson*. His first songs were written during his college days, his last shortly before his death, and throughout a long career their quality remained amazingly consistent: among other exquisite gems were *Après un rêve* (which belonged to his twenties), *Le Secret* (his thirties), *En Prière* (his forties), *Soir* (his fifties), *Veilles-tu, ma senteur de soleil?* (his sixties) and *Diane, Séléné* (his seventies). These six, and many more too numerous to catalogue here, have rarely been surpassed for poetic sensitivity, purity of utterance and polished artistry.

Just after the First World War but before he retired to Annecy, Fauré provided music for a hybrid entertainment (ballet-cum-opera) vaguely based on poems of Verlaine and produced at Monte Carlo; he composed an overture and three other new items, filling in the gaps with transcriptions of some of his earlier works. As originally conceived *Masques et bergamasques* is as dead as a doornail but it survives in the form of an orchestral suite which is light music at its very best, going far to prove that Fauré, had he so wished, could in that field have outpaced Léo Delibes (*Coppélia*) and his own pupil André Messager (*Véronique*); the significance of *Masques et bergamasques* has sometimes escaped the attention of serious-minded musical historians.

In the main however Fauré devoted his last few years to chamber music. He had previously written two violin sonatas, a cello sonata, two piano quartets and a piano quintet, among which the cello sonata alone had enhanced his reputation to any considerable extent. At Annecy, between 1920 and 1923, he composed a second cello sonata, a second piano quintet, a piano trio and a string quartet. All these were imbued with the austerity that had earlier characterized the Requiem and *Pénélope*, and furthermore aroused speculation as to whether deafness affected him to the same degree that it had affected Beethoven. Analogy was justifiable, for despite the incidence of many obscure passages Beethoven's genius reached a summit point in the *cavatina* of his 'deaf' string quartet op. 130 and Fauré's in the first movement of his 'deaf' piano quintet op. 115.

During his lifetime Gabriel Fauré (like Schumann and Bruckner but in sharp contrast to Berlioz) was rarely acclaimed beyond the frontiers of his own country. Even today, one feels, the outside world is reluctant to grant him the recognition which he deserves. It is true that he did not excel as an all-rounder and by that token can perhaps hardly be rated as the most historically important French composer of his generation; as a miniaturist, however, he reigned supreme.

CHAPTER THIRTY-EIGHT

Wolf*

HUGO WOLF (1860–1903) was the son of Philipp Wolf, a
leather-merchant in Windischgraz, a small town midway
between Graz and Laibach. Graz was – and still is – the
capital of the Austrian province of Styria. Laibach was the
largest town in Slovenia, in those days incorporated in the
vast and amorphous Austro–Hungarian Empire; since 1918,
as Ljubljana, it has been the capital of the province of
Carniola in the north-western corner of Yugoslavia. The
composer's birthplace lies some twelve miles on the Yugoslav
side of the present frontier, but his father (unlike many inhabitants of the region) was of unimpeachable Austrian
descent, and although his mother was a Slovene he is
normally reckoned to have been Austrian by birth.

Hugo went to school first at Graz and afterwards at
Marburg (now Maribor); in 1875 he entered the Vienna
Conservatoire of Music, where he made good progress with
his studies but quarrelled with the director and was soon
dismissed for insubordination. His father, whose leather
business had fallen on evil days, was no longer able to support him: over the next few years he earned only an
extremely modest livelihood by teaching and often hardly
knew where his next meal was coming from; a promising
engagement as deputy conductor at Salzburg lasted for
just three months, his excitable temperament rendering
him quite unsuitable for such a post. Prospects looked
brighter when in 1884 he was appointed music critic of the
Viennese journal *Salonblatt*, but this angriest of angry
young men did himself no good by attacking Brahms and

* The longer-lived Janáček, Elgar and Puccini were all older than
Wolf, but since none of the three reached maturity until Wolf was
nearing the tragic end of his active career, discussion of their achievements is postponed to the immediately succeeding chapters.

other eminent senior contemporaries in vitriolic terms – while at the same time lauding to the skies his idol Wagner, still somewhat suspect in 'responsible' musical circles in the Austrian capital.

Compositions that survive from this period include a few songs, a string quartet in D minor and a symphonic poem entitled *Penthesilea*; in 1888, thanks to the generosity of Friedrich Eckstein, a rare (and well-to-do) admirer, he was able to retire from the controversial turmoil of Vienna to a nearby but peaceful country hide-out at Perchtoldsdorf, on the edge of the Wienerwald. Here, during the next two and a half years, he wrote well over two hundred songs, sometimes completing half a dozen or so in a single week and on at least one occasion three in a single day; they included settings of poems by Michelangelo, Goethe, Joseph von Eichendorff, Eduard Mörike and Gottfried Keller, as well as the forty-four of the *Spanish Song-book* (Emanuel von Geibel and Paul Heyse) and the twenty-two in Part I of the *Italian Song-book* (Heyse again). Leaving aside early and immature efforts, this constituted virtually the whole of his lifelong song output except for the twenty-four in Part II of the *Italian Song-book*, which were composed during April and May 1896. His only important instrumental work, apart from the string quartet (see above) was the *Italian Serenade*, first written in 1887 for string quartet and in 1892 transcribed for small orchestra. The opera *Der Corregidor* (*The Magistrate*), based on Pedro de Alarcón's entertaining story *El sombrero de tres picos* (*The Three-cornered Hat*) was completed in 1895 and produced the following year at Munich; although containing much fine music it made little impact on musicians and none at all on the public: it was never played in Vienna, even, until after Wolf's death, and subsequent revivals have been few and far between. It must also be recorded that his songs, many of which have been recognized by posterity as masterpieces, enjoyed only a *succès d'estime* during his lifetime – and that in Germany rather than in Austria.

In 1897, by which time he was settled once again in Vienna

(Schwindgasse), this highly strung composer began to suffer from delusions: for instance, he became convinced in his own mind that *Der Corregidor* – instead of having been a failure, commercially speaking – had been acclaimed as a work of genius, and believed that he, Wolf, not Gustav Mahler (see page 232), had just been appointed artistic director of the Vienna Court Opera. Presently his public behaviour and utterances became so distressingly outrageous that on medical advice he was removed to a private mental home; he never fully recovered his sanity and died there some five years later.

Wolf's reputation depends almost entirely upon his songs. It would be unrealistic to maintain – and perhaps hardly to be expected of a composer who worked in such mercurial spasms of energy – that they were altogether consistent in quality: a fair proportion of them were hurriedly (although not carelessly) written and might well have benefited from second-thought revision. But when he was at his best (which was perhaps more often than not) he combined a lyrical inspiration worthy of Schubert with a *gemütlichkeit* akin to that of Schumann; furthermore he resembled Mahler in showing true appreciation of the proper relationship between poetry and music, admirably demonstrated in (for instance) *Der Gärtner* and *Fussreise* (Mörike), in *Frühling übers Jahr* and *Blumengruss* (Goethe). Some of the songs in the *Spanish Song-book* display considerable powers of characterization; those of the later *Italian Song-book* tend to be dramatic, a noteworthy feature being that the piano accompaniments often hold independent interest, doing much more than provide formal support for the vocal line. One notes, too, that in much the same way the melodic spontaneity of many passages in *Der Corregidor* is helped along by an appropriate and carefully wrought orchestral background; in this ill-fated opera there are also two splendid love-duets as well as note-for-note (and word-for-word) reproductions of two well-known songs from the *Spanish Song-book* – *In dem Schatten meiner Locken* and *Herz, verzage nicht geschwind*. The pity was that the composer, in an enthusiastic determination to emulate his beloved Wagner (and in particular the Wagner of *The Mastersingers*) should have allowed valour to outrun discretion when he accepted an inadequate libretto without due consideration, when he failed to plan the work in advance, and when he dashed off the music in a matter of months.

Hugo Wolf was what would nowadays be called a psychiatric case: he appears to have gone out of his way to acquire personal enemies rather than personal friends, and yet was always prompt to complain that every man's hand was against him; in truth he was pathetically out of tune with the world into which he had been born. But he left an imperishable treasury of lovely *Lieder*, and one may readily concur with the judgement of W. H. Hadow (see page 157) that his eager and hectic genius wore him out before his time.

CHAPTER THIRTY-NINE

Janáček

Leoš Janáček was born on 3rd July 1854 at the village of Hukvaldy in the Beskydy hills of Eastern Moravia, which lie about sixty miles north-east of Brno (Brünn), the capital of the province; his father, Jiří (George) Janáček, was an ill-paid schoolteacher whose numerous children were brought up in somewhat poverty-stricken surroundings. At the age of eleven Leoš became a chorister at the 'Queen's Monastery' in Brno (founded in 1648), where after his voice broke he stayed on for a few terms as deputy choirmaster. At twenty, with a satisfactory diploma in his pocket, and already – like Smetana at the same age (see page 152) – an ardent Czech nationalist, he made his way to Prague to continue his studies at the Organ School there. Two years later he returned to Brno, where he was appointed director of the Beseda Choral Society. Early in 1877 he became acquainted with Antonín Dvořák; the two men got on famously and during the summer months went on a walking tour together. It may be significant that it was at about this time that Janáček composed his early *Suite for String Orchestra*, which showed many traces of his friend's influence. (Long afterwards Janáček wrote: 'You know how it is when someone takes the words out of your mouth; with me it is always like that with Dvořák'.)

Following two short periods of further study at the Conservatoires in Leipzig and Vienna, Janáček settled permanently in Brno and presently fell in love with a young girl named Zdenka Schulzová; she was little more than a child and, indeed, was less than sixteen years old when in 1881 they were married. A year later they had a daughter, Olga, but quarrels were already beginning to break out and they soon parted company, Zdenka taking the baby away with her. There was talk of a divorce, but eventually a reconciliation was effected and they joined forces again. When in 1888 Zdenka gave birth to the son for whom her husband had been longing, prospects for happiness looked brighter, but they were dashed to the ground when, before reaching his third birthday, the boy succumbed to a fatal attack of meningitis. Although the bereaved parents continued thereafter to share the same dwelling, they seem to have done so in a spirit of armed neutrality – which became no less armed when their daughter Olga, who had always been sickly, died at the age of twenty-one. Excuses for the incompatibility of the pair could no doubt be found on both sides. Leoš certainly suffered from 'mother-in-law trouble', for Zdenka's mother, to whom she was devoted, was German by birth and strongly opposed to the Czech national aspirations which had always meant so much to him; he himself (like several other famous composers) was not averse to sympathetic female companionship outside the family circle, and his successive friendships with two married woman – both extremely good-looking and both by coincidence bearing the same Christian name, Kamila – may not have been entirely platonic.

Reverting to Janáček's professional career as distinct from his domestic involvements, mention should be made of his first opera *Šárka* (originally composed in 1887 but later revised – at Dvořák's suggestion); of his growing interest in the folk music of his native land, which led to the *Lachian Dances* of 1891; of the oratorio *Amarus*. It was not until 1903, when he was forty-nine years old, that he completed the opera *Her Stepdaughter* which, renamed *Jenufa*, was eventually to bring him recognition beyond the borders of Moravia, although it did not reach Prague, even, until 1914, nor Vienna until 1918 – when the title role was played by Maria Jeritza (also Moravian by birth) and the composer was able to record that 'at last I have heard and seen the Jenufa of my opera'.

Between 1903 and 1913 Janáček produced little music of importance, but during the First World War (when his sympathies, like those of most Czechs, lay with the Allies rather than with the Central Powers) he completed the orchestral rhapsody *Taras Bulba* and the satirical opera *The Excursions of Mr Brouček*. No sooner did the independent republic of Czechoslovakia come into being after the war than this creative urge was aroused anew: during the ten years that remained to him he composed four more very remarkable operas – *Káta Kabanová, The Cunning Little Vixen, The Makropoulos Case* and *From the House of the Dead* – as well as two cantatas (*The Ballad of Blánik Hill* and *The Wandering Madman*), the *Glagolitic Mass*, and several important instrumental works including an attractive 'sinfonietta' and an enigmatic string quartet subtitled *Intimate Letters*. The Mass and the quartet were both dated 1928. Later that same year Janáček contracted pneumonia while paying a visit to his birthplace, Hukvaldy; he was taken by ambulance to a hospital at Ostrava (a large industrial town some twenty miles away), where he died – following a heart attack – on 12th August.

Like Mussorgsky, the mature Janáček – despite frequent reiterations that his favourite composer was the conservatively minded Dvořák – largely scouted the classical notion that a discreet relationship between melody and harmony was the basis of all respectable music. He rarely wrote what is called a 'good tune': when setting words to music his main endeavour was to reproduce as closely as possible the rise and fall of the verbal accentuation in what has been described as 'speech song'. If this were all it might well be imagined that his operas would only make their full effect when played in the original Czech (a language with which few of us are familiar); some other explanation must be sought for the success they have enjoyed when given in English – and other languages. It may be found in the composer's ability to illustrate and indeed intensify a dramatic impact, to express and partially resolve, in terms of music, some of the problems – religious, political, aesthetic, personal – which were apt to beset his contemporaries and continue, perhaps to an even greater degree, to beset us today. Even the comparatively light-hearted *Cunning Little*

Vixen, ostensibly concerned with the animal world, holds symbolic human undertones; *The Makropoulos Case*, although dealing with legal matters, does not avoid consideration of deeper-lying causes of unrest; *From the House of the Dead* is perhaps even more evocative of man's frustration and suffering than is Beethoven's *Fidelio* with its 'happy ending'.

As has been made clear, Leoš Janáček was a 'late developer' and his fame depends almost entirely upon the music of his maturity; furthermore, the full significance of that music was not generally realized until after his death.

CHAPTER FORTY

Elgar

It is thirty-six chapters since we last met a native English-man. That the Britain of the interim was unmusical is a canard which Haydn, Mendelssohn and Dvořák would have been glad to refute from personal experience, but all this long while creative aspects of the art had admittedly been meagerly realized. However the sixteen-year period 1st May 1842 to 30th April 1858 saw the birth of half a dozen very talented British composers, five of whom (Arthur Sullivan, Alexander Mackenzie, Hubert Parry, C. V. Stanford and Ethel Smyth) later played a part in shaping the musical renaissance which swept the country in the 1880s and 1890s; the sixth, the odd man out, was still comparatively unknown at renaissance-time, but before the twentieth century was well under way his achievements had put those of the other five in the shade and he had clearly established himself as the first really great British-born composer since Henry Purcell. (I say British-*born* because it must always be remembered that Handel, Purcell's junior by twenty-five years, was for practical purposes at least as British as his patron King George I, the Hanoverian *Ursprung* of our present royal dynasty.)

EDWARD ELGAR, born 2nd June 1857 at Broadheath just outside Worcester, was the fourth of seven children of William Henry Elgar (who kept a music shop in the city) and Anne Elgar *née* Greening. The father, although he spent his Sunday mornings playing the organ at a Catholic church, was himself a member of the Church of England, but the mother was a Roman Catholic and it was in that faith that the five children who survived infancy were educated. (The youngest daughter afterwards became a nun.) For a time Elgar, like Handel and Schumann and Tchaikovsky at much the same age, was intended by his parents to join the legal profession, but Worcester (with its triennial Three Choirs Festival – shared with Gloucester and Hereford) was a centre of musical culture and before he was out of his teens he gave up the law in order to play a fuller part in that activity, both as violinist and accompanist. He soon conceived an ambition to become a composer but had to rely entirely on self-tuition and extensive practice. This is a cardinal factor which should always be borne in mind when any attempt is made to assess his achievements: experience is the best of all teachers, and Elgar might not have acquired such practical knowledge of orchestration at a conservatoire as he did as bandmaster of the county mental home, as a first violinist in a Birmingham (semi-professional) orchestra and as conductor of the Worcester (amateur) Orchestral Society. On the concert programmes of all three of these organizations his name figured occasionally as composer; presently he succeeded his father as organist at the nearby Catholic church and furthermore built up a good teaching connexion. By the time he was thirty he had therefore acquired considerable local reputation as an excellent all-round musician.

In 1889 Elgar married one of his pupils, Caroline Roberts. She was eight years older than he was, the daughter of a major-general and appropriately enough a woman of strong character who had unbounded faith in her husband's capabilities and stoked his ambitions. At first they went to live in London (where she presented him with a daughter, Carice), but the Thames proved less easy to set on fire than the Severn, and the only noteworthy happening in the capital, so far as Elgar was concerned, was the sale of the copyright of *Salut d'amour* (which ever since has been a Corner House 'must') for two guineas. So it was back to Worcestershire and the old routine of teaching, conducting and violin-playing. During the next six or seven years, however, Elgar found time to compose a very charming serenade for string orchestra and (on a larger scale) about half a dozen extended choral works (owing something to the Wagner of *Tannhäuser* days) which were played with fair success at music festivals in the midlands and north of England; one or two even reached the Crystal Palace in south London. Unfortunately he was misguided in his choice of librettists, and it must also be admitted that more often than not the music was as uninspired as the words were uninspiring. *King Olaf* was the pick of the bunch: it included the 'challenge of Thor' (a magnificent outburst of pagan energy) and the 'ballad of Thyri', which in its happy combination of fluent lyricism and technical accomplishment was an earnest of what was to come.

Yet the fact remains that Elgar, who by the age of thirty had become by diligence a big fish in a little pond, was by forty, despite further diligence, no more than a medium-sized fish in a medium-sized pond. The transformation scene of 19th June 1899 when the *Variations on an Original Theme, 'Enigma'* ('dedicated to my friends pictured within') had a first performance at St James's Hall in London (under the baton of Hans Richter) was so surprising that one is tempted to mix metaphors and declare that the medium-sized fish in the medium-sized pond became overnight the brightest star in the firmament. *Enigma* made its mark not only on Elgar's career but also on the future of British music. Some have found it, on a first hearing, disconcertingly terse (the fourth variation lasts less than half a minute), but surely all must acknowledge that here Elgar provided a masterpiece – and at the same time a yardstick by which his subsequent compositions of comparable magnitude must be judged.

First among these was his only important collection of songs (*Sea Pictures*); next came the incense-laden oratorio *The Dream of Gerontius*, based on the mystical poem of Cardinal Henry Newman. (Elgar himself) by the way, although his faith never wavered, was not an *ardent* Catholic; indeed at one time – he later changed his mind about this however – he expressed a wish that his body should be cremated.) The first performance of *Gerontius* (Birmingham, 1900) was under-rehearsed and had a mixed reception; a year later it was acclaimed at Düsseldorf (a success for which the composer had to thank the German conductor Julius Buths) but it did not reach London until 1903. Since then it has never looked back; musicians and public alike are right when they rank it higher than either of the two later oratorios – *The Apostles* (1903) and *The Kingdom* (1906) – for although each of these contains some beautiful music (particularly in the choral sections) the white-heat intensity of *Gerontius* is sadly cooled and there is over-reliance on repetition rather than development of the Wagner-like *Leitmotive*. Meanwhile Elgar had also written the *Cockaigne* overture ('capital fun'), the less garish but more original *Introduction and Allegro for Strings* (string quartet plus string orchestra) and the concert overture *In the South* (*Alassio*) – a glowing and impassioned evocation of

> ... lands of palms, of orange blossom,
> Of olives, aloe, and maize and vine.

The first symphony (A flat major, 1908) must also be regarded as a fine piece of work; here and there it is disturbingly redolent of Edwardian opulence but by contrast the slow movement (placed third) is deeply moving.

The violin concerto (1910) fell into a rather different category. It was perhaps the most impersonal of all Elgar's large-scale works : himself a violinist, he was better equipped than most to assess the technical potentialities of the instrument, and yet no important solo passage was finally committed to paper until it had been vetted by Fritz Kreisler, to whom the concerto was dedicated and who was the first to play it. Undoubtedly the composer here made a gallant attempt (like Brahms before him) to reconcile artistic integrity with opportunities for executive virtuosity and in the main he succeeded admirably; it may be significant, however, that in this undeniably great concerto some of the loveliest moments occurred when such problems were cast aside and the composer *per se* came into his own.

Symphony no. 2 (E flat major, 1911) was more consistent than no. 1, yet in performance somehow fails to make the profound impression which a perusal of the score leads one to expect; the first movement is admirable but the others seem to develop out of mechanism rather than inspiration. In any case both symphonies – and even the violin concerto – were surpassed by the symphonic poem *Falstaff* (1913), where spontaneity and technique joined hands in full accord, enabling the composer to achieve resounding and unexpected success in a new field. To appreciate all the detailed subtleties of this work one would have to refer to Elgar's own programmatic analysis published in the September 1913 issue of *The Musical Times*, but for any listener remembering that the hero was the classic knightly scoundrel of *King Henry IV* who was inclined to any form of roguery (rather than the inflated caricature of *The Merry Wives of Windsor* who was interested only in cuckoldry) the music itself should suffice; it gives its own account of Falstaff himself, of Prince Hal, of Mistress Quickly and the rest in a manner which a reincarnated William Shakespeare would surely approve. (I cannot forbear to draw special attention to the characteristic 'Falstaff as cajoling and persuasive' theme, first announced by the cellos between figures 7 and 8, and to the wholly captivating 'dream interlude' – figures 76 to 81.)

Nearly all this while the Elgars had been spending their time at either Malvern or Hereford but Sir Edward (he had been knighted in 1904 and awarded the Order of Merit in 1911) was soon increasingly in demand to conduct his works all over Britain and indeed on the continent and in America. So that he could be more conveniently placed for travel they moved once more to London (Hampstead) – and presently acquired a country retreat in Sussex as well. In August 1914, since his patriotism did not stop short with the provision of imperial marches and coronation odes, Elgar enrolled (at the age of fifty-seven) as a special constable; during the war he produced little music of lasting significance. (It is interesting to note however that although he never wrote an opera his musical play for children, *The Starlight Express*, was played at the Kingsway Theatre in

1915 and a ballet, *The Sanguine Fan*, at the Chelsea Palace in 1917.) During the first year or so of peace came some attractively lyrical chamber music (a violin sonata, a string quartet, a piano quintet) and a cello concerto which was more intimately personal than its counterpart for the violin and, moreover, achieved in the slow movement a level of poetic expression matched only in parts of *Gerontius, In the South* and the slow movement of the first symphony. In effect the cello concerto was Elgar's swan-song, for soon after the death of his devoted wife in 1920 he returned to the county of his birth and lived there in semi-retirement, composing meanwhile only a handful of 'occasional' pieces. Further honours were heaped upon him: he was appointed Master of the King's Music in 1924, a K.C.V.O. in 1928, a baronet in 1931, a G.C.V.O. in 1933. In that year, however, he was attacked by a malignant tumour; an operation to remove it was unsuccessful and the inevitable end came on 23rd February 1934. He died, as he had been born, within sight of the tall tower of Worcester Cathedral and within sound of its bells.

By ancestry and upbringing and temperament Elgar was an open-air-loving countryman: all his life he retained a boyish enthusiasm for fishing, walking, riding, cycling – and later, motoring. He was also a systematic punter, and in his affluent days kept a separate race-going bank account. Nearly all his friends – as distinct from his acquaintances – belonged to this same world; townsfolk and (especially) professional colleagues found him a poor mixer. He was as good-natured a fellow as one could hope to meet in the paddock at Cheltenham or during the course of a day's tramp over the Malvern Hills, but when he strove to uphold the dignity of his art in public company he was apt to appear stand-offish. Matters were not helped when he showed himself extremely sensitive to criticism – which he tended to ascribe to jealousy or vindictiveness. He mellowed as the years went by and his personal relationship with several contemporary musicians eventually became quite cordial, but the only ones admitted to his circle of intimates were W. H. Reed (a fellow violinist), Henry Walford Davies (who later succeeded him as Master of the King's Music) and Percy Hull (organist of Hereford cathedral) – all three, be it noted, of west-country origin. At the other extreme the record of his bitter thirty-year-long feud with a distinguished but more academically minded British musician who came near to rivalling his own eminence makes sorry reading.

The idiosyncrasies of Elgar the composer were as easily recognizable as those of Elgar the man – but less irritating; mannerisms they may have been, but the distinctive flavour which they imparted to nearly every page of his music is by no means unattractive. For instance there is a tendency for melodic phrases, rather than going first up and then down, to proceed by alternate rises and falls; then there is that curious insistence on a steady and indeed often stereotyped rhythmic tread, almost every beat of every bar being emphasized by the actual striking of a note or chord. The first six bars of *Enigma* exemplify what I have in mind; this passage represents Elgar in embryo.

So far I have refrained from specific comment on either the Elgar of *Salut d'amour* or the Elgar of 'Land of Hope and Glory', but since he took very seriously everything that he set down on paper a word or so on these aspects of his work is obligatory: it may suffice to say that in *Salut d'amour* – as in the unexceptionable orchestral suites entitled *Wand of Youth* and *Dream Children* – he appeared as the rich man's Edward German; that in the technically impeccable *Pomp and Circumstance* marches he can be seen in retrospect to have been the tycoon's Eric Coates. Lapses in taste need not be forgotten but they should be forgiven; in any case some of his struggles to reconcile poetry with chauvinism ended with poetry coming out on top. To have consistently maintained the high artistic level of *Enigma, Gerontius, In the South*, the two concertos and *Falstaff* would have been out of this world, and even when his occasional indiscretions are taken into consideration Edward Elgar can be accounted a truly great composer by international standards.

CHAPTER FORTY-ONE

Puccini

A composer of music named Giacomo Puccini, well respected in his day, was born in 1712 at Lucca (twelve miles north-east of Pisa); he died there in 1781. His great-great-grand-son, also named GIACOMO PUCCINI and also a composer of music, was born in the same Tuscan town (at 30 via di Poggio, a narrow street leading off the piazza San Michele) on 22nd December 1858. It was assumed by his parents that, like many of his forbears, he would become a church organ-ist, and so he did – until at the age of twenty-one he secured admittance to the Milan Conservatoire. His leaving exercise, a *Capriccio sinfonico* for orchestra (1883), showed great promise, and presently he completed his first opera *Le Villi* (originally in one act but later, at the instigation of the publisher Giulio Ricordi, expanded to two acts). This was played during the next few years at Turin, Milan, Naples and even abroad; it is still given occasionally. So is *Edgar* (originally Milan, 1889); but the Puccini whom we all know and whom many of us admire did not emerge until *Manon Lescaut* (Turin, 1893).

About the time of *Le Villi* Puccini had set up house with Elvira Gemignani, the wife of a grocer friend, their son Antonio being born in 1886. Since Elvira was a devout Catholic divorce was out of the question and the union was not legalized until after the death of her husband in 1904; long before that (in 1891) Puccini had found a permanent home for the family. This was a villa at Torre del Lago on Lake Massaciuccoli (about midway between Pisa and Via-reggio) where he could refresh himself by indulging in his favourite hobby – duck-shooting. (Today visitors to the shrine, after inspecting the interesting documents which it houses, can refresh themselves at the adjoining 'Butterfly bar'.) Although during the course of his career Puccini travelled widely throughout Europe and America, it was nearly always to Torre del Lago that he retired when he wanted to apply himself seriously in peace and quiet to composition. Not that he always *found* peace and quiet, for life with Elvira – both before and after marriage – was often troublesome and noisy: being (for an Italian) unmusical, she gave him little help or encouragement in his work and moreover was wont to make scenes when, as often happened, she suspected him of infidelity. In nine cases out of ten her suspicions were justified, for although Puccini was no great lover by Liszt or Wagner standards (his only *affaire* to ripen into something more permanent was that with Sybil Seligman, wife of a prominent London banker) he held an extraordinary fascination for pretty women of both high and low estate – who were rarely backward in coming forward to bestow their favours. Though not ill-natured he was extremely self-centred (it may be significant that he was a lifelong hypochondriac) and there was a grain of coarseness in his character to which psychologists inevitably attribute his fondness for depicting scenes not only of sensual passion but also of physical suffering. This is what a large section of the public enjoys; since Puccini was a gifted melodist, a very practical if unscholarly craftsman who chose his libretti with extreme care, and since moreover he was blessed with a superb instinct for making the most of a stage situation, it is small wonder that out of the ten operas he composed between 1892 and his death at Brussels on 29th November 1924 – from cancer of the throat – three rank among the 'top pops' of all time and several others still put in a welcome appearance now and again.

At least six operas (plus one ballet) are known to have been based on Antoine François Prévost's novel *Les Aventures du Chevalier des Grieux et de Manon Lescaut* (published in 1731) but only two are of historical importance – Massenet's *Manon* (1884) and Puccini's *Manon Lescaut* (1893); both are most enjoyable, and for once comparison can be illuminating rather than odious. *Manon* (composed when Massenet was forty-one) was better constructed and in many ways a maturer work of art than *Manon Lescaut* (composed when Puccini was thirty-four), for Massenet had no peer when it came to the delineation of feminine frailty and his heroine was a more sympathetic figure than Puccini's, who remained strangely anonymous; indeed Puccini seems to have lavished more affection on Des Grieux, whose melodic outburst 'Donna non vidi mai' far outshone Manon's aria 'In quelle trine morbide' – which was tuneful but rather insipid. In their respective first acts each composer cleverly captured the bustle and excitement of a stage-coach journey-break in the courtyard of an inn at Amiens. Puccini with his Act III at Le Havre and his Act IV outside New Orleans carried the story a stage further than Massenet – who tactfully allowed Manon to expire before being shipped off to America (which in Prévost's day was evidently regarded as a recognized dumping-ground for convicted prostitutes) – and in Act III displayed a flair for 'atmosphere' which Massenet, for all his talent, was incapable of matching.

La Bohème (Turin, 1896, after Henri Murger) is one of the few full-length operas of the late nineteenth century which are exempt from criticism on the ground that they go on just a shade too long. (Others that spring to mind are Bizet's *Carmen* and Verdi's *Falstaff*.) The first two acts show Puccini in his lightest and most lyrical mood, the quartet that concludes Act III rivals in ingenuity and charm the classic 'Bella figlia dell' amore' from Verdi's *Rigoletto* (see page 134), and even if Act IV is accounted a tear-jerker this is surely tear-jerking at its most gracious.

In *Tosca* (Rome, 1900), closely based on a melodrama by Victorien Sardou, Puccini's workmanship shows itself (from the very first two bars) in a rather grim light, being geared not so much to sentiment as to sadism. (C. V. Stanford has reminded us that 'the torture scene in Sardou's *Tosca*, which in itself is horrible enough, becomes ten times more so when Puccini dots the i's and crosses the t's with his vivid score'.) Among the famous arias Cavaradossi's 'Recondita armonia' and 'E lucevan le stelle' are more satisfying than Tosca's 'Vissi d'arte'; one feels that, as in *Manon Lescaut*, the composer was more in sympathy with his hero than with his heroine.

If so, he made ample amends to the gentler sex in *Madam Butterfly* (Milan, 1904) where the tenor was the merest stooge. (The hero of J. L. Long's magazine novelette on which the opera was based was named Benjamin Franklin Pinkerton; in the opera he is referred to by his initials and in this country, to avoid embarrassment, they are usually transposed and he becomes F. B. instead of B. F.) *Madam Butterfly* on its première was a failure, and it is a tribute to Puccini's determination to maintain his hold on public allegiance that he promptly revised it, whereupon it became – and has ever since remained – a big box-office draw. There can be no denying its appeal, and one's only serious quarrel with the composer over *Butterfly* is that he apparently disregarded the practical difficulty that, whereas the heroine is supposed to be fifteen, both 'Un bel dì' and 'Che tua madre' demand the lung-power of a thirty-five-year-old. At one time or another over the last forty-five years I must have seen and heard at least twenty singers of various nationalities attempting to reconcile this discrepancy, but I recall only two – Isabel Rhys-Parker and Sena Jurinac – who came within measurable distance of making Butterfly credible.

Puccini's music, like Elgar's, is full of mannerisms; so much so that one rarely comes across a passage (other than a piece of deliberate pastiche) which is not immediately identifiable. This does not mean that he stood still. On the contrary: although his methods never changed, no composer was more broadminded in experimenting with – and sometimes permanently adopting – new idioms. In *Madam Butterfly* he flirted with both genuine and spurious orientalisms and *The Girl of the Golden West* (New York, 1910) evidenced a further widening of harmonic and rhythmic outlook: the musical treatment of the exciting moments was often reminiscent of *Tosca* but the handling showed greater technical assurance. Unfortunately, melodic inspiration was at a comparatively low ebb, which probably explains why *The Girl* (as the composer himself used to call it, rather than

229

La fanciulla del West) has failed to rival its immediate predecessors in popularity.

The operetta *La rondine* (Monte Carlo, 1917) was an indiscretion, but by-passing this patchwork of sentiment and banality (redeemed only by one superbly uncharacteristic waltz) we come to *Il trittico* (New York, 1918). The 'triptych' consists of three one-act pieces – *Il tabarro*, *Suor Angelica* and *Gianni Schicchi*. (Nowadays they are rarely played straight off the reel; theatrical evenings aren't long enough.) Puccini's constructional flair was admirably suited to the one-act form and it would be hard to fault any of these three works from the dramatic standpoint; musically they were less consistent. It could have been foreseen that he would deal competently with a sordid tale of animal passion and brute violence which might have been subtitled 'Three on a barge', and technically speaking *Il tabarro* was a fine achievement, a fitting pendant to *Tosca* and *The Girl*. It could also have been foreseen that he would be less at home in a convent than on a barge – and indeed *Suor Angelica* was a somewhat maudlin affair: Puccini's music could be affecting or even moving – but never ennobling. What could not have been foreseen was that he would excel himself in farce, yet *Gianni Schicchi* remains one of the greatest comic masterpieces in musical history. Here the gradually developing freedom of harmonic expression which had served him well in *The Girl* and *Il tabarro* was exploited to even better purpose; at the same time there was a revival of the lyric strain that had lain relatively dormant since *Tosca*. Despite the light-hearted use of *Leitmotive*, a possible quibble is that fetching little tunes sometimes flit across the scene (as in Verdi's *Falstaff*, see page 138) and then vanish for ever.

And so we reach the Puccini apotheosis – *Turandot*. He did not live to complete the last act of this, his last opera, and its first performance (Milan, 1926) ended abruptly when the chorus left the stage after the death of Liù; the conductor, Arturo Toscanini, then turned to the hushed audience and said: 'At this point the Master laid down his pen.'

(The final duet between Turandot and Calaf, as we now know it, was pieced together from Puccini's sketches by his pupil Franco Alfano.) *Turandot* was the culmination of its composer's search for new worlds to conquer and not even the dissonances of *Il tabarro* and *Gianni Schicchi* – most appropriate in their context – had quite prepared one for a stark insistence on bitonality for its own sake, e.g. the frequently reiterated clashes between the common chords of D minor and C sharp major (or their equivalents). There were in *Turandot* passages of surpassing beauty (notably the miraculous chorus 'Perchè tarda la luna' from Act I), but taken as a whole was not the triumph one of brain over heart? All Puccini lovers must decide for themselves whether they prefer the antics of Ping, Pang and Pong to the antics of Marcel, Schaunard and Colline; whether the musical realization of Calaf implanting a kiss on the thin frozen lips of Turandot as they stand on the steps of an exotic oriental palace gives them more pleasure than the musical realization of Rudolph touching Mimi's tiny frozen hand as they pretend to search for a lost key on the floor of a moonlit Parisian attic; to get down to it, whether they really love *Turandot* better than *La Bohème*.

Whether Giacomo Puccini can be regarded as a great as well as a famous composer depends largely upon personal taste and therefore *non est disputandum*; what lies beyond all doubt is that he was an extremely significant figure in the history of opera.

CHAPTER FORTY-TWO

Mahler

GUSTAV MAHLER, born 7th July 1869, was the son of a Moravian Jew who owned a small distillery at Jihlava (Iglau), a medium-sized industrial town, seventy miles south-east of Prague; Jihlava was one of those isolated outposts of German culture dotted over the predominantly Slavonic, Magyar and Roman lands of central and south-eastern Europe (hence the Teutonic conception of *Mitteleuropa*). The composer's actual birthplace was the Bohemian village of Kalište, a few miles away to the west, but it was in Jihlava itself, just in Moravia, that he spent a rather unhappy childhood (unhappy because his father and mother were an ill-suited and quarrelsome pair), had his first music lessons and went to school. From 1875 until 1880 he was in Vienna, studying first at the Conservatoire and then at the University; thereafter his name became associated with opera, for during the next seventeen years he was either chorus master or conductor at the municipal or state theatres of Laibach (Ljubljana), Olmütz (Olomouc), Cassel, Prague, Leipzig, Budapest and Hamburg in turn; in 1897 he was appointed artistic director of the Vienna Court Opera. He held this post until 1907 and although he spent the next three winters in the United States, as conductor of the New York Philharmonic Orchestra, he always returned between-whiles to Vienna; it was there that he succumbed to chronic heart-disease on 18th May 1911. Of his private life it need only be recorded that at the age of about thirty-five (while at Hamburg) he fell in love with a singer named Johanne Richter but nothing came of the affair; that a year or two later he abandoned the faith of his fathers and became, nominally at any rate, a Roman Catholic; that in 1902 he married Alma Maria Schindler, a talented amateur musician who thenceforth until his death was his prop and stay. They had two daughters: the elder died tragically at the age of five; the younger is now the wife of the Russian-born conductor Anatole Fistoulari. After Mahler's death his widow married the author and poet Franz Werfel; she long survived her two husbands and until her death in 1964 remained an unfailing champion of them both.

Taking his other commitments into account, Mahler's output as a composer, though not prodigious, was considerable. He only found time for creative work during the summer months – opera's close season – when he was wont to retire to a hide-out in the Austrian Alps; yet although he destroyed most of his youthful compositions (which he regarded as immature) he left a cantata (*Das klagende Lied*), about forty songs, ten colossal symphonies (including the named but unnumbered *Lied von der Erde*) and copious sketches for an eleventh (no. 10) – recently prepared for performance by the English musicologist Deryck Cooke in a version which displays remarkable insight into the workings of the composer's mind.

Mahler was completely uninhibited: as a man he was outspoken to the point of ill manners; as a conductor he was ruthless and uncompromising; as a composer he went his own sweet way regardless of opposition. Consequently personal acquaintances, opera lovers and concertgoers were either delighted or enraged according to their temperament. Our main concern lies with the composer: why did his music arouse delight in some breasts and anger in others? It was (*a*) because he often flouted convention, e.g. by concluding songs and symphonies in the 'wrong' key; (*b*) because he came under the influence of both Berlioz and Bruckner, who were themselves controversial figures; (*c*) because his thematic material – the basic inspiration – was nearly always simple in the extreme, the simplicity springing at times from impeccable classical models but at others from unfashionable folk song; (*d*) because he adopted an individual approach to the problems of symphonic development, making it episodic rather than continuous; (*e*) because his orchestration, like Rimsky-Korsakov's, was so startlingly brilliant that it sometimes seemed to be the 'essence' of the composition. Either *a, b, c, d* or *e,* taken separately, would have been sufficient to cause a narrow cleft in the ranks of responsible musicians and music critics; taken collectively they caused a nuclear fissure. On the wider issue as to whether Mahler's symphonies proved him a genius who in quick time could raise a huge oak tree from a couple of acorns, or a poseur who regularly used an ostentatious sledge-hammer to crack a modest walnut, I must leave to his listeners and posterity to decide for themselves, contenting myself meanwhile with a less figurative review of his achievements.

Virtually all Mahler's songs were composed during his twenties and thirties (although some were not published until later), and it is in them that his art can be seen in its purest form. He had a fondness for recreating the moods of childhood and drew largely on *Des Knaben Wunderhorn,* an anthology of juvenile folk poetry collected by Joachim von Arno and Clemens Brentano. For the four *Lieder eines fahrenden Gesellen,* however, he supplied his own words, while the five *Kindertotenlieder* were settings of verses by the early nineteenth-century German poet Friedrich Rückert – who had also from time to time inspired Schubert, Schumann and Brahms. In his songs Mahler was consistently successful in capturing atmosphere by directly musical rather than impressionistic methods: impish humour in *Verlorene Muh'* and *Ablösung im Sommer* for instance; simple piety in *Himmlisches Leben* and *Es sangen drei Engel;* deeper religious feeling in *Um Mitternacht* and *Ich bin der Welt abhanden gekommen;* elegiac pathos in *Das irdische Leben* and *Revelge.* Among them all perhaps *Die zwei blauen Augen von meinem Schatz* and *Ich atmet' einen linden Duft* were unrivalled in their happy blending of poetry with melody.

Mahler also appeared as an apostle of nature in his first four symphonies (all composed between 1886 and 1900 and therefore belonging to the song period), but acorn evolution (or sledge-hammer treatment) was very much in evidence –

even in no. 1 (D major) which the composer later described as a youthful try-out. In no. 2 (C minor, known as the 'Resurrection') and no. 3 (D minor) he really let himself go: each required several solo singers and a chorus to help out an orchestra of stupendous proportions; no. 4 (G major) was a comparatively modest affair needing only a single vocalist, triple woodwind, four horns, trumpet, harp, strings, and a battery of percussion. Of the four, no. 3 was in every sense the greatest: not only does it hold the world's symphonic endurance record (two hours); it is also the apotheosis of nineteenth-century Mahler. (We shall come to twentieth-century Mahler presently.) The first movement – itself longer than the entire symphony in the same key by César Franck – is admittedly an aesthetic puzzle, but once one is acclimatized to the scale of the whole conception the remaining five movements, which are played without a break, are consistently satisfying and in places very moving: here the composer is almost (though not completely) successful in conveying to the audience his musical interpretation of the ever-changing miracles of nature – the flowers, the forest, the twilight, human joy, human grief. In these four symphonies there are other (separate) movements that are truly beautiful, notably the second movement of no. 2 and the third of no. 4; but in much of no. 1, in the third and fourth movements of no. 2 and in the finale of no. 4 Mahler fell between two stools: the simple measures of *Des Knaben Wunderhorn* were not at home in the trappings of affluence – nor, for that matter, was the even simpler measure of *Frère Jacques*.

About the time of his first meeting with Alma Schindler (I am not suggesting that this had anything to do with it) Mahler turned from nature to metaphysics, from personal introspection to cosmic speculation, and in his next three symphonies (all restricted to orchestra alone and where the stylistic influence of Bruckner was often in evidence) was feeling his way tentatively in a somewhat unfamiliar world. No. 5 (1902, C sharp minor, and incorporating a haunting *adagietto*), alternated between fiery exuberance and tender passion; no. 6 (1904, A minor) rivalled Tchaikovsky's no. 6 in its undiluted pessimism; the three middle movements of no. 7 (1906, E minor) discovered youthful romanticism anew, but the first and last were inconsequently demoniac. Mahler himself was never really satisfied with these transitional works; he revised them continually and his final intentions with regard to no. 5 are uncertain to this day. With no. 8 (1907, E flat major) he came back into his own. This was 'the symphony of the thousand': for its first performance the sponsors engaged eight soloists, eight hundred and fifty choristers and an orchestra of one hundred and forty-six, so that when the composer/conductor was included the total number of musicians taking part was precisely one thousand and five. This no. 8 certainly showed the composer in more assured and more optimistic mood than nos. 6 and 7, but it was soon overtaken by *Das Lied von der Erde* (1908, a capacious setting of six poems by the Chinese poets Li-Tai-Po, Tchang-Tsi, Ming-Kao-Yen and Wang-Wei, translated by Hans Bethge) and was left behind by no. 9 (1910, orchestral only, nominally in D major), which stood in the same relation to no. 3 as did Berlioz' opera *The Trojans* to his *Symphony fantastique* and Brahms' fourth symphony to his first piano concerto: all three marked a mature culmination of youthful (or comparatively youthful) ardour. In Mahler's case the doubts of the interim were resolved and realization of physical phenomena became imperceptibly merged (so far as a detached listener could judge) with a more recently acquired recognition of spiritual values. Several of Gustav Mahler's massive symphonies were indeed masterworks of their kind, yet although prophecy is a dangerous game I shall for once take it upon myself to play the part of a long-term Old Moore by venturing to foretell, in defiance of many distinguished colleagues, that in years to come this enigmatic composer is less likely to be revered as a symphonist than as a song-writer.

CHAPTER FORTY-THREE

Debussy

No doubt many of my readers will have admired the fine view from the *jardin anglais* at St-Germain-en-Laye, which covers a wide reach of the Seine valley with the Eiffel Tower and Montmartre visible on the distant horizon; they may not have realized that they were within a few minutes' walk of the *maison natale* of CLAUDE DEBUSSY, who was born 22nd August 1862 over a china shop kept by his parents at 38 rue au Pain. Somewhere about 1865 the family moved to Paris. Manuel Debussy and his wife Victorine were evidently a rather disreputable couple, and although they treated their five children kindly it was a well-disposed aunt who taught Claude to read and write and arranged for him to have his first piano lessons. He showed such promise that at ten he was admitted to the Conservatoire, where he made slow but reasonably steady progress and presently began to compose. A stroke of good fortune came in 1880 when he attracted the attention of none other than Tchaikovsky's wealthy patroness Nadezhda von Meck – whom we met in chapter 33; she engaged Debussy to give piano lessons to her younger children and took a personal interest in him that may not have been entirely motherly. That autumn his duties were carried out in such pleasant spots as Interlaken, Arcachon (a seaside resort near Bordeaux), Venice and Florence; in each of the two succeeding summers he joined the von Meck entourage in Moscow itself. Here he became acquainted with the music not only of Tchaikovsky but also of Borodin and possibly of Mussorgsky; moreover, on his way home in 1882 he called at Vienna in order to hear *Tristan and Isolde*. Seeds were being sown. Back in Paris he was befriended by Maurice Vasnier, civil servant by profession but in private life a *littérateur* and lover of the arts, who was sufficiently well-off to maintain both a flat in town and a villa near Versailles. He also had a very pretty wife, Marguerite, and some of Debussy's most enjoyable visits to the Vasnier household took place during Maurice's office hours. This happy association came to an end when, having won the Prix de Rome (see page 100, footnote), he set out for Italy in January 1885.

The work which had gained him the prize was a cantata, *L'Enfant prodigue*, lyrical throughout and almost every bar reminiscent of Massenet, but in Rome itself Debussy never settled down and produced nothing of importance. Soon after his return to Paris in 1887, however, he got into his stride with another cantata (*The Blessed Damozel*), a dozen or so piano pieces and twenty songs – all composed during the next four or five years. *The Blessed Damozel* was a rather restrained setting of the poem by Dante Gabriel Rossetti, none the worse because there was no attempt to capture the preciousness of the original. Of the early piano pieces the popular *Clair de lune* is the best known, but the *Petite suite* for piano duet (sometimes heard in an orchestral version) deserves to be. Here Debussy expressed in practical terms his indebtedness to Lalo, Bizet, Chabrier and early Fauré. More significant were some settings of verses by Charles Baudelaire and Paul Verlaine, two writers with whom he had more temperamental affinity than with Rossetti (although he admired pre-Raphaelite painting); in these songs one can trace the influence of both Wagner and Borodin, but what really matters is that Debussy was by now showing himself to be an impressionist of the first order, whether evoking Baudelaire's voluptuously alternating moods of ecstasy and despair – as in *Le Balcon* – or the unashamed sensuality of Verlaine's *Green*.

His first characteristic masterwork, however, did not come until 1892: this was *Prélude à l'après-midi d'un faune* (inspired by a poem of Stéphane Mallarmé) which might be described in the same words that Rimsky-Korsakov applied to his own *Spanish Capriccio* (see page 204): a brilliant composition for orchestra. Yet the two works were utterly dissimilar: Rimsky-Korsakov deliberately gave each instrumentalist an opportunity to display his executive prowess in contribution to overall brilliance, whereas Debussy exploited the virtuosity of the whole orchestra, individually and collectively, to purvey subtle sound effects; furthermore the *Spanish Capriccio* was based on definable thematic material while *L'après-midi* was based on practically *no* definable thematic material. The excellent string quartet in G minor of 1893 was also largely dependent (like all good string quartets) on the composer's perfect understanding of his medium, but for all its originality in detail the conception, taken as a whole, appears formal when set beside *L'après-midi* and the three so-called *Nocturnes* which followed it. These were originally planned for solo violin and orchestra but in the event were recast for orchestra alone – plus a women's chorus in the last of the three. Debussy may here be allowed, like Rimsky-Korsakov on page 204, to describe his own achievement.

The title is not meant to designate the usual form of nocturne, but rather all the various impressions and the special effects of light that the word suggests. *Nuages* renders the immutable aspect of the sky and the slow, solemn motion of the clouds, fading away in grey tones lightly tinged with white. *Fêtes* gives us the vibrating atmosphere with sudden flashes of light. There is also the episode of the procession (a dazzling fantastic vision) which passes through the festive scene and becomes merged in it. But the background remains persistently the same: the festival, with its blending of music and luminous dust, participating in the cosmic rhythm. *Sirènes* depicts the sea and its countless rhythms and presently, amongst the waves silvered by the moonlight, is heard the mysterious song of the Sirens as they laugh and pass on.

(It is interesting to compare this with Berlioz' analysis of his own *Symphonie fantastique* – see page 102; both composers took themselves seriously, but it will be noticed that

Debussy's approach to the problems of programme music was very different from that of Berlioz.)

Although *L'après-midi d'un faune*, the quartet and *Nocturnes* – together with a further handful of songs and piano pieces – were the only compositions which Debussy completed during the 1890s, for most of the decade he was simultaneously engaged on a more ambitious work – the opera *Pelléas et Mélisande*. The drama of the great Belgian poet and essayist Maurice Maeterlinck was first published in 1892; Debussy picked up a copy at a bookstall and promptly conceived the idea of setting it to music. After seeing the play performed on a Paris stage in May 1893 he made a few preliminary sketches; the following autumn he journeyed to Ghent to discuss his proposition with the author (who incidentally was exactly the same age – thirty-one). No one could have been more cooperative than Maeterlinck; he knew nothing of music, but instinct told him that *Pelléas* cried out for musical treatment (which it did) and that Debussy was the right man to provide it (which he was). Having been given virtual *carte blanche* to make any cuts he wished to fit the work for operatic production, the composer returned home in high good humour. It was eight years before the opera was finished, but it was then almost immediately accepted by the Opéra Comique, thanks largely to the interest and good offices of the theatre's principal conductor, André Messager. At this juncture, however, a storm-cloud passed across the sky. Maeterlinck, who now lived in the Paris outskirts and was married to a French soprano named Gabrielle Leblanc, had apparently assumed that his wife would play Mélisande. When he learnt that the role had been allotted to the young Scottish singer Mary Garden (who had recently made a big hit in Gustave Charpentier's opera *Louise*) his fury knew no bounds and drove him to dissociate himself from the whole venture. As it might have been embarrassing for him to disclose the true cause of vexation, he adopted a different line of attack: at this late stage in the proceedings he shrugged aside his earlier assurances to Debussy by publicly declaring that the opera was a travesty of his play and that he could only pray 'for its immediate and decided failure'. So far as the première (30th April 1902) was concerned his prayer was answered, but with each succeeding performance there was a growth in public interest and it was not long before *Pelléas et Mélisande* became – by Opéra Comique standards – a money-spinner.

This unusual opera is not everyone's cup of tea, and many music lovers find themselves unable to appreciate its shadowy and elusive quality: there are no 'good tunes' and although the whole is held together by a discreet use of *Leitmotive* the influence of Wagner is stylistically almost indiscernible (except perhaps in the sharply abrupt endings of Acts III and IV). Debussy's purpose – admirably suited to the libretto and splendidly translated into practice – was to intensify in song (not necessarily in melody) the underlying rhythm and meaning and emotion of the words and to provide an orchestral accompaniment which, while remaining judiciously subservient, would be more than mere background and would help to point the unfolding of the drama. The term 'operatic realism' is often applied to high-pressure works like Mascagni's *Cavalleria rusticana*, but *Pelléas et Mélisande* is in truth far more 'realistic' – by reason of its reticence.

It was during the 1890s that Debussy first began to exploit the potentialities of the whole-tone scales: *viz.* C, D, E, F♯, G♯, A♯, C; and D♭, E♭, F, G, A, B, D♭. These were a logical if somewhat artificial evolution of 'equal temperament' (see page 37). It would be virtually impossible to construct any but the most monotonous piece of music *entirely* on a whole-tone scale because of the limited opportunities for modulation, but it can be used with great effect to add characteristic touches of melodic or harmonic colour-contrast. The opening of *Pelléas et Mélisande* exemplifies Debussy's methods: bars 1 to 4 are strictly diatonic, bars 5 to 7 strictly whole-tone, bars 8 to 11 diatonic again; from bar 12 onwards the whole-tone melodic pattern of bars 5 to 7 is retained, but it is both softened and enriched by harmonic treatment that might be called compromise-chromatic.

Meanwhile Debussy's domestic affairs were becoming more tangled than those of any operatic character. From 1888 until 1898 he had lived – on and off – with a green-eyed blonde named Gabrielle Dupont, but in 1899 he married Rosalie Texier, an unaffected and rather simple country girl who came from Montereau-fault-Yonne and was working in Paris as a dressmaker's assistant. Soon afterwards he entered into a simultaneous *liaison* with Emma Bardac, the wife of a wealthy banker, a woman-of-the-world, an enthusiastic musician and an excellent cook. When the desirable attributes of his latest *inamorata* led him to leave poor ineffective little Rosalie for ever, she tried to commit suicide and wounded herself so seriously that she had to be taken to hospital. The next complication was that Emma Bardac became pregnant – and it was common knowledge who was responsible. By this time Debussy's personal friends and acquaintances, even the most broadminded among them, were beginning to raise eyebrows and display cold shoulders; to get away from it all he crossed the Channel and spent the summer of 1905 at Eastbourne, where no doubt he was regarded as an eccentric but amiable foreigner. He returned to Paris just in time to attend (*a*) the birth of an illegitimate daughter and (*b*) the first performance of a recently completed orchestral work which shared the frigid reception accorded by press and public alike to the composer himself. Indeed it was only after Debussy's death that *La Mer* came to be recognized as the masterpiece that it is. In construction (three separate movements subtitled 'De l'aube à midi sur la mer', 'Jeux de vagues' and 'Dialogue du vent et de la mer') it reverts to something like the form of a classical symphony: the instrumental effects, as skilfully planned as ever, are even more varied than in *Nocturnes* but the whole is based on identifiable themes – many of them of striking vitality – which are subjected to the process of exposition, development and recapitulation almost in accordance with the tenets of sonata form. To paraphrase Rimsky-

Korsakov once again, *La Mer* is something more than a brilliant composition for orchestra; it is a magnificently orchestrated composition. (About the same time Debussy wrote two of his most characteristically impressionistic piano pieces – *Jardins sous la pluie* and *Reflets dans l'eau*.)

Soon after the arrival of his little daughter two divorce decrees were made absolute and Claude was able to marry his Emma. During the next seven or eight years he paid several more visits to Britain and one each at least to Italy, Austria, Hungary and Russia, and seems to have lost the taste for tackling large-scale compositions with the old integrity and determination. Admittedly the pseudo-Spanish *Iberia* (one of three 'Images' for orchestra) was a clever piece of work of its kind; so was the almost surrealistic ballet *Jeux* (the 'jeux' concerned being 'l'amour' and 'le tennis'); so too was the incidental music for Gabriele d'Annunzio's play *Le Martyre de Saint Sébastien*, in which the composer was surprisingly successful in reconciling his own pantheistic outlook with a background of Christian suffering and sacrifice. But the most representative works of this period were the late piano pieces ranging from *Golliwog's Cakewalk* to *La Cathédrale engloutie*, from *La Fille aux cheveux de lin* to a set of *étude*s dedicated to the memory of Chopin. The best of the last few songs (*Trois ballades de François Villon*) were touched with irony; the last of all (*Nöel des enfants qui n'ont plus de maison*) was written and composed during the autumn of 1915 in a mood of bitterness engendered by French sufferings under enemy invasion: here the innocent victims of war implore Father Christmas in carol-like phrases not to take presents to *German* children.

But now Debussy was attacked by cancer; he worked intermittently on a projected opera based on Edgar Allan Poe's *Fall of the House of Usher* – but it was never completed. From the end of 1917 onwards he was confined to his house (near the Porte Dauphine), presently to his room, eventually to his bed. He died on 25th March 1918 (while Paris was undergoing long-range artillery bombardment by the Germans). Pathetically enough, his daughter Emma-

Claude (nicknamed Chou-chou) followed him a year later – at the age of fourteen. They had always been devoted to one another and at the risk of being accounted a sentimentalist I make so bold as to suggest that Debussy the man, always a hedonist, was more to be admired as an affectionate father than as a semi-reluctant husband.

What of Debussy the composer? One will start by saying that his style, in the first instance, was influenced by Bizet and Fauré and several other compatriots (notably Massenet and Chabrier), all of whom played an honourable part in striving to make France a first-class power in the world of music; one will go on to say that Debussy – when he struck out on a line of his own – clinched the issue, thereby earning the gratitude of all Frenchmen imbued with a sense of national pride (and what Frenchman isn't?). On an international level his achievements were no less significant: Elgar, Puccini and Mahler, for all that they provided plenty of contrast, each inherited a measure of the classical tradition; Claude Debussy, in his maturity, belonged to a different world, since he relied to a large extent upon his extraordinary flair for impressionism. The only close contemporary of perhaps comparable calibre to adopt a similarly individualistic approach to the problems of composition comes up for discussion in the next chapter.

CHAPTER FORTY-FOUR

Delius

FREDERICK DELIUS was born at Bradford on 29th January 1862 and educated at Bradford Grammar School. His father (half-Dutch and half-German by birth and British by naturalization) originally intended him to follow in parental footsteps and become a wool-merchant, but since Frederick was inclined to indulge in a different sort of wool-gathering he dispatched him, early in the year 1884, to Florida, in the hope that he would settle down when placed in charge of an orange grove there. But young Delius was already keenly interested in music and now, listening each evening, intently and enthralled, to the improvised part-songs of his Negro workers on the plantation, he felt an urge to make it his career. Presently he persuaded his elder brother to take over the management of the estate, and after two short spells endeavouring to teach the rudiments of music to small boys (first at Jacksonville, Florida, and then at Danville, Virginia) returned to Europe and for a time studied at the conservatoire in Leipzig – where he met Edvard Grieg;* the two men got on very well together and Delius later went to stay with his new friend in Norway. Next he made his way to Paris, where he was resident on and off for eight years, for the most part leading the sort of gay and promiscuous life commonly associated in those days with the artistic *coterie* of Montparnasse. In 1897 he married Jelka Rosen (a granddaughter of the pianist Ignaz Moscheles); they settled at Grez-sur-Loing, a small village not far from Fontainebleau, which was to remain their home for the rest of their lives. (Perhaps Delius had read R. L. Stevenson's *Essays of Travel*, in which there is a characteristic and inimitable description of the charms of Grez-sur-

---

* This was, of course, long after Grieg's student days there, but he revisited the town while touring Germany in 1886 (see page 199).

Loing in the year 1875.) The self-centred Delius, who completely rejected the idea of God and accepted *in toto* the philosophy of Friedrich Nietzsche, was far from being an ideal husband, but Jelka, confident that she had married a genius, regarded it as both a privilege and a duty to minister to his material welfare. So much – for the moment – about Delius the man; there have been others of similar character and holding similar beliefs. But there has never been another composer quite like him: it is remarkable enough that hardly a page of the music of his maturity could have been written by anybody else; it is astonishing that his highly individual style should have blossomed from such a variegated assortment of implanted seeds.

As has already been noted, he was fascinated by the Negro music which he heard in the 'deep south' of the United States of America. He would hardly have been human had he emerged from the Leipzig Conservatoire uninfluenced by the Wagner tradition. (The only opera of which at any time of his life he possessed a full score was *Tristan and Isolde*.) Grieg, too, came well into the picture: for no other composer (apart from himself) did Delius ever express more than qualified admiration, although while in Paris he was attracted by the romantic attributes of Chopin's music and almost overwhelmed by the impressionistic attributes of Debussy's. Yet throughout all these formative years of *absorbing* music he set comparatively little of his own on paper: life was too hectic. It was only after his marriage that he began to devote most of his time to composition: in the quietude of Grez-sur-Loing works poured forth in which there was an unconscious weaving together of the diverse and contrasted threads into a homogeneous tapestry. It could indeed be said that Delius' most characteristic music, like Wordsworth's most characteristic poetry, was born of 'emotion remembered in tranquillity'.

But compositions which – however uniform they may have sounded – sprang from such a curious amalgam of sources as Negro music, Wagner, Grieg, Chopin and Debussy, could hardly be expected to appeal to more than a comparatively small proportion of the music-loving public. Despite having some initial success in Germany (where nearly all his early works were originally published) Delius' music was in the long run found to be too French for German taste, too German for French taste and too 'exotic' for British taste – although some listeners descried therein an 'English pastoral quality'. Fortunately that broad-minded and unconventional cosmopolitan Sir Thomas Beecham quickly recognized Delius' unusual talent and was soon directing performances of his operas, choral works and orchestral pieces. But for Beecham's championship perhaps only a limited number of connoisseurs would ever have heard of the operas *Koanga* (with its attractive 'Colinda' sequences) and *A Village Romeo and Juliet* (with its evocative 'Walk to the Paradise Garden'), of the lovely choral work *Sea Drift* (the setting of a poem by Walt Whitman), or of the short orchestral tone-poems among which particularly honourable mention might be made of *Paris, Brigg Fair, On Hearing the First Cuckoo in Spring*, the two *Dance Rhapsodies*, and *Summer Night on the River*. Of the ambitious *Mass of Life* (1905) it can be said that in many ways it was a tremendous achievement, and I am not surprised that Philip Heseltine, who was one of the composer's comparatively few intimate friends and shared his Nietzschean outlook on life, should have rated it as 'the most essentially *religious* work of our time' (my italics). It might be added that except perhaps in *Sea Drift* Delius did not display any exceptional talent in his handling of voices, either solo or choral, his *forte* lying, rather, with the orchestra. Yet even in the purely orchestral pieces there are rarely any brilliantly instrumented climaxes, and sometimes one becomes oppressed by the prevailing sameness of mood. For that reason, possibly, there are those who find themselves unable to appreciate Delius' music and many others who understandably prefer to take it in sips rather than gulps: with all respect to Beecham's memory, a whole evening of typical Delius (and there is hardly such a thing as untypical Delius) is apt to have a somewhat cloying effect upon the nerves of any but the most ardent devotee.

Delius died at Grez-sur-Loing on 13th November 1934, his widow surviving him by little more than a year. Since the early 1920s syphilis had rendered him half-paralysed and totally blind; that any music coming into his head thereafter was ever transcribed was entirely due to the conscientious and selfless devotion of Eric Fenby, who modestly described himself as an amanuensis but was in truth more of a collaborator; without him, the world would never have known (for instance) *A Song of Sunset* or the choral work entitled *Songs of Farewell*. His task was no easy one and was made the more frustrating for him because he was totally out of sympathy with Delius' Nietzschean philosophy of life; mercifully both men hailed from Yorkshire and (like all Yorkshiremen) always enjoyed a chat about cricket – almost the only topic they could argue over without tempers becoming strained. In his sensitively written and in places deeply moving account of his life at Grez-sur-Loing, Fenby recorded how at their very first meeting Delius brought up the subject of Scarborough Festivals and even boasted of his own youthful prowess on the field; during the summer of 1930, when the Australians were touring England, the blind composer insisted that Fenby should read aloud to him the scores, and a full account of each day's play in the Test Matches.

A mention of music and cricket in the same breath almost inevitably brings to mind the name of Sir Neville Cardus, who when discussing cricket has often had recourse to a musical analogy.* Curiously enough, I cannot recall having come across a cricketing analogy in his writings about music; Fenby was more venturesome, and I hope he will forgive another lover of the great game if this brief review of the life and achievements of Frederick Delius concludes with the quotation of a passage from his *Delius as I knew him*.

---

* e.g. 'Sobers' immense power is concealed by a rhythm which has in it as little obvious propulsion as a movement by Mozart – who could be dramatically as strong as Wagner.' (*Wisden*, 1967)

No music is more difficult to interpret convincingly, or requires more rehearsal, than that of Delius, and no music sounds duller when it is badly played. Consummate artistry and skill are needed to give it life. Delius is like that delightful member of the team who goes in to bat fairly well down in the list and requires a great deal of fuss and attention. One must fasten his pads for him, help him into his batting-gloves, adjust his cap, and sometimes even run for him, but somehow it is worth it; he always manages to score. Some of his shots may be flukes, and, where a crack batsman would play a defensive stroke to a ball pitched well up on his middle stump, Delius, serene and unruffled, with a mixture of bat, pad, and glove, will steer the same pitched ball dangerously through the slips for a boundary, then fall to a silly catch from a ball that he should have hit out of the field. And the amazing thing about it all is that it never occurs to him that his escapades have given the others some anxiety, or that he takes more looking after than all the rest of the team put together.

CHAPTER FORTY-FIVE

Strauss

Munich has always been noted for the baroque splendour of its public buildings (among them the opera house, now rebuilt after suffering bomb damage in 1944), for the excellence of its beer and for the ability of its citizens to reap a financially satisfactory harvest from their manifold activities. These three traditions were fused when the opera house's leading horn-player, Franz Strauss, married Josephine, daughter of Georg Pschorr, the city's wealthiest brewer. Their son RICHARD STRAUSS (1864–1949) may have given up serious beer-drinking at an early age, but he spent most of the rest of his life composing and conducting music and making money thereby (it has been estimated that he was a millionaire by the time he was fifty), so that, take him for all in all, he can be accounted a Münchener through and through.

He composed his first piano piece (a polka) at six, his first symphony at sixteen; then, after two years' study at Munich University, he went to Berlin, where he was befriended by the conductor Hans von Bülow – long since rid of his erstwhile helpmeet Cosima who by now (1883) was widow Wagner (see page 125). Presently young Strauss took over his patron's directorship of a small but expert orchestra at Meiningen (in the south-western corner of Thuringia), where he had the satisfaction of conducting several of his own works, including a second symphony – which showed the influence of both Brahms and Wagner. In the following year, 1886, Strauss the conductor and Strauss the composer each reached a turning-point in his career, for the former was appointed deputy at Munich opera house (how appropriate!) and the latter completed the comparatively mature *Symphonie aus Italien* – which contained some original ideas and owed less to Brahms or Wagner than had his two previous essays in that form. In 1889 the composer/conductor moved to Weimar, where in 1894 he produced his first opera, the one-act *Guntram* – and married its leading soprano, Pauline de Ahna. Not long afterwards Strauss again succeeded von Bülow, but this time in a more remunerative job – conductorship of the Berlin Philharmonic Orchestra. Meanwhile, he had completed the first four of the eight symphonic tone-poems, which he composed during youth and early middle-age. The eight were:

Don Juan (first played at Weimar in 1889)
Tod und Verklärung (Eisenach, 1890)
Macbeth (Weimar, 1890)*
Till Eulenspiegel (Cologne, 1895)
Also sprach Zarathustra (Frankfort, 1896)
Don Quixote (Cologne, 1898)
Ein Heldenleben (Frankfort, 1899)
Symphonia domestica (New York, 1904).

In these remarkable works (some in one movement only, others in more than one) Strauss was brilliant enough to combine a descriptive power that was all his own with the inspiration of a Berlioz, the initiative of a Liszt and the technique of a Wagner; also apparent was the influence of Berlioz the mixed-up kid, Liszt the flashy showman and Wagner the second-hand philosopher. I shall confine myself to very brief comment on those which to my mind were pre-eminent among them.

If one remembers that *Don Juan* (based neither on the old legend directly, nor on Mozart's librettist Lorenzo da Ponte, nor on Byron, but on the more idealistic conception of the German poet Nikolaus Lenau) was composed at the age of twenty-four, one must acclaim it as a masterpiece. The superbly virile opening, the lovely oboe *cantabile* (which in performance is sometimes almost overwhelmed by the weight of the throbbing orchestral accompaniment – a rare instance, for Strauss, of instrumental miscalculation), the

* *Macbeth* was the first in order of composition.

rousing horn tune which heralds the peroration; these were all the stuff of which youthful genius is made. *Till Eulenspiegel*, a venture into the field of humour, was a *tour de force*; fastidious musicians should excuse the brass-band intrusions (cf. Elgar's *Cockaigne*) which after all were a programmatic necessity. There was also plenty of humour in *Don Quixote* ('fantastic variations on a theme of knightly character' in which a solo cello represented the Don and a solo viola Sancho Panza), notably in variation no. 7 'the adventure of the magic horse' and no. 9 'the adventure of the two monks'. *Ein Heldenleben* was admittedly a bit of a hotch-potch, but anyone who disparages it thereby disparages Strauss himself, since its inconsequence was utterly characteristic: the nostalgic recollections of voluptuous love-making *à la* Don Juan and the bitterly clever allusions to nattering critics did at least as much to illumine the composer's attitude to his own life and work as did the allegedly autobiographical *Symphonia domestica*.*

It was during this period that Strauss earned distinction as a song-writer, distinction comparable with that of his predecessor Johannes Brahms and of his contemporaries Gustav Mahler and Hugo Wolf. Like Brahms' and Wolf's and by contrast with Mahler's, Strauss' songs (about a hundred and fifty all told) were uneven in quality, but singers and the world at large would be poorer without *Ständchen* ('Mach' auf!'), *Heimliche Aufforderung*, *Frühlingsgedränge*, *Morgen* (is there not an echo here of Brahms' *Feldeinsamkeit*?), *Traum durch die Dämmerung* and a good few others. Many of the best belonged to the 1890s: after the turn of the century Strauss was fully occupied in other pastures. From 1898 until 1910 he was director of the Berlin Opera, and although his second essay in the genre, *Feuersnot* (Dresden, 1901), made little more impression than had *Guntram*, it was on opera that he thereafter concentrated his attention. *Salome* (Dresden, 1905, based on Oscar Wilde and

---

* Perhaps the composer himself would have included his later *Alpine Symphony* in the same category as the tone-poems, but this work (dated 1915) has found few admirers.

comprising one act lasting an hour and three-quarters) displayed great dramatic sensitivity; subject and treatment alike helped to earn it a *succès de scandale*, and much of the music, too, was appropriately luscious. About the same time Strauss became acquainted with the Austrian dramatist Hugo von Hofmannsthal, with whom he soon found himself completely *en rapport*: between them they fashioned:

Elektra (first played at Dresden in 1909)
Der Rosenkavalier (Dresden, 1911)
Ariadne auf Naxos (final version, Vienna, 1916)
Die Frau ohne Schatten (Vienna, 1919)
Die ägyptische Helena (Dresden, 1928)
Arabella (Dresden, 1933).

Of these six operas the first three, in their different ways, were masterpieces. *Elektra* was an electrifying assault on the nerves: some adjudged it depraved and gruesome, others vivid and realistic, for librettist and composer forced their own interpretation of Sophocles on listeners who were at first too startled either to accept or reject it. By complete contrast *Der Rosenkavalier* – 'not only very long but also very broad' (Ernest Newman) – was an operatic comedy standing in the category of Wagner's *Mastersingers* and Verdi's *Falstaff*; that in this work Strauss tried here and there, very successfully, to emulate his namesake Johann the younger – no relation – should in theory be beside the point but in practice cannot be disregarded, since its Viennese waltzes have certainly helped to further the opera's popularity.

In *Der Rosenkavalier* Strauss had paid tribute not only to the waltz king but also to Mozart, Schubert and Mendelssohn. He did so again, with even greater panache, in *Ariadne auf Naxos*; this is one of the most engaging of his large-scale compositions. Unfortunately, that cannot be said of any of three subsequent Hofmannsthal operas, nor of *Intermezzo* (1924), where the composer provided his own libretto and once again inclined towards autobiography. The melancholy truth must be faced that the plush world to which Strauss' art belonged collapsed in 1918 along with the German Empire: nothing was ever again the same. Before chronicling what some regard as his decline, let us take a quick look at one or two of the fingerprints embossed on the representative works of his heyday.

It would perhaps be unfair to call Strauss an eclectic, yet although he was a great composer he was not, in essence, a very original one: his mentality was imbued with late nineteenth-century and early twentieth-century sophistication but his aesthetic consciousness was partly that of a late eighteenth-century classic and partly that of an early nineteenth-century romantic. A flair for conceiving (or contriving) sensuously expressive tunes was his strongest card, and he was more successful than Wagner in superimposing pleasing vocal lines on a significant and often turbulent orchestral background. No less than Elgar and Puccini, he had easily recognizable mannerisms – for intance, that characteristic upward melodic sweep of a major sixth or an octave at an anacrusis, and the somewhat facile tendency to settle on a comfortable 'six-four' or 'dominant seventh' chord at a climax – but generally speaking his approach to chromaticism showed more initiative than Elgar's and was less crude than Puccini's: his polytonal effects derived less from setting two or more keys against one another (so typical of late Puccini) than from setting them in close sequence, e.g. the common chords of D sharp major, B minor and F minor at Elektra's first entrance. This gambit recalled Liszt's *Psalm XIII* (see page 118) but one hopes that Strauss may be remembered as something more than 'Liszt plus one' – which is what Vaughan Williams called him.

From 1909 onwards Strauss lived at Garmisch-Partenkirchen in the Bavarian Alps, where he owned a luxurious villa and could compose to his heart's content, but during the years of the Weimar Republic after the First World War he made several tours abroad and, apart from a few unconsidered trifles, wrote only *Intermezzo, Die ägyptische*

Helena, Arabella and a ballet entitled *Schlagobers* (*Whipped Cream*), which was produced at Vienna in 1924. After Hitler came to power Strauss faced a situation fraught with difficulty, even danger: his latest opera – *Die schweigsame Frau* – had a première at Dresden in 1935 but was almost immediately withdrawn because the librettist, Stefan Zweig, was a Jew; the composer himself was under suspicion, too, because his son Franz had married a Jewess. Furious at first, Strauss was presently obliged to compromise with authority: in return for undertaking that in future he would collaborate with Josef Gregor – beyond question an Aryan – he was allowed to remain in untroubled peace and quiet at Garmisch. The arrangement suited both sides: the Nazis could (and did) claim that the greatest living German composer supported the régime; Strauss could (and did) claim that so long as he stayed in Germany German culture was protected. In Britain and the United States, either of which would no doubt have been proud to grant him asylum as a refugee, his equivocal behaviour was widely criticized, an understandable attitude but one which failed to take into consideration a point of cardinal importance. Virtually all the thousands of men and women – including many distinguished writers, artists, musicians and scientists – who voluntarily left or escaped from Germany during those dark years had the shadow of the concentration camp looming over them because they were either Jewish or left-wing. Strauss was neither, and once the Government had agreed to overlook the indiscretion of his short-lived association with Zweig no shadow loomed over *him*; he thus had no strong incentive (as had the Jews and left-wingers) to uproot himself. Had he done so it would have been welcomed abroad as the magnificent gesture of a world-famous composer more than seventy years old, but anyone who feels inclined to blame Strauss for lack of moral courage should search deep in his own conscience before glibly asserting that at that age and in similar circumstances he would have acted differently.

Strauss spent the war years at Garmisch (where in 1944 he celebrated his golden wedding), but when in 1945 the United

States Army of Occupation in the American zone of Germany established divisional headquarters at that attractive tourist centre its most distinguished inhabitant was unable to convince the ruling guests that he was no Nazi sympathizer; finding the atmosphere uncongenial, he betook himself to Switzerland. (Although a very old man he was by no means either decrepit or penurious and came and went as he pleased between Zürich, the Engadine and Lac Léman.) In 1948, however, his political record was examined by an international court which ultimately exonerated him from the charge of active participation in the Nazi movement, and so at last he felt free to return to Garmisch; he died there the following year at the ripe age of eighty-five. (His widow survived him by only a few months.)

The three operas in which Strauss had collaborated with Gregor – *Friedenstag, Daphne, Die Liebe der Danae* – hardly showed him at his best and none of them is likely to enjoy frequent revival; nevertheless (like *Arabella* and *Die schweigsame Frau*) all three contained some pleasant music. More satisfying on the whole were (*a*) a symphony for sixteen wind-instruments subtitled 'a light-hearted piece of work' and composed as a tribute to his beloved Mozart; (*b*) his last opera of all, *Capriccio* (libretto by the conductor Clemens Krauss), which holds certain features in common with *Ariadne auf Naxos* although the music is more often reminiscent of *Der Rosenkavalier*; (*c*) a work for twenty-three solo stringed instruments entitled *Metamorphosen*; (*d*) an oboe concerto; (*e*) the noteworthy *Four Last Songs*. These works were all composed during or just after the Second World War and, as might have been expected from a musician of vast experience who was still in full possession of his faculties, they were well-constructed, fluent and highly polished – while belonging in spirit to a bygone age. Richard Strauss, the one-time *enfant terrible*, was, as things turned out, the last famous composer to fly the flag of nineteenth-century romanticism – and he flew it to the end.

CHAPTER FORTY-SIX

Sibelius

Johan Julius Christian Sibelius (1865–1957), known to posterity simply as JEAN SIBELIUS, was born at Hämeenlinna,
chief town in the province of Hämeenlääni in south-western
Finland and lying some sixty miles north of the Baltic port
of Helsinki, today the country's capital.* Sibelius was the
longest-lived of our fifty composers, but unlike the runners-
up, Saint-Saëns, Verdi, Strauss and Vaughan Williams, who
were all still at work during their eighties, he virtually abandoned composition at the age of sixty-five: his first piece of
music to be published was dated 1888, the last 1930, so that
his active career may be said to have covered little more
than forty years. They were forty very productive years,
however. Small-scale compositions included about thirty
pieces for violin and piano, nearly a hundred for piano alone,
and more than a hundred songs and part-songs. His only
completed opera, *The Maiden in the Tower*, received a
single performance and was never published, but the incidental music that he wrote for half a dozen stage-plays –
among them *King Christian II* (Adolf Paul), *Swanwhite*
(Strindberg) and *The Tempest* (Shakespeare) – survives in
the form of concert suites. It was in major orchestral works
that he showed his true strength; not merely in seven sym-

* It was only after the Bolshevik Revolution of 1917 that Finland
achieved political independence, having been since 1809 a semi-
autonomous grand-duchy owing allegiance to the Czar of all the
Russias, and prior to that part of the kingdom of Sweden. At the
time of Sibelius' birth some Finns spoke Swedish (basically a Germanic language) and others Finnish (belonging to the rare Finno-
Ugric etymological group and akin to Hungarian); his parents were
bilingual, but being of Swedish origin normally used that language
in the home and would therefore refer to Helsingfors rather than
Helsinki, to Tavastehus rather than Hämeenlinna. Throughout this
chapter, however, I have adopted the Finnish place-name styles and
spellings which have been officially recognized since 1918.

phonies (now in the standard repertory of every self-respecting symphony orchestra) but also in a dozen or so characteristic tone-poems ranging from *En Saga* (1892) to *Tapiola* (1926), the majority of which were inspired by the *Kalevala* or some other treasury of traditional Finnish folk lore.

When Sibelius was two years old his father (a doctor) died in a typhus epidemic, but his mother saw to it that he received a good education, and at the age of nineteen he entered Helsinki University with a view to becoming a lawyer. But as with Handel, Schumann, Tchaikovsky and Elgar before him, a love of music overrode a love of the law, and a year later he transferred himself from the University to the Conservatoire – recently founded by the enthusiastic all-round musician Martin Wegelius. He remained there for three years, eventually winning a travelling scholarship which enabled him to continue his studies first in Berlin (where he learnt little but heard plenty of music) and then in Vienna, where he learnt a lot from those excellent teachers Carl Goldmark and Robert Fuchs and composed a song-cycle, a piano quartet and his first orchestral work – a concert overture in E major. On returning to Finland in 1891 he married Aino Järnefelt, sister of the dramatist Arvid Järnefelt and the composer Armas Järnefelt; the marriage was a happy one and eventually produced five children – all girls.* For the next nine or ten years Sibelius held a teaching appointment at the Helsinki Conservatoire, but meanwhile found time to compose the tone-poem *En Saga* and some admirably tuneful incidental music for a students' entertainment held at Viipuri – on the 'Karelian Isthmus' separating the Gulf of Finland from Lake Lagoda – which later reached the outside world as the *Karelia* suite; also the

* Armas Järnefelt (1869–1958) and Selim Palmgren (1878–1951) remain the only Finnish composers apart from Sibelius to have acquired an international reputation, and curiously they shared – in turn – the same wife. She was Maikki Pakarinen, a well-known singer in her day, who was evidently as partial to eminent composers as was Camille Moke (see page 102, footnote); she allied herself first with Järnefelt and then, after a divorce, with Palmgren.

'Four Legends' for orchestra, among them *The Swan of Tuonela*, which comprise the *Lemminkäinen* suite.

Around the turn of the century the Russian Government introduced some repressive measures designed to curb growing political unrest in Finland; this resulted in a combative upsurge of nationalistic fervour, to which Sibelius contributed a patriotic tone-poem entitled *Finland Awakes*; as *Finlandia*, it became the earliest of his compositions to make a big impact in Britain, where for many years it was regarded, somewhat erroneously perhaps, as representative. (If *Finlandia* was Sibelius' *Pomp and Circumstance*, then the inescapable *Valse triste* – the only item to survive from the music he composed for a play written by his brother-in-law Arvid Järnefelt – was his *Salut d'amour*.) Next, having been granted a pension by the enlightened Finnish Senate and with additional financial assistance from his good friend the concert-promoter Axel Carpelan, Sibelius embarked upon a round of foreign travel, taking his family with him. He visited Berlin again and then Prague, where he met Dvořák and conceived a great admiration for him; the autumn and winter of 1901–2 he spent in Italy. Meanwhile he completed two symphonies (E minor and D major) and revised *En Saga*, originally composed ten years previously.

Before the outbreak of the First World War Sibelius paid three visits to Britain and one to the United States of America; in both countries he was warmly welcomed and lavishly entertained, although much to his regret as a *bon viveur* (having recently undergone an operation in which a cancerous growth in the throat had been successfully removed) he was obliged to abstain from alcoholic refreshment. His most important compositions of this period were the tone-poem *Pohjola's Daughter*, his single violin concerto (which, despite its popularity, hardly ranks as one of his finest achievements) and his third and fourth symphonies (C major and A minor); the fifth (E flat major) was completed during the war years, the sixth (D minor) in 1923, the seventh (C major) in 1924, and the tone-poem *Tapiola* in 1926. He came to Britain for the last time in 1921 and went to Italy for the last time in 1924; thereafter he rarely left his home at Järvenpää in the quiet countryside of southern Finland – which, however, may not have been so quiet when occupied by the invading troops of Soviet Russia during the Second World War. After the war Sibelius, who continued to enjoy good health, took a great interest in what was going on in the contemporary world of music, but virtually abandoned composition; although he allowed a British friend, the conductor Basil Cameron, to see some of the manuscript sketches for a projected eighth symphony, he later became dissatisfied with its progress and the work was never completed. He died of a cerebral haemorrhage at the age of ninety-one.

Although Sibelius rarely made use of an actual folk tune, much of his music, notably in the songs and in the tone-poems, was cast in folk idiom and by that token 'national'. His symphonies, however, may fairly be accounted in every respect 'international'; furthermore, they were on a scale which enabled him to adopt a somewhat new approach to symphonic composition: instead of presenting a theme in the classical manner and then developing its melodic, harmonic and rhythmic potentialities, he often allowed fragmentary constituents to coalesce bit by bit until eventually a definable theme emerged from the assorted embryos. This method of construction was to a certain extent in evidence in the first movements of nos. 1, 2 and 5, in the last movement of no. 3, in the first and last of no. 4, in the second and last of no. 6 (both of which works, by the way, were by Sibelius standards unusually introspective) and in the one-movement no. 7. Nevertheless, in the quicker movements he rarely lost sight altogether of the tenets of sonata form, although it would not always be at all easy to analyse their content satisfactorily on that basis. Many musicians regard nos. 3 and 5, each of which comprises three movements only, as his masterpieces. No. 3 was specially composed for the Royal Philharmonic Society, was dedicated to Granville Bantock, and had its world première at the Queen's Hall in London, the composer conducting. It has been suggested that the whirling violin passages in the first movement represent 'fog-banks drifting along the English coast', but personally I find this notion fanciful: similar 'fog-banks' build up in the typically 'Nordic' finale of no. 5 and elsewhere in Sibelius' music; indeed, this form of string figuration was one of the most characteristic features of his highly individual approach to the problems of orchestration. The dance-like middle movement of no. 3 – like the scherzo of Dvořák's no. 7 (see page 195) – depends upon an ambiguous hovering between 3/2 time and 6/4; so, to a lesser degree, does the fascinating tacked-on section at the end of the first movement of no. 5, which was originally intended to be a short separate movement. The unassuming but delightful *Andante mosso quasi allegretto* which follows is one of Sibelius' most original creations: it consists largely of a succession of simple but varied little tunes all based on the same rhythmic formula.

Perhaps what helped more than anything else to raise this extremely talented composer to a level of true greatness was his astonishing flair for conjuring up 'atmosphere' – the romantic atmosphere of a near-Arctic and sparsely populated land, its fundamental bareness tempered by innumerable pine-bordered lakes dotted with pine-studded islets. I have never been to Finland and I hesitate to go there – fearing disillusionment; I remain content to envisage it as pictured so vividly in the amazingly evocative music of Jean Sibelius.

CHAPTER FORTY-SEVEN

Vaughan Williams

Few well-known composers have been able to boast such a varied and distinctive ancestry as could RALPH VAUGHAN WILLIAMS. His maternal grandparents were Josiah Wedgwood, master potter and grandson of the founder of the famous Staffordshire firm, and Caroline Darwin, sister of Charles Darwin, author of *The Origin of Species*. His paternal grandfather, of Welsh descent, was Sir Edward Vaughan Williams, an eminent judge, and his father a Church of England clergyman, from 1868 onwards vicar of Down Ampney near Cirencester in Gloucestershire. It was there that Ralph, the youngest of three children, was born on 12th October 1872.

The Reverend Arthur Vaughan Williams died two years later, whereupon his widow took the children to her father Josiah Wedgwood's stately home, Leith Hill Place on the wooded southern slopes of Leith Hill, the highest 'mountain' (965 feet) in Surrey. After his death in 1880 she stayed on there with her unmarried sister Sophie, who gave Ralph piano lessons and fostered a love for music. Beginning to compose while a schoolboy at Charterhouse, he subsequently studied for two years at the Royal College of Music in London with Hubert Parry before going up to Trinity College, Cambridge, where so far as music was concerned he was in the care of Charles Wood. He left Cambridge with the Degrees of Bachelor of Music and Bachelor of Arts (second-class honours in history) and promptly returned to the Royal College for a further course of lessons, this time with Charles Villiers Stanford. One of his fellow-students was Gustav Holst (1874–1934); the two young men found much in common and were to remain lifelong friends, their association proving as mutually rewarding, both in private life and in their professional activities, as that of Haydn and

Mozart. In 1897 Vaughan Williams married Adelina Fisher, and shortly afterwards, since he did not feel that his formal musical education was as yet satisfactorily completed, carried her off to Germany and spent three months at the Berlin Academy of Music under Max Bruch (who was well known in Britain not only for his violin concerto in G minor but also for having been for several years permanent conductor of the Liverpool Philharmonic Orchestra). Even after this visit to Berlin, Vaughan Williams remained dissatisfied with his progress, and (after earnest consultation with Holst) destroyed much of the music he wrote almost as soon as it was put on paper : his only composition of this period known today is the charming little song *Linden Lea*.

Although he himself may have been only subconsciously aware of it at the time, one cannot help feeling that he was probably out of sympathy with the artistic ideals of his distinguished preceptors, all of whom had lived their lives in an inherited belief that Germany was the sole cradle of great music, and based their teaching, however broadminded it might be in other respects, on the assumption that the German masters were more worthy than any others of a student's serious attention. Now Vaughan Williams regarded Bach (not Beethoven, one notes) as the greatest musician of all time and was a discriminating admirer of both Wagner and Brahms; no doubt his technique benefited from a close study of their works, but he never had any inner urge to compose their sort of music, being indeed far more attracted by that of Byrd and Purcell. This concern with the sixteenth and seventeenth centuries soon led him to throw aside Germanic ties and interest himself in English folk song, a field hitherto explored only superficially by contemporary musicians. During the next few years he visited many country districts in his search for folk tunes, which he took down from the lips of farm labourers and their wives, finding the predominantly agricultural regions of East Anglia particularly productive. Many of these tunes were well worth rescuing from the mists of the past for their own sakes; others held no special appeal for any but an enthusiast for folk music *per se*. (A few may have been spurious. Unsophisticated countrymen can sometimes be unexpectedly and disconcertingly shrewd when asked to do a favour for a 'musical gent from the city'. A later collector of folk songs, E. J. Moeran, was aware of this danger: he once told me that he always found it prudent to ignore such superficially tempting taproom suggestions as 'When I was a little 'un my old gran'dad used to sing a good tune; I ain't heard it since, but I reckon that another tankard might revive my memory.') What matters is that the folk tradition, together with the Byrd/Purcell tradition, soon became part of Vaughan Williams' musical make-up, perhaps not to so great an extent as has sometimes been made out, but nevertheless to a sufficient extent for him to rank as a truly 'national' composer.

During the early years of the century he published about twenty original songs (in addition to some folk-song arrangements), among them the collections entitled *The House of Life* (verses by D. G. Rossetti and including *Silent Noon*) and *Songs of Travel* (R. L. Stevenson and including *The Vagabond* and *The Roadside Fire*). None the less a certain sense of frustration lingered on, and nothing could have been more indicative of his determination to improve his prospects than his decision, in 1908, to go to Paris and study with Maurice Ravel (for whom see chapter 49). This time Vaughan Williams was taking lessons from a composer of alien culture and a very different outlook, who furthermore was several years younger than himself – on the face of it an incongruous proceeding. (It was as though that other great 'national' composer, Antonín Dvořák, had gone to Paris at the same age to study with his junior contemporary Gabriel Fauré.) Nevertheless, Ravel seems to have instilled into Vaughan Williams renewed confidence in his latent talent, and during the next six years he completed a succession of works showing considerably more assurance than any which had preceded them. For instance: the incidental music for *The Wasps* (Aristophanes); the song-cycle *On Wenlock Edge* (A. E. Housman); for voices and orchestra

A Sea Symphony (Walt Whitman); for violin and orchestra *The Lark Ascending*; for orchestra alone *Fantasia on a Theme by Thomas Tallis* and *A London Symphony*; and the so-called ballad opera *Hugh the Drover*. Then came the war, and Vaughan Williams enlisted at the age of forty-two as a private in the Royal Army Medical Corps. At first he was stationed in this country, but in June 1916 was posted to France and six months later to Greece (Salonika); in January 1918, after a short spell at an officers' training camp in England, he was commissioned in the Royal Field Artillery and sent back to France. There was no E.N.S.A. in the First World War, but it is interesting to note that before being demobilized 2nd Lieut. Vaughan Williams was gazetted 'Director of Music, First Army, British Expeditionary Force'.

Not long after the war Vaughan Williams was appointed a professor of composition at the Royal College of Music and conductor of the London Bach Choir, but he relinquished these posts when in 1927 he moved from London (Cheyne Walk, Chelsea) to a bungalow near Dorking, only a few miles from his boyhood home on Leith Hill. (His wife suffered from severe arthritis and was unable to climb stairs.) Meanwhile – that is to say during the 1920s – he composed at least nine works of importance: *A Pastoral Symphony* for voice and orchestra; a Mass in G minor and a sacred cantata entitled *Sancta Civitas*; a violin concerto; *Flos Campi* for viola, chorus and orchestra; *Job, a Masque for Dancing*; and three more operas – *Sir John in Love* (after Shakespeare), *Riders to the Sea* (J. M. Synge) and *The Poisoned Kiss* (which, however, was more by way of being an operetta and was not performed until six years later).* Presently he became engrossed in a fourth (unnamed) symphony (in F minor), which was more forcefully dramatic than any of his previous orchestral works; the marked

* Several items in *The Poisoned Kiss* owed something to Sullivan, of whom Vaughan Williams once wrote that 'he was potentially the right man born at the wrong time; had he not been thwarted by mid-Victorian inhibitions he might have written a *Figaro*'.

change of style may have reflected the composer's abhorrence of the 'might is right' policies then being pursued by Mussolini and Hitler. This symphony, a piano concerto and the choral work *Dona nobis pacem* were his only large-scale compositions of the 1930s. The next decade was more productive: a fifth symphony (in E minor) and a sixth (in D major); an oboe concerto; music for half a dozen films – among them *Forty-ninth Parallel*, *Coastal Command* and *Scott of the Antarctic*; and another opera, *The Pilgrim's Progress* (after John Bunyan), which was partly based on an earlier work, *The Shepherds of the Delectable Mountains*.

Vaughan Williams' wife Adelina died in 1951; in 1953, at the age of eighty, he married Ursula Wood, an old friend, and left Dorking to settle once again in London (Hamilton Terrace, St John's Wood). About the same time he completed the *Sinfonia antartica* (which incorporated music lifted from the film *Scott of the Antarctic*); health and vigour unimpaired, he went on to compose, besides many smaller pieces, a tuba concerto (to the best of my knowledge the only specimen in existence), two more symphonies (in D minor and E minor) and the oratorio *Hodie*. By 1958 Sir Adrian Boult and the London Philharmonic Orchestra had almost completed their gramophone recordings of his symphonies, and he arranged to attend the first recording session of the ninth and last, which was to be held on 26th August. Conductor and orchestra waited in vain for him to put in an appearance; he had died suddenly that very morning.

To many music lovers Vaughan Williams remains something of an enigma: they never quite know what to expect from him. They may be able to trace the Beethoven of the early sonatas in the Beethoven of the late quartets, the Verdi of *Nabucco* in *Otello*, the Elgar of the *String Serenade* – or even of *Salut d'amour* – in the cello concerto; but what on earth is there in common between (say) *Songs of Travel* and the *Sinfonia antartica*? Well, stylistically speaking, perhaps nothing at all, or at best some factor that is so obscure as to be hardly worth searching for. Vaughan Williams' music was dictated by the heart rather than the head, and what *Songs of Travel*, the *Wasps* overture, *Sancta Civitas*, the symphonies early and late, *The Pilgrim's Progress* and the rest had in common was the composer's heart-felt determination to demonstrate that British music, whether simple or complex, whether in traditional or contemporary idiom, could spring from roots buried deep in native soil. However, this was by no means a straightforward case of *plus ça change plus c'est la même chose*: if a man says that he loves Mozart – or Wagner, or Puccini – one has a fair idea of what sort of music he enjoys; if anybody were to say that he loved Vaughan Williams one would be left in the dark as to his preferences, because the flowering from those deep-buried roots was of almost infinite variety. For that reason, rather than attempt to squeeze a comprehensive review of his output into a few pages, I shall restrict myself to exemplifying his versatility by drawing attention to the varied characteristics of a representative handful of individual works.

Hugh the Drover (completed in 1914 but not played on the stage until 1924) might be regarded as an apotheosis of his folk-song style; here was a simple tale of love and jealousy in the Cotswolds at the time of the Napoleonic wars, and the characters of Mary the village maiden, the conventionally heroic Hugh and his cowardly rival John the Butcher were admirably delineated in a light-hearted 'folk-tuny' manner which would have been entirely inappropriate in the later and impressively dramatic one-act opera *Riders to the Sea* where, indeed, the word-setting (often against the background of a wordless chorus) was somewhat suggestive of Janáček's 'speech song' approach (see page 217).

That extraordinary work *Job, a Masque for Dancing*, based on William Blake's interpretation of the Book of Job, was largely devoid of anything resembling folk music or even formal musical characterization: as James Day put it, 'we have here in choreographic terms a quest into the nature of man's place in the universe and his eternal spiritual destiny'. Man's eternal destiny was, of course, also the subject of the Mass in G minor, but this work was written for solo voices and chorus without accompaniment of either organ or orchestra, and one feels that Vaughan Williams was here reaching back in spirit to the Elizabethan age.

Among the nine symphonies – so unpredictably contrasted in style and mood – certain significant features of the fifth, sixth and eighth may be pointed out. No. 5 (D major) requires only a modest orchestra and almost suggests a small-scale bringing-up-to-date of Bruckner – a romantic Bruckner transplanted from the romantic banks of the Danube to the romantic banks of the Thames. On the other hand no. 6 (E minor), scored for a very large orchestra, is a disturbingly violent, impetuous, warlike affair – until disturbance is quietened and violence quelled in its slow-moving, peaceful and yet curiously tense last movement. By comparison no. 8 (D minor) appears almost frivolous in conception; at any rate the composer here reverts to the eighteenth-century notion that the primary function of music is to entertain rather than to provoke discussion or pose aesthetic problems.

I hope enough has been said to make clear the many-sidedness of Vaughan Williams' immense talent as a composer; mention must now be made of his splendid work in an allied field. In 1905, in collaboration with Percy Dearmer and Martin Shaw, he sponsored the publication of the *English Hymnal*, a marked improvement upon *Hymns Ancient and Modern*. The later *Songs of Praise* (1925, and an enlarged edition in 1931, containing over seven hundred tunes) was an even more commendable production. The joint editors wrote in their preface that 'the bulk of the tunes [to which hymns were sung in the Victorian era] illustrated a period of British music which the musicians of today are anxious to forget, and which, fortunately for our reputation, has been superseded by a national revival that has now given our music a foremost place in Europe again.' They went on: 'It is therefore a hopeful sign that our newer hymnals have shown courage in replacing many weak and poor hymns by words and music more worthy of our great traditions and more suitable to be used in the worship of God.'

Of several famous composers (Delius being perhaps an example) it has been said that either one likes their music or one doesn't: there is no halfway position; exactly the opposite could be said of Ralph Vaughan Williams. Although he had little time for composers who persistently piled discord upon discord to secure artificially contrived 'effects', it may be admitted that he himself sometimes made experiments along similar lines – experiments which were successful or unsuccessful according to the individual listener's point of view; therefore, instead of tending (like Delius) to please some of the people all of the time, he tended to please all of the people some of the time. Even in his most provocative moments, however, he never lost touch with 'our great traditions'.*

* Sturdily democratic and detesting any form of class distinction, Vaughan Williams several times turned down the offer of a knighthood, but in 1935 he was prevailed upon to accept the far greater honour of the Order of Merit.

CHAPTER FORTY-EIGHT

Rachmaninov

SERGEI RACHMANINOV (1873–1943) was born at Oneg in the Novgorod province of Russia (well to the north-west of the Nizhny-Novgorod province where Rimsky-Korsakov was brought up), and as a small boy showed great musical promise. When he was nine years old the family moved to St Petersburg (now Leningrad) and he attended elementary classes at the conservatoire there, but three years later, on the advice of his cousin Alexander Siloti, a concert pianist, he was sent to the Conservatoire at Moscow where he studied the piano with Nikolai Sverev (one of the finest teachers in Russia) and composition with Sergei Taneiev and Anton Arensky; he also attracted the attention of Tchaikovsky, who took considerable interest in his progress and exerted a profound influence over him. While still a student Rachmaninov began to make his mark as a virtuoso pianist. Meanwhile he composed a one-act opera, *Aleko*, and a piano concerto in F sharp minor owing nearly everything to Tchaikovsky; this remained in manuscript until 1917 and was not performed until long after concertgoers had become acquainted (if not as yet familiar) with the better-known no. 2 and no. 3. By contrast, his first composition after leaving the Conservatoire (at the age of twenty, and loaded with prize-winning awards) was the immediately and fabulously successful Prelude in C sharp minor, which has probably been played more frequently, both in public and in private, than any other piano piece ever written. Thus far everything had gone right for him, but disillusionment was in store. A performance at St Petersburg in 1897 of his first symphony (D minor) was an utter fiasco and ended in uproar, members of the audience demanding their money back. César Cui later referred to its 'devilish discords' but, whatever Rachmaninov's shortcomings, a proneness to devilish discords was not one of them, and indeed when the work was unearthed and revived after the Second World War no clue could be found as to why there should have been such a rumpus over it; one is almost inclined to think that the composer must have been right when he asserted that Glazunov, who conducted, was hopelessly drunk at the time. Be that as it may, this unfortunate experience completely destroyed the sensitive young man's self-confidence, and indeed it seems likely that he might have lost his reason had he not been persuaded to undergo a prolonged course of treatment from Dr Nikolai Dahl, an enlightened psychologist and early practitioner of hypnotic auto-suggestion. The cure that he effected, although very welcome, was only partial: for the rest of his life Rachmaninov continued to suffer from periodic attacks of depression amounting almost to melancholia – his state of mind being often reflected (to an even greater degree than in the case of Tchaikovsky) in his music.

If the Prelude in C sharp minor remains the best known of Rachmaninov's small-scale compositions, it would be fair to say that over the years its popularity has been rivalled by that of his piano concerto no. 2 in C minor, of which the slow movement and the finale were completed in 1900 (not long after his withdrawal from the ministrations of Dr Dahl), the first movement being added a year or so later. In many ways derivative from Tchaikovsky's in B flat minor, this concerto is comparable with its predecessor in the opportunity it gives for displays of pianistic virtuosity, in the expertness of its construction, and in the extremely subjective, not to say self-pitying, nature of much of its content, notably in the first movement and in the 'second subject' of the last. Highbrow musicians, of course, have no use for this sort of emotional gush, but Rachmaninov's C minor concerto, in which his quintessence is revealed, holds considerable appeal for many less inhibited although not necessarily unsophisticated music lovers.

In 1902 Rachmaninov married Natalia Satin (a first cousin) and in 1903 was appointed musical director of Moscow's

Imperial Theatre. Ten years previously his student opera *Aleko* (see page 270) had been favourably received there, but the two operas which he now composed and produced – *The Miser Knight* (1904) and *Francesca da Rimini* (1905) – met with no success. In a fit of pique he decided to shake Russian dust off his boots and took his wife and baby daughter first to Italy and then to Germany, where they settled for a time in Dresden. It was in Dresden that he completed his technically impeccable but inordinately long second symphony (E minor), his third piano concerto (D minor) – which, while reproducing many features of no. 2, was more mixed in style, being in places almost as reminiscent of Liszt as of Tchaikovsky – and a mournfully weird tone-poem entitled *The Isle of the Dead*, inspired by the painting of Arnold Böcklin. Next came a concert-tour of America, during which he played his third piano concerto (twice) in New York, conducted his second symphony in Philadelphia, and was enthusiastically acclaimed everywhere both as pianist and as composer. In 1910, after an absence of four years, he returned to Russia and was presently appointed conductor of the Moscow Philharmonic Orchestra, but nevertheless found time to compose numerous songs and short piano pieces – about fifty of each. The Bolshevik Revolution of 1917 drove him to seek sanctuary in Scandinavia, and a year later he crossed the Atlantic again to reach the United States, where for the time being he was content to abandon composition and devote himself to giving piano recitals. However, he subsequently formed the habit of taking his family each summer to western Europe (not Soviet Russia). While in France in 1926 he completed his fourth piano concerto (G minor) – which has never attained quite the same popularity as no. 2 or even no. 3; on visits to Switzerland, where for several years he maintained a *pied-à-terre* on the shore of Lake Lucerne, he composed the characteristic *Rhapsody on a Theme of Paganini* (1934) and the less well-known third symphony (A minor, 1936). During the winter months, although ailing in health, he continued to tour the North American continent as a concert pianist but eventually fell seriously ill; he died at his home in Beverly Hills, California, five days short of his seventieth birthday.

From student days onward Sergei Rachmaninov (like Camille Saint-Saëns) remained stylistically static: not even Rimsky-Korsakov (whom he admired) made the slightest impact upon him; as for younger contemporaries such as Igor Stravinsky and Sergei Prokofiev, on the internal evidence of his music he might never even have heard of them. It would hardly be an over-simplification to describe him as a Tchaikovsky *manqué*, who escaped less frequently than did his predecessor from the vale of tears, but it is perhaps to his credit that in a catalytic world he unswervingly maintained the traditions of Russia's *ancien régime* as pictured in literature by Dostoievsky, Tolstoy and Tchekhov.

CHAPTER FORTY-NINE

Ravel

On the Basque coast of the Bay of Biscay, some twelve miles south of Biarritz, lies one of the most popular bathing-resorts in south-western France – St-Jean-de-Luz. Separating the town from its suburb Ciboure is a small harbour confined on the St-Jean-de-Luz side by the quai de l'Infante, while facing it across the water in Ciboure is the quai Maurice Ravel, originally the quai de la Nivelle but renamed in 1929 in honour of an illustrious composer who, through a curious chain of circumstances, had chanced to be born there. This is how it had come about.

The composer's father, Pierre-Joseph Ravex, was born at Versoix – on the Swiss side of Lac Léman just north of Geneva. He was keenly interested in music and as a boy gained a prize for piano-playing at the Geneva Conservatoire, but later he became by profession a mechanical engineer. Unlike many of his compatriots he had the initiative to seek his fortune abroad and worked for long periods in several western European countries. It was in Spain, during the early 1870s (having by now changed the spelling of his name to Ravel), that he met and married Marie Deluarte. Although resident in Spain at the time, his bride had been born in the French Basque country (the *département* of Pyrénées-Atlantique), and when during the last few months of her first pregnancy Pierre-Joseph was away in Paris – where he soon secured further employment – she went to stay with an aunt who lived in a timber-framed house (still standing) on the quayside at Ciboure; it was there that on 7th March 1875 she gave birth to a son. MAURICE RAVEL was only three months old when his mother took him to Paris and introduced him to his father, but although he lived in the French capital for the next forty-six years he always regarded himself as a Basque rather than as a Parisian, and in later life spent nearly all his holidays in or near his birthplace.

Inheriting from his father a love of music (as well as that logically precise outlook on affairs so typical of Swiss nationals whatever language they may speak), young Maurice entered the Paris Conservatoire at the age of fourteen and studied there for about nine years. He found some of the preceptors too conservative for his liking and was delighted to be eventually admitted to the 'advanced composition' class of Gabriel Fauré – who was considerably more broadminded than many of his colleagues. As pointed out on page 208, Fauré's roots lay in the classical tradition, but he himself was always ready to make novel experiments in melody and harmony and rhythm, and allowed his pupils to do likewise – within reason; Ravel benefited greatly from his tuition. Meanwhile he had become acquainted with that bizarre character Erik Satie, whimsical *enfant terrible* in the artistic world of *fin-de-siècle* Paris, whose influence lay along what were at the time considered to be extremely unconventional lines. And this applied not only in music: Ravel tried to imitate his friend by cultivating a beard – an almost indispensable attribute for anyone who aspired to be recognized as a member of the *avant-garde*; unfortunately he found that no type of beard suited a man of his unimposing physique (he was very short in stature and somewhat sensitive on the point) and soon decided to revert to being clean-shaven. His music, too, always remained clearcut, innocent of trendy affectations analogous to shoulder-length hair, extravagant side-whiskers, curled mustachios or even a modest goatee.

In the earliest of Ravel's compositions familiar to present-day listeners – *Pavane pour une infante défunte*, originally written in 1899 for piano but subsequently transcribed for orchestra – the impact of Satie was less noticeable than that of Fauré. Neither of them can have had much to do with another early piano piece, *Les Jeux d'eau* (1901) – although it was dedicated to Fauré; the impetus would seem more likely to have been provided by 'Les Jeux d'eaux à la villa d'Este' from Liszt's *Années de pèlerinages* (see page 117), but in descriptive imagery this brilliant little work surpassed anything of the same type that Liszt ever wrote and went far to prove that musical impressionism need not be solely an orchestral preserve. One imagines that Debussy, although Ravel's senior by thirteen years, took careful note of it.

The many piano pieces which Ravel composed over the next ten years or so all displayed that meticulous attention to detail which was one of the most noteworthy characteristics of his music, but they were by no means all alike in mood. They included the elegantly neo-classical 'Sonatine', the grimly fantastic three-movement cycle entitled *Gaspard de la nuit*, and the eight *Valses nobles et sentimentales* in which an audacious attempt was made to bring Schubert up to date; *Ma Mère l'Oye* (*Mother Goose*), comprising musical interpretations of a set of fairy-tales, was first written for piano duet but is better known to most listeners in its orchestral version. During the same period Ravel was also active in other fields of composition. *Shéhérezade* – not to be confused with Rimsky-Korsakov's symphonic suite *Scheherazade* (page 203) – was a setting for voice and orchestra of three poems by Tristan Klingsor (the plausibly Wagnerian pseudonym adopted by a French writer named Léon Leclère). An intriguing and attractively luscious contribution to chamber music was the 'Introduction et allegro' for the unusual combination of flute, clarinet, harp, two violins, viola and cello, at one time known as the 'harp septet' but nowadays sometimes given with a slightly fuller complement of string-players. In 1907 Ravel concentrated attention upon Spain (where his mother had lived for many years), composing the emotionally evocative *Rapsodie espagnole* for orchestra and the enchanting operetta *L'Heure espagnole* – which, however, was not granted a production until four years later.* In 1912 came the ballet *Daphnis et Chloë*, whose

* In case I should be gently chided – as I have been before now – for referring to this work as an operetta, let me point out that the composer's firm friend Roland-Manuel, in the December 1938 issue of *La Revue musicale*, recalled that Ravel had told him that in *L'Heure espagnole* his intention was 'to join up again with the tradition of *opéra bouffe*'.

primary instigator was Sergei Diaghilev; the composer was not on particularly good terms with the choreographer, but the alluring music represented him at his best and is still frequently played in concert halls.

By the time he reached the age of thirty-nine Ravel had established a reputation among contemporary French composers second only to that of Debussy, but the outbreak of the 1914–18 war caused an interruption in his creative activity. In August 1914 he was (as usual) spending his summer holiday at St-Jean-de-Luz, and immediately made his way to the nearest garrison-town, Bayonne, to volunteer as an infantryman; he was rejected on the grounds that he was two kilograms under the regulation minimum weight for a French soldier, but presently, thanks partly to the influence of his friend Paul Painlevé, a Cabinet minister, he was drafted into the army as an ambulance driver and served close behind the front line for eighteen months before being discharged as medically unfit. Shy by nature and perhaps slightly introspective, he had hitherto been able to detach himself, so to say, from human problems, but it would seem that his wartime experiences engendered a more objective outlook. It is hard to believe that the pre-war Ravel could have conceived the tone-poem *La Valse* (1920), which was headed with this note.

An imperial court, about 1855. Clouds wheel about. Occasionally they part to allow a passing glimpse of waltzing couples. As they gradually lift, one can discern a gigantic hall, filled by a crowd of dancers in motion ...

Now at the time *La Valse* was composed the inhabitants of Vienna, as Ravel well knew, were suffering from near-starvation, and it was (tragically) the psychological moment for his masterly re-creation of a ghostly Schönbrunn peopled by ghostly dancers of the Johann Strauss era. *La Valse* is technically impeccable; moreover, for any listener endowed with a sense of historical perspective its poignancy can be overwhelming.

Having meanwhile settled in a new country home at Montfort-l'Amaury (thirty miles west of Paris), Ravel reverted to something more like his earlier manner in parts of the ballet-opera *L'Enfant et les sortilèges* (1925) – which, however, was somewhat mixed in style – and while touring the United States of America in 1927–8 scored a great popular success with his *Bolero*. Far more significant, to my mind, were the two piano concertos dated 1931, in the second of which (the D major) the piano part was restricted to the player's left hand; in both these works – as well as here and there in *L'Enfant et les sortilèges* – Ravel exploited the potentialities of contemporary jazz. (His old friend Satie would no doubt have approved.)

Maurice Ravel the man was as fastidious as Maurice Ravel the composer – apart perhaps from the curious fact that throughout his life he was a confirmed chain-smoker of the cheap cigarettes then known as Caporals and now known as Gauloises. In 1935 he suffered slight concussion in a motor accident and thereafter was subject to periodic bouts of locomotor ataxia, eventually being sent to Paris to undergo an operation. This was only partially successful and he died in hospital there on 28th December 1938, widely mourned by many good friends as well as by all those in the outside world who very properly admired his achievements as a composer.

CHAPTER FIFTY

Falla

Spain, although never producing a Schubert, a Verdi, a Wagner or a Debussy, deserves no more than does Britain to be described as a 'Land ohne Musik'. Indeed, the national characteristics of much of its music date back further than do those of any other European country (Russia not excepted): that is to say to about six centuries ago, when roving bands of itinerant gipsies from the Asian regions now known as Afghanistan and Turkestan found their way across Persia, Syria and north Africa, eventually reaching the Iberian peninsular across the Straits of Gibraltar and settling there permanently. Despite the fact that the dominating influence in Spain was that of the Church, whose music always tended to adhere to prevailing western European trends (Tomás Luis de Victoria, for instance, belonged to the same School as did his Italian contemporary Palestrina), oriental gipsy-traits became embedded in the music of Spanish folk song and folk dance, music that during the eighteenth century became part and parcel of the *zarzuela*, a very loosely fashioned form of stage-entertainment in which the audience often joined in the fun, bawling the lusty choruses and indulging in impromptu cross-talk with the actors and actresses.* Bit by bit, as generation succeeded generation, a greater degree of formality was introduced to *zarzuela* proceedings, and the genre received official recognition when in 1857 the Teatro de la Zarzuela was opened in Madrid and reputable composers like Joaquín Gaztambide, Francisco Barbieri and Tomás Breton were encouraged to write for it. The nineteenth-century *zarzuela*, at its best, was a colourful affair, introducing the villainous bandits, glamorous bull-fighters, starving beggars, well-padded prelates and other

* The origin of the term *zarzuela* was fortuitous; anyone interested should read chapter 6 in Gilbert Chase's *Music of Spain* (1941).

picaresque oddities that have been part of the Iberian scene since the days of Cervantes, and the melodic and rhythmic characteristics of the frequent boleros, seguidillas, jotas and so on made a great impression upon many composers of other nationalities, for example Bizet, Chabrier and Rimsky-Korsakov.* That any Spanish composer born during the late nineteenth century, or even during the early twentieth, ever ventured upon music of a more ambitious nature was almost entirely due to the fervent and effective propaganda spread by Felipe Pedrell (1841–1922), himself a composer, but better remembered as a musical historian and theorist – and better still as an idealistic and forward-looking teacher, among whose most illustrious pupils were Isaac Albéniz (1860–1909), Enrique Granados (1867–1916) and MANUEL DE FALLA (1876–1946).

Falla was a native of Cadiz (Andalusia) and received his first music lessons from his mother (a Catalan). During his youth he composed a *zarzuela* or two almost as a matter of course, but after studying with Pedrell at Madrid he entered in 1907 for a nation-wide opera competition and won a prize with *La vida breve* (*Life is short*) – although no production eventuated at the time. From 1907 until 1914 he lived in Paris where, like Delius before him (see page 246), he concentrated not so much upon writing music as upon listening to and absorbing it; again like Delius, he felt the impact of the impressionistic methods of Debussy. 'The spirit, the aesthetics and the technique of modern music [he wrote] were not established in a precise, lasting and definite manner until the appearance of the *Nocturnes*, the G minor quartet, *L'Après-midi d'un faune* and *Pelléas et Mélisande*.' During this period Falla did however complete his ballet *El amor brujo* (*Love the Magician*), and for piano and orchestra *Nights in the Gardens of Spain* ('In the Gardens of the Generalife', 'A Dance heard in the distance' and 'In the Gardens of the Sierra de Cordoba'). He had the further satisfaction that *La vida breve* was produced at Nice in 1913 and at the Opéra Comique in Paris a year later.

* See footnote on opposite page.

On the outbreak of the 1914–18 war Falla returned to Spain and settled in Madrid, where there shortly took place the first performances of *El amor brujo* and his second ballet *The Three-cornered Hat*, based on the same story by Alarcón as was Wolf's opera *Der Corregidor* (see page 212).* Subsequently he divided his time between Granada and Majorca, meanwhile composing the puppet-opera *Master Peter's Puppet-show*; *Psyché* for mezzo-soprano and chamber orchestra; 'Four Spanish pieces' for piano – *Aragonese, Cubana, Montañesa* and *Andaluza*; a few songs; a harpsichord concerto (for Wanda Landowska) with very light woodwind and string accompaniment; and *Homenaje*, an orchestral work. Although an ardent supporter of Franco during the Spanish Civil War, Falla became disillusioned when the Generalissimo subsequently became Spain's ruling dictator, and in 1940 betook himself to Argentina, where he spent the rest of his days at the small town of Alta Gracia in the province of Cordoba, some two hundred and fifty miles to the north-west of Buenos Aires; here he worked spasmodically on an ambitious oratorio entitled *L'Atlantída*, but never completed it.

Falla was painstakingly self-critical and in consequence his output was small, but what it lacked in quantity was made up in quality. His whole approach to music was conditioned partly by his great interest, as a patriotic Spaniard, in the folk songs and folk dances of his native land; partly by his admiration, as a cultured and knowledgable historian, for the polyphonic masters of the sixteenth and seventeenth centuries; partly by his lifelong devotion, as a pious Catholic, to the artistic ideals which found expression in Church ritual. It was from these sources that he largely derived his inspiration – and to a certain extent evolved his technique. ('To a certain extent' because in this respect the influence of

* It is remarkable how often the music of *The Three-cornered Hat* recalls passages from Bizet's *Carmen* (1875), Chabrier's orchestral rhapsody entitled *España* (1883) and Rimsky-Korsakov's *Spanish Capriccio* (1887), a sure indication of the successful manner in which both French and Russian composers were able to capture the authentic Spanish atmosphere.

Debussy cannot be altogether discounted.) Let me quote Falla's own recorded words.

> The wonderful musical treasure previous to J. S. Bach is systematically ignored and despised as if the art of sound had not had a worthy existence until the arrival of the great cantor. Beethoven employs the Lydian mode in his *canzona* [the short *molto adagio* of the string quartet in A minor, op. 132] to give it a religious character, since it is written as a hymn of thanksgiving to the Divinity. Wagner also makes use of modal formulae, and even themes from the Catholic liturgy, in *Parsifal*. Yet he does not abandon the Protestant tradition – that tradition of ill omen which has been the principal, if not the only, cause of the contempt that the music of the so-called classical period had for that of the sixteenth century ... Mussorgsky was the true initiator of the new era in music : thanks to him the melodic forms and ancient scales which (being despised by composers) had taken refuge in the Church and the people, were restored to musical art ... The belief that modernity in music depends upon a prodigality of harmonic dissonances is a widespread error. This is to such an extent untrue that I make bold to declare that the modern spirit in music can subsist in a work in which only consonant chords are used, and, what is more, in music consisting solely of an undulating melodic line.

Fair enough from his own point of view – despite the somewhat unexpectedly appreciative reference to Mussorgsky.

It is perhaps slightly ironic that Manuel de Falla, the youngest of the fifty composers discussed in this book, should have gloried in being to such an extent a traditionalist that he harked back to Palestrina (our chapter 1) and took little account of the 'so-called classical period'. Yet when listening to his vivid and evocative music one cannot but feel that he must also have been fully aware (subconsciously perhaps) of contemporary requirements and expectations.

Index

Index

Agapit, Saint, 1
Agoult, Marie d', 116
Ahna, Pauline de, 251
Alarcón, Pedro de, 212, 281
Albéniz, Isaac, 115, 280
Alexander II, Czar, 182
Alfano, Franco, 231
Alheim, Pierre d', 185
Andersen, Hans, 200
Anne, Queen, 15, 27
Annunzio, Gabriel d', 243
Anzalone, Antonia, 19
Arensky, Anton, 270
Ariosti, Attilio, 27
Aristophanes, 264
Arno, Joachim von, 234
Avenarius, Cäcilie, 120

Bach, Anna, 37–8
Bach, C. P. E., 33, 37, 48
Bach, J. Christian, 33, 37
Bach, J. Christoph, 33–4
Bach, J. S., 8, 17, 23, 29, 33–40,
   63–4, 94, 112–13, 136, 143n, 166,
   179, 263, 282
Bach, Maria, 34, 37
Bach, W. F., 33, 37
Balakirev, Mily, 171–4, 181, 183–
   184, 188, 201–2
Bantock, Granville, 260
Barbaia, Domenico, 88
Barbieri, Francisco, 279
Bardac, Emma, 242–3
Barezzi, Antonio, 131–2
Barezzi, Margherita, 131–2
Barnett, J. F., 83
Bartók, Béla, 69
Barzun, Jacques, 105

Baudelaire, Charles, 238
Bax, Arnold, 157
Beaumont, Francis, 16
Beecham, Thomas, 247
Beethoven, Karl, 67–8
Beethoven, Ludwig van, 48, 51,
   53, 55n, 61–9, 73, 75, 79–80,
   83–4, 100–1, 112, 115, 122, 143–
   144, 150, 164–5, 167, 174, 190,
   196, 198, 206–7, 210, 218, 263,
   266, 282
Bellini, Vincenzo, 88–91, 93, 130,
   133–4
Berlioz, Harriet, 103–4
Berlioz, Hector, 62, 64, 73, 99–
   105, 110, 115–16, 145, 151, 161,
   177, 208, 210, 233, 236, 239–40,
   251
Berlioz, Louis, 103, 105
Berlioz, Marie, 104
Bethge, Hans, 236
Beyer, Frants, 199
Birley, Joanna, 5
Bizet, Geneviève, 139, 141
Bizet, Georges, 139–45, 147, 179,
   228, 238, 244, 280, 281n
Bjørnson, Bjørnstjerne, 200
Blake, William, 267
Blom, Eric, 116
Blow, John, 15
Böcklin, Arnold, 272
Boïeldieu, François, 76n
Boito, Arrigo, 136, 138
Bononcini, Giovanni, 27, 39
Bordoni, Faustina, 27–8
Borodin, Alexander, 139n, 170–6,
   181, 188, 201, 205, 237–8
Borodin, Ekaterina, 171–2

Borodin, Porphyri, 171
Bortniansky, Dimitri, 170
Boschot, Adolphe, 105
Boult, Adrian, 84, 266
Brahms, Johannes, 64, 79, 139n,
    157, 163–9, 191, 193–6, 200,
    211–12, 222, 234, 236, 250, 252,
    263
Brandt, Caroline, 72
Brentano, Clemens, 234
Bretón, Tomás, 279
Britten, Benjamin, 77, 98
Browne, Count, 67
Bruch, Max, 263
Bruckner, Anton, 79, 139n, 147,
    157–63, 165, 210, 233, 235,
    268
Bruneau, Alfred, 151
Brunner, Franz, 159
Bull, Ole, 198
Bülow, Cosima von, 121n, 125,
    250
Bülow, Hans von, 125, 250–1
Bunyan, John, 266
Buths, Julius, 221–2
Buxtehude, Dietrich, 34, 39
Byrd, Joanna, 5
Byrd, William, 2, 5–8, 263–4
Byron, George Gordon, 103, 112,
    251

Calzabigi, Raniero da, 43
Cameron, Basil, 260
Campion, Thomas, 5
Cardus, Neville, 248
Carpelan, Axel, 259
Cattaneo, Claudia, 10
Cavour, Camillo, 133
Cecilia, Saint, 18
Čermáková, Anna, 192
Cervantes, Miguel de, 280
Chabrier, Emmanuel, 142, 238,
    244, 280, 281n
Charles II, King, 15

Charles V, Holy Roman Emperor,
    1, 9
Charpentier, Gustave, 240
Chase, Gilbert, 279n
Chausson, Ernest, 151
Cherubini, Luigi, 100, 177
Chopin, Frederic, 17, 102n, 106–
    110, 113, 115–17, 149, 171,
    208–9, 243, 246
Christian Ludwig, Margrave of
    Brandenburg, 36
Clement VII, Pope, 1
Clement VIII, Pope, 2
Coates, Eric, 225
Colbran, Isabella, 75–6
Colloredo, Hieronymus von, 55–6
Congreve, William, 16
Cooke Deryck, 233
Cooper, Martin, 150
Corelli, Arcangelo, 23
Cornelius, Peter, 116
Cromwell, Richard, 15
Cui, César, 172, 181, 270
Cuzzoni, Francesca, 27–8

Dahl, Nikolai, 271
Dante Alighieri, 122, 136
Darwin, Charles, 262
Daudet, Alphonse, 142
Davies, Henry Walford, 224–5
Day, James, 267
Dearmer, Percy, 268
Debussy, Claude, 97, 172–3, 177,
    208n, 237–44, 246, 276–7, 279–
    282
Debussy, Emma, 242–3
Debussy, Emma-Claude, 242–4
Debussy, Manuel, 237
Debussy, Rosalie, 242
Debussy, Victorine, 237
Delibes, Léo, 209
Delius, Frederick, 244–9, 269, 280
Delius, Jelka, 245–6, 248
Deluarte, Marie, 274

Diaghilev, Sergei, 276–7
Dent, E. J., 21–2, 91
Dohnanyi, Ernö, 148
Donizetti, Andrea, 91
Donizetti, Domenica, 91
Donizetti, Gaetano, 89–93, 130, 133–4
Donizetti, Virginia, 92
Dormuli, Virginia, 2
Dostoievsky, Feodor, 273
Dowland, John, 5
Dryden, John, 16
Dudevant, Aurore, 107
Dudevant, Casimir, 107
Dudevant, Maurice, 107
Dudevant, Solange, 107
Dunhill, Thomas, 51
Dupin, Aurore, 107
Dupont, Gabrielle, 242
Dvořák, Antonín, 157, 168, 192–197, 199–200, 202–3, 215–17, 219, 258–9, 261, 264
Dvořáková, Anna, 192
Dvořáková, Magda, 200n

Eckstein, Friedrich, 212
Eichendorff, Joseph von, 212
Einstein, Alfred, 58, 161–2
Elgar, Anne, 219
Elgar, Carice, 220
Elgar, Caroline, 220, 223–4
Elgar, Edward, 211n, 219–25, 229, 244, 252, 254, 258–9, 266
Elgar, William, 219–20
Elizabeth I, Queen, 5
Elsner, Joseph, 106
Erben, Karel, 196
Ernst August, Duke, 35
Esterházy, Johann, 79
Esterházy, Nicolas (1), 46–7, 49
Esterházy, Nicolas (2), 115
Esterházy, Paul Anton, 46, 49

Falla, Manuel de, 8, 279–82

Fauré, Gabriel, 177, 179n, 206–10, 238, 244, 264, 275
Fauré, Marie, 207
Fauré, Toussaint, 206
Fellowes, Edmund H., 4, 7–8
Fenby, Eric, 248–9
Ferdinandi, Barbara, 153
Fisher, Antonia, 263
Fistoulari, Anatole, 233
Flaubert, Gustave, 184
Fletcher, John, 16
Fox-Strangways, A. H., 52
Francesco, Duke of Mantua, 12
Franck, César, 139n, 146–51, 158, 168, 177, 179, 235
Franck, Félicité, 146
Franco, Francisco, 281
Frederick, King of Würtemberg, 71
Frederick Augustus, King of Saxony, 72
Fremiet, Emmanuel, 207
Fremiet, Marie, 207
Fricken, Ernestine von, 111
Friederica, Princess of Anhalt, 37
Fuchs, Robert, 258
Fuller-Maitland, J. A., 16–17
Fürnberg, Baron von, 46, 49

Gade, Niels, 198
Garborg, Arne, 200
Garden, Mary, 240
Gasparini, Francesco, 24
Gay, John, 28
Gaztambide, Joaquín, 279
Gedeanev, Luka, 170
Geibel, Emanuel von, 212
Gemignani, Elvira, 226
George I, King, 15, 27, 219
German, Edward, 225
Geyer, Cäcilie, 120
Geyer, Johanna, 120
Geyer, Ludwig, 120
Gibbons, Orlando, 5, 8

Glazunov, Alexander, 175, 271
Glinka, Mikhail, 170, 172–3
Gluck, A. J., 41
Gluck, C. W., 41–4, 53, 57, 59, 67, 79, 100, 163
Gluck, Marianne, 42
Goethe, J. W. von, 53, 86, 101, 110, 112, 212–13
Gogol, Nikolai, 184, 186, 202–3
Goldberg, J. C., 38
Goldmark, Carl, 157, 258
Gori, Lucrezia, 1
Gounod, Charles, 30, 140–1, 146–7
Granados, Enrique, 280
Gregor, Josef, 255–6
Gregory XIII, Pope, 2
Gregory XIV, Pope, 2
Grétry, André, 146
Grieg, Alexander, 198
Grieg, Edvard, 115, 198–200, 245–246
Grieg, Gesine, 198
Grieg, Nina, 199
Grisi, Giulia, 89
Grove, George, 61–2, 65
Guidarini, Anna, 74
Guiraud, Ernest, 141, 143
Gyrowetz, Adelbert, 65

Haas, Robert, 161
Hadow, W. H., 91, 101, 157, 214
Hagerup, Gesine, 198
Hagerup, Nina, 199
Halévy, Fromental, 139, 142n, 178
Halévy, Geneviève, 139
Halévy, Ludovic, 144
Hallé, Charles, 104
Hallström, Ivar, 198
Handel, Dorothea, 26
Handel, G. F., 8, 13, 18, 25–32, 36, 38–9, 42–3, 48, 96, 143n, 166, 219, 258
Hanslick, Eduard, 160
Harding, James, 178

Hartmann, J. P. E., 198
Hartmann, Victor, 183
Haydn, Joseph, 8, 45–53, 57–60, 65, 67, 71, 77, 79–80, 83–4, 112, 115, 166–7, 219, 262–3
Haydn, Maria, 46, 58
Haydn, Michael, 45, 71
Heine, Heinrich, 86
Hensel, Fanny, 95
Hensel, William, 95
Heseltine, Philip, 247
Heyse, Paul, 212
Hitler, Adolf, 255, 266
Hoffmann, E. T. A., 110
Hofmannsthal, Hugo von, 253
Holmès, Augusta, 178–9
Holst, Gustav, 262–3
Housman, A. E., 264
Hughes, Rosemary, 46
Hugo, Victor, 103, 117
Hull, Percy, 224–5

Ibsen, Henrik, 200
Indy, Vincent d', 151
Ingegneri, M. A., 9
Innocent IX, Pope, 2

Jahn, Otto, 56
James II, King, 15
Janáček, Jiři, 215
Janáček, Leoš, 211n, 215–18, 267
Janáčeková, Olga, 215–16
Janáčeková, Zdenka, 215–16
Järnefelt, Aino, 258
Järnefelt, Armas, 258
Järnefelt, Arvid, 258–9
Järnefelt, Maikki, 258n
Jeanrenaud, Cécile, 95
Jeppesen, Knud, 7
Jeritza, Maria, 216
Joachim, Joseph, 81–2
Joseph II, Emperor of Austria, 56
Julius III, Pope, 2
Jurinac, Sena, 229

Keitel, Wilhelm, 34n
Keller, Gottfried, 212
Keller, Maria, 46
Khatchaturian, Aram, 186
Kinsky, Prince, 67
Kleinecke, Avdotya, 170
Klingsor, Tristan (Léon Leclère), 276
Köchel, Ludwig von, 58
Kolařová, Kateřina, 152
Krauss, Clemens, 256
Kreisler, Fritz, 222
Kurz, Joseph, 46

Lablache, Luigi, 89
Lalo, Édouard, 142, 238
Landowska, Wanda, 281
Lassus, Orlando de, 14
Lavigna, Vincenzo, 131
Leblanc, Gabrielle, 240
Leclère, Léon, 276
Legrenzi, Giovanni, 23
Lenau, Nikolaus, 251
Leo, Leonardo, 22
Leonova, Daria, 181
Leopold, Prince of Anhalt, 35–6
Lesueur, J. F., 100
Lévy, Roland (Roland-Manuel), 276n
Lichnowsky, Prince Charles, 67
Liszt, Cosima, 125
Liszt, Franz, 62, 64, 102n, 115–19, 123, 146, 153, 155, 159, 165, 171, 173, 199n, 207, 227, 251, 254, 272, 275–6
Li-Tai-Po, 236
Lobkowitz, Prince (1), 41, 67
Lobkowitz, Prince (2), 67
Loeffler, C. M., 157
Logroscino, Nicola, 22
Long, J. L., 229
Lorenz, Alfred, 22
Louis XIV, King, 14

Ludwig II, King of Bavaria, 124–5
Lully, J. B., 14–15

Macdowell, Edward, 157
Mackenzie, Alexander, 219
Maeterlinck, Gabrielle, 240
Maeterlinck, Maurice, 208, 240–1
Mahler, Alma, 232–3
Mahler, Gustav, 79, 157–8, 190, 213, 232–6, 244, 252
Mallarmé, Stephane, 238
Manzoni, Alessandro, 135
Marcellus II, Pope, 2
Maria Theresa, Empress of Austria, 42–3
Marie Antoinette, 43
Mary, Queen (of 'William and Mary'), 15
Mascagni, Pietro, 241
Massenet, Jules, 147, 208, 227–8, 238, 244
Matinsky, Mikhail, 170
Mayr, Simone, 92
Mayrhofer, Johann, 79
Meck, Nadezhda von, 189, 237
Meilhac, Henri, 144
Melzi, F. S., 41–2
Mendelssohn, Abraham, 94
Mendelssohn, Cécile, 95
Mendelssohn, Fanny, 95
Mendelssohn, Felix, 23, 94–9, 113–14, 123, 130, 148, 159, 165, 173–174, 193, 198–9, 201–2, 219, 253
Mercadante, Saverio, 89
Merelli, Bartolomeo, 131–2
Mérimée, Prosper, 144
Messager, André, 209, 240
Meyerbeer, Giacomo (Jakob), 123–4, 134
Michelangelo, Buonaroti, 141, 212
Milton, John, 51
Milyukova, Antonina, 188
Min-Kao-Yen, 236

Moeran, E. J., 264
Moke, Camille, 102
Monteverdi, Baldassare, 9
Monteverdi, Claudia, 10
Monteverdi, Claudio, 2, 8–14, 130
Montgomery, Bernard, 34n
Mörike, Eduard, 212–13
Morlacchi, Francesco, 72
Morley, Thomas, 5, 8
Morris, R. O., 7
Morzin, Count, 46, 49
Moscheles, Ignaz, 245
Mozart, Anna Maria, 54–5
Mozart, Constanze, 57–60, 70
Mozart, Leopold, 54–7, 60, 70
Mozart, Maria Anna, 54–5
Mozart, W. A., 8, 13, 20–2, 25, 30, 54–60, 63–4, 67, 70–1, 73, 79, 83–4, 90, 94, 112, 118, 122, 143–144, 167, 170, 177, 198, 248n, 253, 256, 262–3, 267
Müller, Wilhelm, 86
Murger, Henri, 172, 228
Musset, Alfred de, 107, 142
Mussolini, Benito, 266
Mussorgsky, Modest, 172, 181–8, 194–5, 202, 205, 217, 237, 282

Napoleon Bonaparte, 48, 74n, 120, 130
Newman, Ernest, 116, 120, 143, 181, 253
Newman, Henry, 221
Niedermeyer, Louis, 179, 206
Nietzsche, Friedrich, 128–9, 246–248
Nordraak, Rikard, 198–9

Offenbach, Jacques, 139, 153–4, 179

Paganini, Niccolò, 103, 272
Painlevé, Paul, 277
Pakarinen, Maikki, 258n
Palestrina, Angelo da, 1–2

Palestrina, Giovanni da, 1–4, 6–9, 14, 68, 279, 282
Palestrina, Iginio da, 1–2
Palestrina, Lucrezia da, 1–2
Palestrina, Rodolfo da, 1–2
Palestrina, Virginia da, 2
Palmgren, Maikki, 258n
Palmgren, Selim, 258n
Parry, Hubert, 45, 219, 262
Paskevitch, Vassily, 170
Pasquati, Baron, 67
Paul IV, Pope, 2
Paul, Adolf, 257
Paul, Jean (J. P. F. Richter), 110
Paul, Saint, 40
Pedrell, Felipe, 280
Pélissier, Olympe, 76–7
Pepusch, J. C., 28
Pergin, Marianne, 42
Peri, Jacopo, 10–11
Philidor, François, 42–3, 76n
Philip of Hesse–Darmstadt, Prince, 24
Piccinni, Nicola, 44, 76n, 163
Pierluigi, Giovanni, 1
Pierluigi, Palma, 1
Pierluigi, Sante, 1
Pierné, Gabriel, 151
Pius IV, Pope, 2
Pius V, Pope, 2
Pius IX, Pope, 116
Planer, Minna, 123
Pleyel, Camille (1), 102
Pleyel, Camille (2), 102
Poe, Edgar Allan, 243
Ponte, Lorenzo da, 251
Porpora, Niccola, 46
Prévost, A. F., 227–8
Prokofiev, Sergei, 157, 273
Protopopova, Ekaterina, 171
Provesi, Ferdinando, 131
Prunières, Henri, 177
Pschorr, Georg, 250
Puccini, Antonio, 226

Puccini, Elvira, 226–7
Puccini, Giacomo (1), 226
Puccini, Giacomo (2), 1n, 144, 211n, 226–31, 244, 254, 267
Purcell, Daniel, 15
Purcell, Frances, 15, 17
Purcell, Henry (1), 14
Purcell, Henry (2), 14–18, 139, 219, 263–4
Purcell, Thomas, 14
Purgold, Nadezhda, 202
Pushkin, Alexander, 184, 203

Rachmaninov, Natalia, 271–2
Rachmaninov, Sergei, 270–3
Racine, Jean, 43
Raff, Joachim, 116
Rameau, J. P., 42–3
Ravel, Marie, 274, 276
Ravel, Maurice, 183n, 264, 274–8
Ravex or Ravel, Pierre-Joseph, 274–5
Recio, Marie, 104
Reed, W. H., 224–5
Reményi, Eduard, 164
Renoir, Jean, 62–3, 65–6
Resphigi, Ottorino, 77
Rhys-Parker, Isabel, 229
Richter, Hans, 159, 221
Richter, J. P. F., 110
Richter, Johanne, 232
Ricordi, Giulio, 226
Rimsky-Korsakov, Andrey, 202
Rimsky-Korsakov, Nadezhda, 202
Rimsky-Korsakov, Nikolai, 172, 175–6, 181, 184–6, 201–5, 233–4, 238–9, 242–3, 270, 273, 276, 280, 281n
Roberts, Caroline, 220
Röckel, August, 121, 124
Roland-Manuel (Roland Lévy), 276n
Rolland, Romain, 63–4
Romani, Felice, 89–90

Rosen, Jelka, 245
Rossetti, D. G., 238, 264
Rossini, Anna, 74
Rossini, Gioacchino, 74–8, 83, 89–93, 130, 133–4, 143–4
Rossini, Giuseppe, 74
Rossini, Isabella, 75–6
Rossini, Olympe, 76–7
Rubini, Giovanni, 89
Rubinstein, Anton, 187–8
Rubinstein, Nikolai, 187–8
Rückert, Friedrich, 234
Rudolph II, Holy Roman Emperor, 9
Rudolph of Habsburg, Archduke, 67

Sabin, Robert, 90n
Saillot, Félicité, 146
Saint-Saëns, Camille, 139, 148, 177–80, 206–8, 257, 273
Salomon, J. P., 47, 50
Sand, George, 107
Sankovsky, Brambeus, 203
Sardou, Victorien, 228
Satie, Erik, 275, 278
Satin, Natalia, 271
Sayn-Wittgenstein, Caroline, 116
Scarlatti, Alessandro, 14–15, 19–22, 30, 43, 88
Scarlatti, Antonia, 19
Scarlatti, Domenico, 19, 22
Scarlatti, Pietro, 19
Schenck, Johann, 65
Schikaneder, Emanuel, 59–60
Schiller, Friedrich, 53, 86, 110, 122, 134
Schindler, Alma, 232, 235
Schober, Franz von, 79–80
Schopenhauer, Arthur, 120
Schrade, Leo, 10
Schrattenbach, Sigismund von, 54
Schröder-Devrient, Wilhelmine, 88

291

Schubert, Franz, 52, 55n, 78–88, 95, 97, 100, 118, 130, 135, 139–141, 158, 167, 170, 194–6, 200, 209, 213, 234, 253, 276, 279

Schulzová, Zdenka, 215

Schumann, Clara, 111–12, 164

Schumann, Robert, 39–40, 100, 110–16, 149, 164–5, 167–8, 171, 198–9, 206–8, 213, 219, 234, 258

Schütz, Heinrich, 14

Seligman, Sybil, 227

Shadwell, Thomas, 16

Shakespeare, William, 16, 20, 86, 88, 101–3, 105, 122, 136, 141, 208, 223, 257, 265

Shaw, Martin, 268

Shostakovitch, Dmitri, 186

Sibelius, Aino, 258

Sibelius, Jean, 173, 257–61

Silito, Alexander, 270

Sinding, Christian, 198

Sixtus V, Pope, 2

Smart, George, 73

Smetana, Bedřich, 139n, 152–7, 193, 202–3

Smetanová, Barbara, 153

Smetanová, Kateřina, 152–3

Smithson, Harriet, 101, 103

Smyth, Ethel, 219

Sobers, Garfield, 248n

Somis, Lorenzo, 23

Sophia Charlotte, Electress, 26

Sophocles, 122, 253

Spitta, Philip, 33

Spontini, Gasparo, 77

Stanford, C. V., 16–17, 219, 228, 262

Stassov, Vladimir, 175

Stephanie, C. G., 56

Stevenson, R. L., 196, 245–6, 264

Strauss, Franz (1), 250

Strauss, Franz (2), 255

Strauss, Johann (1), 157

Strauss, Johann (2), 143–4, 157, 253, 277

Strauss, Pauline, 251, 256

Strauss, Richard, 30, 143–4, 250–257

Stravinsky, Igor, 205, 273

Strepponi, Giuseppina, 132–3

Striggio, Alessandro, 11

Strindberg, August, 257

Suckling, Norman, 62–3

Suk, Josef (1), 193

Suk, Josef (2), 193

Sullivan, Arthur, 219, 265n

Svendsen, Johan, 198

Sverev, Nikolai, 270

Swieten, Gottfried von, 51–2

Synge, J. M., 265

Tallis, Thomas, 5, 265

Tamburini, Antonio, 89

Taneiev, Sergei, 270

Tartini, Giuseppe, 23

Taust, Anna, 26

Tchaikovsky, Alexandra (1), 187–8

Tchaikovsky, Alexandra (2), 188

Tchaikovsky, Anatole, 188

Tchaikovsky, Antonina, 188

Tchaikovsky, Ilya, 187

Tchaikovsky, Peter, 62, 170, 174, 181, 187–91, 219, 235–7, 258, 270–3

Tchang-Tsi, 236

Tchekhov, Anton, 172, 273

Tell, William, 76

Texier, Rosalie, 242

Thomson, James, 51

Thun, Leopold, 152

Tolstoy, Leo, 273

Tomkins, Thomas, 5

Torelli, Giuseppe, 23

Toscanini, Arturo, 230

Tovey, Donald, 61–2, 68–9, 102, 195

Turina, Giuditta, 89
Tye, Christopher, 5

Vasnier, Marguerite, 238
Vasnier, Maurice, 237–8
Vasseli, Virginia, 92
Vaughan Williams, Adeline, 263,
  265–6
Vaughan Williams, Arthur, 262
Vaughan Williams, Edward, 262
Vaughan Williams, Ralph, 190,
  254, 257, 262–9
Vaughan Williams, Ursula, 266
Vecchi, Orazio, 10
Verdi, Carlo, 130–1
Verdi, Giuseppe, 3, 130–8, 143–4,
  159, 192, 228, 230, 253, 257,
  266, 279
Verdi, Giuseppina, 136–7
Verdi, Luigia, 130–1
Verdi, Margherita, 131–2
Verdi, Romano, 132
Verdi, Virginia, 132
Verlaine, Paul, 209, 238
Viardot, Marianne, 207
Viardot-Garcia, Pauline, 207
Victoria, T. L. de, 14, 279
Villon, François, 243
Vincenzo, Duke of Mantua, 9–10,
  12
Vinci, Leonardo, 21
Vinci, Leonardo da, 21
Vivaldi, Antonio, 8, 23–5
Vivaldi, G. B., 23–4

Wagner, Cosima, 125, 250
Wagner, Johanna, 120
Wagner, Minna, 123, 125–6
Wagner, Richard, 33, 52, 73, 88,
  97, 116, 120–30, 135, 137–8,
  143–5, 153–4, 156, 159–62, 165,
  177, 192–4, 200, 207, 209, 211–
  212, 214, 220, 227, 237–8, 241,
  246, 248n, 250–1, 253–4, 263,

Wagner, Richard (cont.)
  267, 279, 282
Wagner, Siegfried, 126
Walker, Ernest, 62–3
Walker, Frank, 22
Wang-Wi, 236
Weber, Aloysia, 55–7
Weber, C. M. von, 55n, 70–3, 94–5,
  97, 101, 122–3, 130, 144, 170
Weber, Caroline von, 72
Weber, Constanze, 57, 70
Weber, F. A. von, 70–1, 94
Wedgwood, Caroline, 262
Wedgwood, Joseph, 262
Wedgwood, Sophie, 262
Weelkes, Thomas, 5, 8
Wegelius, Martin, 258
Weingartner, Felix, 83, 140
Werfel, Alma, 233
Werfel, Franz, 233
Wesendonck, Mathilde, 125–6
Westrup, J. A., 14
Whitman, Walt, 247, 264–5
Widor, C. M., 207
Wieck, Clara, 110–11
Wieck, Friedrich, 110–11
Wilbye, John, 5
Wilcken, Anna, 37
Wilde, Oscar, 252–3
Wilhelm Ernst, Duke, 35–6
William III, King, 15
Wilson, Steuart, 52
Wodzińska, Marie, 106–7
Wolf, Hugo, 79, 157, 211–14, 152,
  281
Wolf, Philipp, 211
Wood, Charles, 262
Wood, Ursula, 266
Wordsworth, William, 246

Ysaÿe, Eugène, 149

Zingarelli, Niccolò, 88
Zweig, Stefan, 255

Arts

BALLET FOR ALL   40p

Peter Brinson and Clement Crisp

Describes in detail over 100 ballets by 38
choreographers – complete with production
credits including original dancers, synopsis
and commentary.

Contains chapters on the historical background
of ballet, Pre-Romantic ballet and a short survey of modern Soviet ballet.

THE PAN BOOK OF OPERA   40p

Arthur Jacobs and Stanley Sadie

'These authors are not afraid of being thought
individual and this is a book that one will be
consulting not just to rehearse the details of a
plot but to find out what the authors themselves think. One has confidence in them as
guides and provokers, and the musical comments are particularly good.' – *The Guardian*

Pan Biography

KATHLEEN FERRIER (illus.)   50p
Comprises her biography by Winifred Ferrier
and a memoir edited by Neville Cardus.

Hester Chapman
LADY JANE GREY (illus.)   35p

Robert K. Massie
NICHOLAS AND ALEXANDRA
   (illus.)   50p

Violet Bonham Carter
WINSTON CHURCHILL AS I
   KNEW HIM (illus.)   37½p

David Cecil
MELBOURNE (illus.)   75p

Vincent Cronin
LOUIS XIV (illus.)   62½p